CLYMER®

SUZUKI

GS750 FOURS • 1977-1982

The world's finest publisher of mechanical how-to manuals

CLYMER®

P.O. Box 12901, Overland Park, Kansas 66282-2901

Copyright ©1985 Penton Business Media, Inc.

FIRST EDITION
First Printing February, 1978
Second Printing April, 1978

SECOND EDITION
Revised by David Sales to include 1978-1979 models.
First Printing March, 1979

THIRD EDITION
Revised by David Sales to include 1980 models
First Printing April, 1981

FOURTH EDITION
Revised by David Sales to include 1981-1982 models
First Printing March, 1983
Second Printing March, 1985

FIFTH EDITION
Revised by Ed Scott
First Printing September, 1985
Second Printing December, 1986
Third Printing April, 1988
Fourth Printing July, 1989
Fifth Printing February, 1991
Sixth Printing August, 1992
Seventh Printing April, 1994
Eighth Printing March, 1996
Ninth Printing November, 1997
Tenth Printing September, 1999
Eleventh Printing January, 2002
Twelfth Printing September, 2004
Thirteenth Printing June, 2008

Printed in U.S.A.

CLYMER and colophon are registered trademarks of Penton Business Media, Inc.

ISBN-10: 0-89287-667-0

ISBN-13: 978-0-89287-667-9

Library of Congress: 95-81993

MEMBER

COVER: GS750E owned and photographed by Ron Hurd, Lakewood, CO.

CLYMER®

Publisher Shawn Etheridge

EDITORIAL

Editorial Director
James Grooms

Editor
Steven Thomas

Associate Editor
Rick Arens

Authors
Jay Bogart
Michael Morlan
George Parise
Mark Rolling
Ed Scott
Ron Wright

Technical Illustrators
Steve Amos
Errol McCarthy
Mitzi McCarthy
Bob Meyer

Group Production Manager
Dylan Goodwin

Production Manager
Greg Araujo

Senior Production Editor
Darin Watson

Production Editors
Holly McComas
Adriane Roberts
Taylor Wright

Production Designer
Jason Hale

MARKETING/SALES AND ADMINISTRATION

Sales Managers
Justin Henton
Matt Tusken

Marketing and Sales Representative
Erin Gribbin

Director, Operations–Books
Ron Rogers

Customer Service Manager
Terri Cannon

Customer Service Account Specialist
Courtney Hollars

Customer Service Representatives
Dinah Bunnell
April LeBlond

Warehouse & Inventory Manager
Leah Hicks

Penton Media

P.O. Box 12901, Overland Park, KS 66282-2901 • 800-262-1954 • 913-967-1719

More information available at *clymer.com*

CONTENTS

QUICK REFERENCE DATA

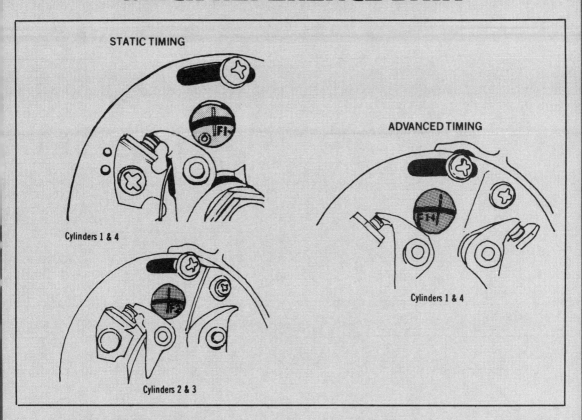

STATIC TIMING

Cylinders 1 & 4

Cylinders 2 & 3

ADVANCED TIMING

Cylinders 1 & 4

TUNE-UP SPECIFICATIONS

Recommended spark plugs	
All TSCC engines	NGK D8EA or ND X24ES-U
All other models	NGK B8ES or ND W24ES
Spark plug gap	0.6-0.7 mm (0.024-0.028 in.)
Breaker point gap	0.3-0.4 mm (0.012-0.016 in.)
Ignition timing	
All TSCC engines	
(preset—non-adjustable)	15 degrees B.T.D.C. below 1,500 rpm
	35 degrees B.T.D.C. above 2,350 rpm
All other models	17 degrees B.T.D.C. below 1,500 rpm
	37 degrees B.T.D.C. above 2,500 rpm
Valve clearance	
All TSCC engines	0.09-0.13 mm (0.004-0.005 in.)
All other models	0.03-0.08 mm (0.0012-0.0031 in.)
Idle speed	950-1,150 rpm
Carburetor air screw	
All models manufactured after January 1978	Preset (non-adjustable)
All earlier models	2 turns open

LAMP RATINGS

	Watts
Headlamp*	
1979 and earlier	**50/40**
TSCC models	**60/55**
Meter lamp	3.4
Turn signal indicator lamp	3.4
High beam indicator lamp	3.4
Oil pressure indicator lamp	3.4
Neutral indicator lamp	3.4
Turn signal lamp	23
Rear combination lamps	
Tail and parking	8 (3 cp)
Stop	23 (32 cp)

ADJUSTMENTS

Drive chain deflection	20-30mm ($\frac{13}{16}$-1$\frac{3}{16}$ in.)
Clutch lever free play	4mm ($\frac{3}{16}$ in. approx.)
Throttle cable free play	1-1.5mm (0.04-0.06 in.)
Brake pedal	10mm ($\frac{3}{8}$ in.) below top of foot rest

CYLINDER LOCATION

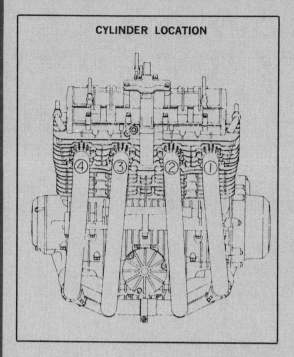

TORQUE SPECIFICATIONS

	Mkg	Ft.-lb.
Oil pan bolt and drain plug	1.0	7
Oil filter cover nut	0.6-0.8	4-6
Camshaft cover bolts	0.7-1.1	5-8
Cylinder head nuts	3.5-4.0	25-29
Spark plug	1.9	14
Engine mounting bolts		
10mm	4.0	29
8mm	2.0	15
Front axle nut	3.6-5.2	26-38
Rear axle nut	8.5-11.5	62-83

RECOMMENDED FUEL AND LUBRICANTS

Fuel	Unleaded or low-lead; 85-95 octane
Engine/transmission oil	SAE 10W/40 SE or SD rated
Fork oil	SAE 10 or 20 fork oil or A.T.F. (automatic transmission fluid) mixed 1:1 with SAE 10W/30
Brake fluid	Rated DOT 3 or DOT 4

WARNING: Use only glycol based brake fluid rated DOT 3 or DOT 4. Mixing silicon or petroleum based fluids can cause brake component damage leading to brake system failure.

CAPACITIES

Fuel tank	liters	U.S. gal.	Imp. gal.
LN	13	3.4	2.9
LT, LX	15	4.0	3.3
TZ	16	4.2	3.5
ET, EX, EZ	19	5.0	4.2
All others	18	4.8	4.0

Engine/transmission oil	liters	U.S. qt.	Imp. qt.
Without filter change			
TSCC engine	3.2	3.4	2.8
All others	3.4	3.6	3.0
With filter change	3.8	4.0	3.3
After overhaul			
TSCC engine	4.0	4.2	3.5
All others	4.2	4.4	3.7

Front fork oil	cc	U.S. oz.	Imp. oz.
LN	280	9.5	9.9
ET, LT, LX	237	8.0	8.3
EX	191	6.5	6.7
TZ	209	7.1	7.4
EZ	214	7.2	7.5
All others	180	6.0	6.3

Fork oil level*	mm	in.
LN	202	8.0
ET, LT, LX	229	9.0
EX	227	8.9
EZ	201	7.9
TZ	180	7.1
All others	206	8.1

* Remove spring and measure oil level from top of fork leg with fork leg held vertically and fully compressed.

CLYMER®

SUZUKI

GS750 FOURS • 1977-1982

CHAPTER ONE

GENERAL INFORMATION

This book provides service and maintenance procedures for all the Suzuki GS750 motorcycles manufactured since 1977. Chapters One through Twelve contain general information on all models and specific information on 1977-1980 models. The Supplement at the end of the book contains specific information on 1981 and later models that differs from earlier years.

Repairing and maintaining your own motorcycle can be an enjoyable and rewarding experience. The following topics provide information on how to use this book as well as general hints and techniques to make the work as easy and enjoyable as possible.

HOW TO USE
THIS MANUAL

This manual has been specifically written and formatted for the amateur home mechanic. All procedures, tables, photos, etc., in this manual assume that the reader may be working on the bike or using this manual for the first time. This section is included to acquaint the home mechanic with what is in the manual and how to take best advantage of the information.

For the most frequently used general information and maintenance specifications refer to the *Quick Reference Data* pages. These colored pages in the front of the book represent a compilation of the most commonly "referred to" facts. The *Quick Reference Data* pages save you from searching each chapter of the manual every time this information is needed. Readily accessible information can help prevent serious and expensive mechanical errors.

To save time on all maintenance tasks, use the *Index.* The *Index* in the back of this manual has been carefully prepared and lists all major maintenance tasks by paragraph heading. Whether you want to remove a piston or simply adjust the drive chain, a quick look in the *Index* will tell you exactly what page it is on.

For a better understanding of manual contents refer to the section on *Chapter Organization* in this chapter.

To save yourself time, energy and possible future aggravation, finish reading this entire chapter. If you acquaint yourself with all the special features of this manual it can become a valuable and indispensable tool. This manual can help you achieve a better maintained and more reliable machine.

CHAPTER ORGANIZATION

This chapter provides general information on how this manual is organized as well as special information and maintenance tips to aid all repair tasks. Read this entire chapter before performing any maintenance procedure.

Chapter Two, *Troubleshooting*, contains many suggestions and tips for finding and fixing troubles fast. Troubleshooting procedures discuss symptoms and logical methods to pinpoint the trouble.

Chapter Three, *Lubrication, Maintenance and Tune-up*, includes all normal periodic and preventive maintenance tasks designed to keep your machine in peak operating condition.

Subsequent chapters describe specific systems such as engine, clutch and fuel system. Each chapter provides complete disassembly, repair and reassembly procedures in easy to follow, step-by-step form. If a repair is impractical for home mechanics, it is so indicated. Usually, such repairs are more economically done by a dealer or qualified specialist.

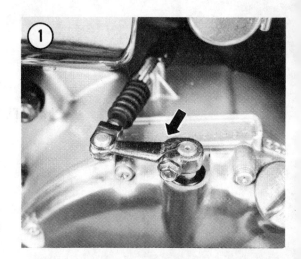

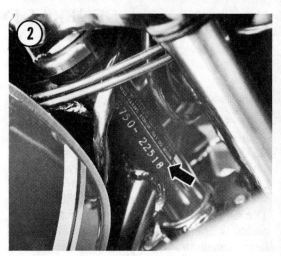

NOTES, CAUTIONS AND WARNINGS

NOTES, CAUTIONS and WARNINGS appear throughout this manual and provide specific and important information for the reader. A NOTE usually provides extra or special information to make a step or procedure clearer. Disregarding a NOTE might cause inconvenience but will not cause damage or personal injury.

A CAUTION is provided in a procedure wherever mechanical damage of any type may occur. Failure to heed a CAUTION will most certainly result in some form of damage to the machine; however, personal injury is unlikely. WARNINGS are the most serious and are included in a procedure where personal injury may occur if the WARNING is not heeded. Mechanical damage may also occur.

PHOTOS, DRAWINGS AND TABLES

This manual contains literally hundreds of photos, drawings and tables that are used to support and clarify maintenance procedures. Each photo, drawing and table is referenced at least once within a specific procedure. When using a procedure, take full advantage of all the support data provided to make your job easier and help avoid costly errors.

MODEL IDENTIFICATION

Suzuki will often make modifications and improvements during a model year. The changes are generally minor, however, if you are performing repair work you will want to install the latest improved parts possible. It is

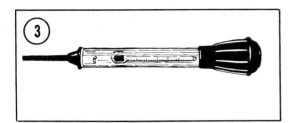

important to keep a record of your engine number and frame number when ordering parts. The applicability of all improved parts is always referenced by the engine number and/or the frame number. The engine number is stamped on the top of the crankcase (**Figure 1**). The frame number is stamped on the steering head (**Figure 2**). When purchasing new parts, if possible, always compare them to the old parts. If the parts are not alike, have the parts or service manager explain the difference to you.

SAFETY FIRST

A safe mechanic, amateur or professional, can work for years and never sustain a serious injury. If you observe a few rules of common sense and safety, you too can enjoy many hours safely servicing your motorcycle. Ignoring some of these basic rules, however, can cause some serious injuries.

1. Never use gasoline as a cleaning solvent.
2. Never smoke or use a torch around flammable liquids, such as cleaning solvent or many spray lubricants.
3. Never smoke or use a torch in areas where batteries are being charged. Highly explosive hydrogen gas is formed during the charging process. Never arc the terminals of a battery to see if it has a charge; the sparks could ignite the explosive hydrogen as easily as an open flame.
4. If welding or brazing is required on the motorcycle, remove the fuel tank and set it a safe distance away—at least 50 feet.
5. Always use the correct size wrench for turning nuts and bolts, and when a nut is tight, think for a moment what will happen to your hand if the wrench should slip.
6. Keep your work area clean and uncluttered.

7. Wear safety goggles in all operations involving drilling, grinding or use of a chisel or air hose.
8. Do not use worn-out tools.
9. Always allow yourself sufficient time to do a thorough and complete job. Many accidents happen as a direct result of "being in a hurry to finish."
10. Keep a fire extinguisher handy. Be sure it is at least rated for Class B and Class C fires (gasoline/oil and electrical).

EXPENDABLE SUPPLIES

Certain expendable supplies are also required. These included grease, oil, gasket cement, wiping rags, cleaning solvent and distilled water. Ask your dealer for the special locking compounds, silicone lubricants and commercial chain lube products which make motorcycle maintenance simpler and easier. Solvent is available at most service stations and distilled water for the battery is available at most supermarkets.

TOOLS

For proper servicing, you will need an assortment of ordinary handtools. As a minimum, these include:

    a. Metric combination wrenches
    b. Metric sockets
    c. Plastic mallet
    d. Small hammer
    e. Snap ring pliers
    f. Gas pliers
    g. Phillips screwdrivers
    h. Slot (common) screwdrivers
    i. Feeler gauges
    j. Spark plug gauge
    k. Spark plug wrench
    l. Dial indicator

Engine tune-up and troubleshooting procedures require a few more tools, described in the following sections.

Hydrometer

This instrument (**Figure 3**) measures state of charge of the battery and tells much about battery condition. Such an instrument is

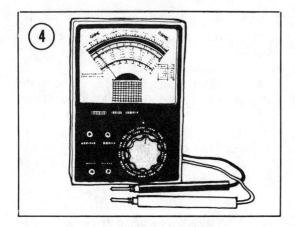

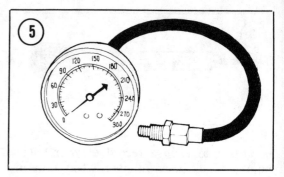

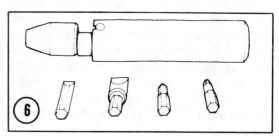

available at any auto parts store and through most larger mail order outlets.

Multimeter or VOM

This instrument (**Figure 4**) is invaluable for electrical system troubleshooting and service. A few of its functions may be duplicated by locally fabricated substitutes, but for the serious hobbyist, it is a must. Its uses are described in the applicable sections of this book.

Compression Gauge

An engine with low compression cannot be properly tuned and will not develop full power. A compression gauge measures engine compression. The one shown in **Figure 5** has a flexible stem which enables it to reach cylinders where there is little clearance between the cylinder head and frame. Compression gauges are available at auto accessory stores or by mail order from large catalog order firms.

Impact Driver

This tool might have been designed with the motorcyclist in mind. It makes removal of engine cover screws easy and eliminates damaged screw slots. See **Figure 6**.

Carburetor Gauge Set

A gauge set which can display manifold vacuum for all cylinders simultaneously will greatly simplify carburetor synchronization. **Figure 7** shows the Suzuki gauge set. Other after-market versions are available.

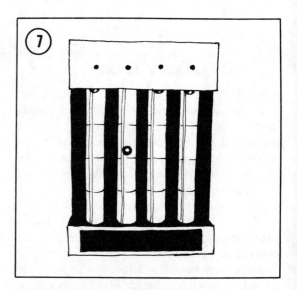

Strobe Timing Light

This instrument is necessary for tuning on all 1979 and earlier models. It permits very accurate ignition timing by flashing a light at the precise instant the cylinder fires. Marks on the ignition advance governor are lined up with the timing plate mark while the engine is running.

Suitable lights range from inexpensive neon bulb types to powerful xenon strobe lights. See **Figure 8**. Neon timing lights are difficult to see and must be used in dimly lit areas.

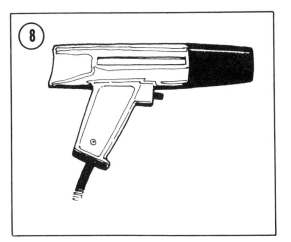

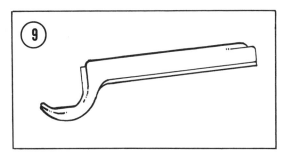

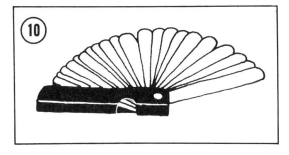

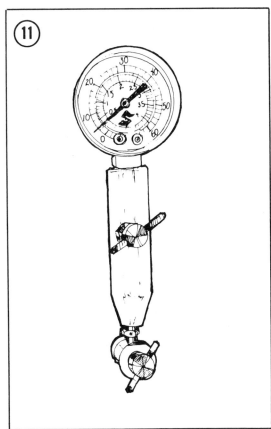

Xenon strobe timing lights can be used outside in bright sunlight. Both types work on this motorcycle; use according to the manufacturer's instructions.

Tappet Depressor
(1979 and Earlier Models)

The Suzuki tappet depressor (**Figure 9**) is absolutely necessary for performing valve adjustments with the camshafts installed. It is used to hold valve tappets down so the adjustment shims can be removed. If you plan to do your own valve adjustments, order this tool (part No. 09916-64510) from your local Suzuki dealer.

Valve Clearance
Feeler Gauge

Valve clearances on GS models are critical and have a very small tolerance (0.03-0.08 mm). This Suzuki special tool (part No. 09900-20803) is particularly useful for setting valve clearances because it contains gauges ranging from 0.02-1.00 mm with many small sizes not usually available in most feeler gauge sets (**Figure 10**). This tool can be purchased from your local Suzuki dealer.

Pressure Gauge

This special tool (part No. 09940-44110) is available from Suzuki to service air forks (**Figure 11**). This tool allows air pressure to be set exactly without air loss when the gauge is removed.

Compothane Mallet

This plastic covered "dead-blow" mallet is virtually indestructable and has become a favorite tool among professional and amateur motorcycle mechanics. This mallet can be used on most metal surfaces without causing any damage to the surface. The mallet is available in a variety of shapes and weights and can be purchased from professional tool distributors such as Snap-On and Mac.

GENERAL MAINTENANCE HINTS

Most of the service procedures provided in this book can be performed by anyone reasonably handy with tools. It is suggested, however, that you carefully consider your own capabilities before attempting any repair task which involves major disassembly of the engine and transmission.

Crankshaft repairs, for example, require the use of a heavy-duty hydraulic press. This type of repair work must be performed by a competent machine shop or authorized dealer. Other procedures require precision measurements and, unless you have the skills and equipment to make them, it would be better to have a motorcycle shop do the work.

Repairs can be made faster and easier if the motorcycle is clean before you begin work. Good soap and pressurized water is usually the best to clean all but the most stubborn dirt or grease. High-pressure coin-operated car washes do a good job of cleaning; however, the bike must be completely dried and lubricated after washing. High-pressure water and detergent can easily enter the wheels, swinging arm and other critical areas and cause corrosion if not treated immediately after cleaning.

Clean all oily and greasy parts with cleaning solvent. An approved solvent is usually available in bulk form from many automobile service stations and parts stores. *Never use gasoline as a cleaning agent.* It presents an extreme fire hazard. Always work in a well-ventilated area when using cleaning solvent. Keep a fire extinguisher, rated for gasoline and oil fires, handy just in case. If you are not used to working with cleaning solvent wear rubber gloves, if possible, or treat your hands with a good skin lotion immediately after cleaning parts. Solvent will remove the skin oils from your hands and cause painful and irritating "solvent burns" if left untreated.

Special tools are required for some service procedures. All special tools necessary are referenced by a Suzuki part number and are available from an authorized dealer. If you are on good terms with the dealer's service department or know a professional motorcycle mechanic, you may be able to borrow what you need. Naturally much of the labor charge made for repairs by a dealer is for removal and disassembly of other parts to reach the defective area. It is usually possible to perform much of the preliminary work yourself and then take the affected part or assembly to the dealer for repair.

Once you decide to tackle a job yourself, read the entire section pertaining to the task. Study the procedures, illustrations, tables and other support data until you have a thorough idea of what is involved in the job. If special tools are required, make arrangements for them before beginning the work. It is very frustrating to get partway into a job and then discover you do not have the necessary parts or tools to complete it.

Simple wiring checks can easily be made at home; but knowledge of electronics is almost a necessity for performing tests with complicated electronic testing gear.

During disassembly of parts keep a few general cautions in mind. Force is rarely needed to get things apart. If parts are a tight fit, like a bearing in a case, there is usually a tool made to separate them. Never use a screwdriver to pry apart parts with machined surfaces such as crankcase halves and valve covers. You will mar the surfaces and end up with leaks.

Make diagrams wherever similar-appearing parts are found. For instance, case cover screws are often not the same length. You may think you can remember where everything came from—but mistakes are costly. There is also the possibility you may be sidetracked and not return to work for days or even weeks—in which interval carefully laid out parts may become disturbed.

Tag all similar internal parts for location and mark all mating parts for position. Record the number and thickness of any shims as they are removed. Small parts such as bolts can be identified by placing them in plastic sandwich bags. Seal and label the bags with masking tape.

Wiring should be tagged with masking tape and marked as each wire is removed. Again, do not rely on memory alone.

Use a locking compound such as blue Loctite No. 242 on all bolts and nuts, even if they are secured with lockwashers. This type of Loctite does not harden completely and allows easy removal of the bolt or nut. A screw lost from an engine cover or bearing retainer could easily cause serious and expensive damage before its loss is noticed.

When applying Loctite, use a small amount. If too much is used, it can squeeze out and stick to parts that are not meant to be stuck.

When replacing missing or broken bolts, particularly on the engine or frame

components, always use Suzuki replacement bolts. They are specially hardened for each application. The wrong 25 cent bolt could easily cause many dollars worth of serious damage, not to mention rider injury.

When installing gaskets in the engine, always use Suzuki replacement gaskets *without* sealer, unless specifically designated. Suzuki gaskets are designed to swell when in contact with oil. Gasket sealer prevents the gaskets from swelling as intended, which can also result in oil leaks. Suzuki gaskets are also cut from material of the precise thickness needed.

Disconnect battery ground cable before working near electrical connections and before disconnecting wires. Never run the engine with the battery disconnected; the alternator could be seriously damaged.

Protect finished surfaces from physical damage or corrosion. Keep gasoline and brake fluid off painted surfaces.

Avoid flames or sparks when working near a charging battery or flammable liquids such as brake fluid or gasoline.

No parts, except those assembled with a press fit, require unusual force during assembly. If a part is hard to remove or install, find out why before proceeding.

Cover all openings after removing parts to keep dirt, small tools, etc., from falling in.

When assembling 2 parts, start all fasteners, then tighten evenly.

Heavy grease can be used to hold small parts in place if they tend to fall out during assembly. However, keep grease and oil away from electrical components or brake pads and discs.

Carburetors are best cleaned by disassembling them and soaking the parts in solvent or a commercial carburetor cleaner. Never soak gaskets and rubber parts in these cleaners. Never use wire to clean out jets and air passages; they are easily damaged. Use compressed air to blow out the carburetor only if the float has been removed first.

A baby bottle (**Figure 12**) makes a good measuring device for adding oil to forks and transmissions. Get one that is graduated in ounces and cubic centimeters.

Take your time and do the job right. Do not forget that a newly rebuilt motorcycle engine must be broken in the same as a new one. Keep the rpm within the limits given in your owner's manual when you get back on the road.

CHAPTER TWO

TROUBLESHOOTING

Diagnosing mechanical problems is relatively simple if you use orderly procedures and keep a few basic principles in mind.

The troubleshooting procedures in this chapter analyze typical symptoms and show logical methods of isolating causes. These are not the only methods. There may be several ways to solve a problem, but only a systematic approach guarantees success. Never assume anything. Do not overlook the obvious. If you are riding along and the bike suddenly quits, check the easiest, most accessible problem spots first. Is there gasoline in the tank? Is the gas petcock in the ON or RESERVE position? Has a spark plug wire fallen off? Check ignition switch. Sometimes the weight of keys on a key ring may turn the ignition off suddenly.

If nothing obvious turns up in a cursory check, look a litle further. Learning to recognize and describe symptoms will make repairs easier for you or a mechanic at the shop. Describe problems accurately and fully. Saying that "it won't run" isn't the same as saying "it quit on the highway at high speed and wouldn't start," or that "it sat in my garage for 3 months and then wouldn't start."

Gather as many symptoms together as possible to aid in diagnosis. Note whether the engine lost power gradually or all at once, what color smoke (if any) came from the exhaust, and so on. Remember that the more complicated a machine is, the easier it is to troubleshoot because symptoms point to specific problems. After the symptoms are defined, areas which could cause the problems are tested and analyzed. Guessing at the cause of a problem may provide the solution, but it can easily lead to frustration, wasted time and a series of expensive, unnecessary parts replacement.

You do not need fancy equipment or complicated test gear to determine whether repairs can be attempted at home. A few simple checks could save a large repair bill and time lost while the bike sits in a dealer's service department. On the oher hand, be realistic and do not attempt repairs beyond your abilities. Service departments tend to charge heavily for putting together a disassembled engine that may have been abused. Some won't even take on such a job—so use common sense, don't get in over your head.

OPERATING REQUIREMENTS

An engine needs 3 basics to run properly: correct gas/air mixture, compression and a spark at the right time. If one or more are missing, the engine won't run. The electrical system is the weakest link of the three basics. More problems result from electrical breakdowns than from any other source. Keep that in mind before you begin tampering with carburetor adjustments and the like.

If a bike has been sitting for any length of time and refuses to start, check the battery for a charged condition first, then look to the gasoline delivery system. This includes the tank, fuel valve, lines and the carburetors. Rust may have formed in the tank, obstructing fuel flow. Gasoline deposits may have gummed up carburetor jets and air passages. Gasoline tends to lose its potency after standing for long periods. Condensation may contaminate it with water. Drain old gas and try starting with a fresh tankful.

TROUBLESHOOTING INSTRUMENTS

Chapter One lists many of the instruments needed and detailed instructions on their use.

EMERGENCY TROUBLESHOOTING

When the bike is difficult to start or won't start at all, it does not help to grind away at the starter or kick the tires. Check for obvious problems even before getting out your tools. Go down the following list step-by-step. Do each one; you may be embarrassed to find your kill switch off, but that is better than

wearing your battery down with the starter. If the bike still will not start, refer to the appropriate troubleshooting procedures which follow in this chapter.

1. Is there fuel in the tank? Remove the filler cap and rock the bike; listen for fuel sloshing around.

> *WARNING*
> *Do not use an open flame to check in the tank. A serious explosion is certain to result.*

2. Turn fuel petcock to RESERVE or PRIME to be sure that you get the last remaining gas.
3. Make sure the kill switch is in the RUN position.

> *NOTE*
> *Remember, on 1979 and later models, the clutch lever must be pulled in or the starter will not operate.*

4. Is the choke in the correct position? The choke lever on earlier models should be down, on later models the choke knob should be pulled up.
5. Is the battery dead? Check the battery connections and the state of charge as outlined in Chapter Eight.
6. Check the main fuse. All 1977 and 1978 models use a single main fuse (**Figure 1**). All later models have a fuse panel as shown in **Figure 2**.

STARTER

Starter system troubles are relatively easy to isolate. The following are common symptoms and cures. **Figure 3** shows a wiring diagram of the starting system. Use it to help isolate troubles.

1. *Engine cranks very slowly or not at all*—If the headlight is very dim or not lighting at all, most likely the battery or its connecting wires are at fault. Check the battery using the procedures described in Chapter Eight. Check the wiring for breaks, shorts and dirty connections.

If the battery and connecting wires check good, the trouble may be in the starter, solenoid or wiring. To isolate the trouble, short the 2 large solenoid terminals together (not to the ground); if the starter cranks normally, check the starter solenoid wiring. If the starter still fails to crank properly, remove the starter and test it.

2. *Starter engages but will not disengage when switch is released*—Usually caused by a faulty starter solenoid or switch.

CHARGING SYSTEM

Troubleshooting an alternator system is somewhat different from troubleshooting a generator system. For example, *never* short any terminals to ground on the alternator or voltage regulator.

The following symptoms are typical of alternator charging system troubles.

1. *Battery requires frequent charging*—The charging system is not functioning, or it is undercharging the battery. Test the alternator rectifier and voltage regulator as described in Chapter Eight.

2. *Battery requires frequent additions of water or lamps require frequent replacement*—The alternator is probably overcharging the battery. Have the voltage regulator checked or replaced.

3. *Noisy alternator*—Check for a loose alternator rotor bolt.

IGNITION

Locating an ignition system miss or complete failure is a relatively simple and logical procedure. Check the obvious first. Is ignition switch on and kill button in the RUN position?

1. Remove one or two spark plugs and reconnect the plug wires.

2. Lay the plug against the cylinder head so its base makes a good connection with the head and crank the engine over. A fat blue spark should be visible at the plug electrode. On 1979 and earlier models, if there is no spark or a very weak spark, perform *Contact Breaker Point and Timing Adjustment* as outlined in Chapter Three. On later models, refer to Chapter Eight for ignition system troubleshooting.

3. After points have been cleaned and properly gapped, turn on the ignition switch and spring points open repeatedly with a screwdriver. A small spark should be seen each time the points are opened and a fat blue spark should be visible at the spark plug electrode. A no-spark condition at the points indicates a possible fault in the battery circuit or a bad connection or broken wire in the ignition primary circuit. Remove the fuel tank as outlined in Chapter Seven and examine the breaker point wire connector (black and white wires) and check for shorted or broken wires.

4. If a small spark is visible at each breaker point set, but no spark or a very weak spark is visible at the spark plug, the malfunction is probably in an ignition coil or condenser. Special test equipment is required to properly test these components. Remove the coil/condenser units as outlined in Chapter Eight and have them tested by a dealer.

ENGINE

These procedures assume the starter cranks the engine normally. If not, refer to *Starter* in this chapter.

Poor Performance

1. *Engine misses erratically at all speeds*—Intermittent trouble like this can be difficult to find and correct. The fault could be in the ignition system, exhaust system (restriction) or fuel system. Follow troubleshooting procedures for these systems to isolate the trouble.

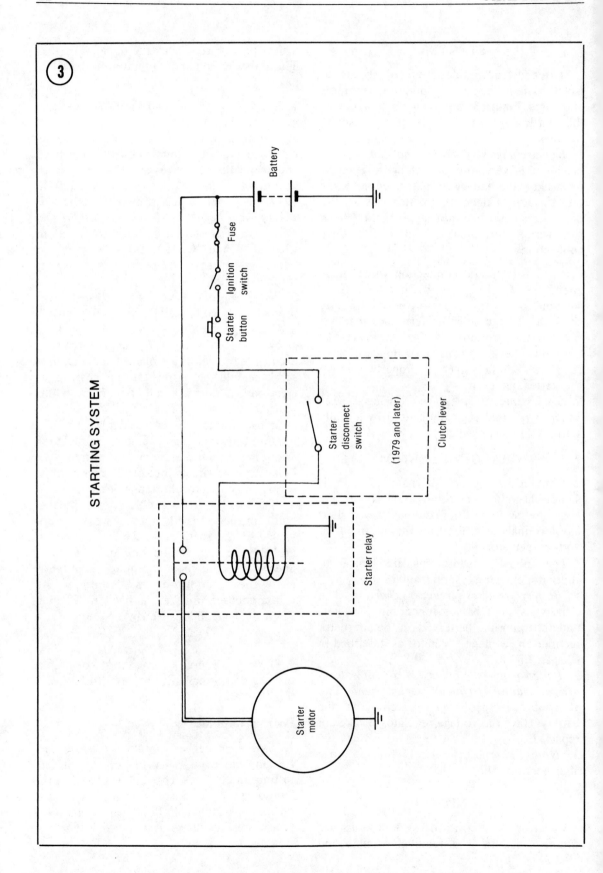

STARTING SYSTEM

2. *Engine misses at idle only*—Trouble could exist anywhere in the ignition system. Follow the *Ignition* troubleshooting procedure carefully. Trouble could exist in the carburetor's idle circuits. Check idle mixture adjustments (Chapter Three, *Carburetor Adjustments*) and check for restrictions in the idle circuits.

3. *Engine misses at high speed only*—Trouble could exist in the fuel system or ignition system. Check the fuel lines and valve as described under *Fuel System* in this chapter. Also check spark plugs and high-tension leads (see *Ignition* in this chapter).

4. *Poor performance at all speeds, lack of acceleration*—Trouble usually exists in ignition or fuel system. Check each with the appropriate procedure. Also check for dragging brakes, tight or bound wheel bearings and correct tire pressure.

5. *Excessive fuel consumption*—This can be caused by a wide variety of seemingly unrelated factors. Check for clutch slippage, dragging brakes and defective wheel bearings.

Check tire pressure. Check ignition and fuel systems.

ENGINE NOISES

1. *Valve clatter*—This is a light to heavy tapping sound from the cambox. It is usually caused by excessive valve clearance. Adjust the clearance as described in Chapter Three. If the noise persists, disassemble the valve drive system as described in Chapters Four and Five and check for worn or damaged cam lobes, broken springs, missing adjustment shims, etc.

2. *Knocking or pinging during acceleration*—May be caused by lower octane fuel than recommended or by poor fuel available from some "discount" service stations. It may also be caused by incorrect ignition timing or spark plugs of wrong heat range. See Chapter Three *Spark Plug Replacement* and *Ignition Timing.*

3. *Slapping or rattling noises at low speed or during acceleration*—May be caused by piston slap, i.e., excessive piston-to-cylinder wall clearance.

4. *Knocking or rapping during deceleration*—Usually caused by excessive rod bearing clearance.

5. *Persistant knocking and vibration*—Usually causd by excessive main bearing clearance.

6. *Rapid on-off squeal*—Compression leak around cylinder head gasket or spark plug.

EXCESSIVE VIBRATION

This can be difficult to locate without disassembling the engine. Usually this is caused by loose engine mounting hardware or worn engine and transmission bearings.

LUBRICATION TROUBLES

1. *Excessive oil consumption*—May be caused by worn rings and bores. Overhaul is necessary to correct this. See Chapters Four and Five. It may also be caused by worn valve guides or defective valve guide seals. Also check for exterior leaks.

2. *Oil pressure lamp does not light when ignition switch is on*—Locate the oil pressure sensor. On 1979 and earlier models, the sensor is on top of the engine as shown in **Figure 4**. On all TSCC models, the oil pressure sensor is

installed in the oil filter cover (**Figure 5**). Ensure that the wire is connected and makes good contact. Pull off wire and ground it. If the lamp lights, replace the sensor. If the lamp does not light, replace the lamp.

3. *Oil pressure lamp lights or flickers when engine is running*—This indicates low or complete loss of oil pressure. *Stop the engine immediately,* coast to a stop with the clutch disengaged. This may simply be caused by a low oil level; check the oil level. Check for a shorted oil pressure sender with an ohmmeter or other continuity tester. Listen for unusual noises indicating bad bearings, etc. Do not restart the engine until you know why the light went on and the problem has been corrected.

FUEL SYSTEM

Fuel system trouble must be isolated to the carburetor or fuel lines. These procedures assume that the ignition system has been checked and correctly adjusted.

1. *Engine will not start*—First determine that fuel is being delivered to the carburetors. Disconnect the fuel line at the carburetor. Insert the end of the line in a small container to catch the fuel. Turn the tap to RUN. Fuel should run from the line. If not, remove the tap from the tank and clean and check it. See Chapter Seven.

2. *Rough idle or engine misses and stalls frequently*—Check carburetor adjustments. See Chapter Three.
3. *Stumbling when starting from idle*—Check idle speed adjustment. See Chapter Three.
4. *Engine misses at high speed or lacks power*—Possible fuel starvation. Check fuel delivery. Clean main jets and float needle valves.
5. *Black exhaust smoke*—Black exhaust smoke indicates a badly overrich mixture. Make sure the chokes disengage. Check idle mixture and idle speed. Check for leaky float needle valves and correct float level. Make sure jets are correct size. See Chapter Seven.

CLUTCH

All clutch work except adjustment requires removal of the right rear engine cover. See Chapter Six.
1. *Slippage*—This is most noticeable when accelerating in a high gear from low speed. To check slippage; start the engine, select 2nd gear and release the clutch as if riding off in 1st gear. If the clutch is good, the engine will slow and stall. If the clutch slips, increased engine speed will be apparent.

Slippage results from insufficient clutch lever free play, worn plates or weak springs.
2. *Drag or failure to release*—This usually causes difficult shifting and gear clash, particularly when downshifting. The cause may be excessive clutch lever free play, warped or bent plates, broken or loose lining or lack of lubrication in clutch actuating mechanism.
3. *Chatter or grabbing*—Check for worn or warped plates. Check clutch lever free play.

TRANSMISSION

Transmission problems are usually indicated by one or more of the following symptoms:
   a. Difficulty shifting gears
   b. Gear clash when downshifting
   c. Slipping out of gear
   d. Excessive noise in neutral
   e. Excessive noise in gear
   f. Transmission symptoms are sometimes hard to distinguish from clutch

symptoms. Be sure that the clutch is not causing the trouble before working on the transmission.

BRAKES

1. *Brake lever or pedal goes all the way to its stop*—There are numerous causes for this including excessively worn pads, air in the hydraulic system, leaky brake lines, leaky calipers or leaky or worn master cylinder. Check for leaks and thin brake pads. Bleed the brakes. If this does not cure the trouble, rebuild the calipers and/or master cylinder.

2. *Spongy lever or pedal*—Normally caused by air in the system; bleed the brakes.

3. *Dragging brakes*—Check for swollen rubber parts due to improper brake fluid or contamination an obstructed master cylinder bypass post. Clean or replace defective parts.

4. *Hard lever or pedal*—Check brake pads for contamination. Also check for restricted brake lines and hoses

5. *High speed fade*—Check for contaminated brake pads. Ensure that recommended brake fluid is installed. Drain entire system and refill if in doubt.

6. *Pulsating lever or pedal*—Check for excessive brake disc runout. Undetected accident damage is also a frequent cause of this.

LIGHTING SYSTEM

Bulbs which continuously burn out may be caused by excessive vibration, loose connections that permit sudden current surges, poor battery connections or installation of the wrong type bulb.

A majority of light and horn or other electrical accessory problems are caused by loose or corroded ground connections. Check those first and then substitute known good units for easier troubleshooting.

FRONT SUSPENSION AND STEERING

1. *Too stiff or too soft*—Make sure forks have not been leaking and oil is correct viscosity. If in doubt, drain and refill as described in Chapter Three.

2. *Leakage around seals*—There should be a light film of oil on fork tubes. However, large amounts of oil on tubes means the seals are leaking. Replace seals. See Chapter Nine.

3. *Fork action is rough*—Check for bent tube.

4. *Steering wobbles*—Check for correct steering head bearing tightness. See Chapter Nine.

NOTE: If you own a 1981 or later model, first check the Supplement at the back of the book for any new service information.

CHAPTER THREE

PERIODIC MAINTENANCE

A motorcycle, like any other precision machine, requires a certain amount of routine and preventive maintenance to ensure its safety, reliability, and performance.

The maintenance and lubrication intervals specified in **Table 1** are recommended by Suzuki for the average rider. Harder than average riding may require more frequent service to maintain peak reliablity and performance. **Tables 1-8** are found at the end of this chapter.

If you ride less than 500 miles per month, the engine oil should be changed every 3 months regardless of miles.

If the motorcycle is used primarily in stop-and-go traffic, it is a good idea to change the oil more often than is recommended. This is also true for frequent short trips. Acids tend to build up rapidly under these conditions and if allowed to remain in the engine, they will accelerate engine wear.

This chapter describes all periodic maintenance and lubrication required to keep your bike running properly. Routine checks are easily performed at each fuel stop. Other periodic maintenance appears in the order of frequency.

Engine tune-up is treated separately from other maintenance tasks because the various tune-up procedures interact with each other. All tune-up procedures should be performed together and in the specified order.

Plan ahead for all servicing and tune-ups. Make sure you have all the supplies such as engine and fork oil, chain lubricant and spark plugs before starting the service work. Nothing is more aggravating or time consuming than having to stop in the middle of a job and pick up some forgotten item. This is particularly important when performing a valve adjustment. The engine must be dead cold, that is, not run for at least 12 hours prior to adjustment.

NOTE
The following procedures provide coverage for the 2 types of GS750 machines. All 1979 and earlier models share one style engine as well as most frame and suspension components.

Starting with 1980 models ("T" models), all GS750 machines are fitted with a TSCC (Twin Swirl Combustion Chamber) engine. Throughout this manual these machines are identified as "TSCC" models. All TSCC models also share other components that differ slightly from earlier models.

Most maintenance and repair procedures are very similar for motorcycles with both engine types. All minor differences, where applicable, are specified within the procedures. Where significant differences exist, a separate procedure is provided for each type of motorcycle. Before starting any

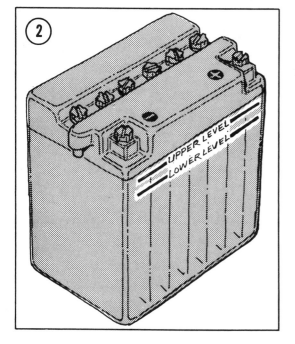

repair or maintenance work, read completely all applicable procedures and note the differences between the models.

ROUTINE CHECKS

Develop a habit of making the following basic checks at each fuel stop. A few minutes spent may prevent personal injury and/or damage to the motorcycle. Correct any problem found before riding.

Engine Oil Level

Place the motorcycle on the centerstand and check the engine oil level through the inspection window (**Figure 1**). Maintain the oil level between the "F" and "L" marks. Use the appropriate oil recommended in **Table 2**.

General Inspection

1. Examine the fuel line and the fuel valve for signs of leakage.
2. Check the control cables for fraying or kinks. All controls must operate smoothly.
3. Inspect the tires, rims and spokes for damage.
4. Check the engine and frame for loose bolts and nuts, wiring, etc.
5. Check the drive chain slack and ensure that the chain is properly lubricated.
6. Ensure that both front and rear brakes operate correctly.
7. Make sure that the lights work properly and that the engine kill switch will shut off the engine.

Battery and Connections

Remove the right side cover and check the electrolyte level in the battery. The electrolyte level must be between the upper and lower level marks on the battery case (**Figure 2**). Top up the level, if necessary, with distilled water.

On all 1979 and earlier models, to add water to the battery it is necessary to open the seat. On all TSCC models, the air filter chamber must be removed.

To clean the battery connections and check the specific gravity of the electrolyte, refer to *Battery Service* in Chapter Eight.

To add water to the battery on all TSCC models, perform the following:
1. Remove the seat.
2. Loosen the clamp securing the front of the filter chamber (**Figure 3**).
3. Remove the bolt securing the rear of the filter chamber (**Figure 4**).
4. Loosen the clamp securing the rear master cylinder reservoir (**Figure 5**).
5. Carefully lift up and remove the air filter chamber.
6. Add enough distilled water to the battery to bring the electrolyte level between the upper and lower marks as shown in Figure 2.
7. Clean the battery connections as outlined in Chapter Eight.
8. Install the air filter chamber. Make sure the rubber coupling is positioned properly on the neck of the chamber.
9. Tighten the clamp securing the rear master cylinder reservoir.

Tire Pressure

Tire pressures should be checked and adjusted when the tires are cold. A simple, accurate gauge (**Figure 6**) can be purchased for a few dollars and should be carried in your motorcycle tool kit. The type of gauge shown in **Figure 6** is generally preferred over the "dial" type gauge since the indicator does not automatically return to zero when the gauge is removed. Refer to **Table 3** for the recommended tire pressures.

Tire Inspection

Check the tread for excessive wear, deep cuts and imbedded objects such as nails or bits of broken glass. If you find a nail in a tire, mark its location with a light crayon before pulling it out. This will help locate the hole in the inner tube. Check local traffic regulations concerning minimum tread depth. Measure with a tread depth gauge (**Figure 7**) or a small ruler. Suzuki recommends tire replacement when the tread depth is less than 1.6 mm (1/16 in.) in the front and 2.0 mm (3/32 in.) in the rear. Tread wear bars or indicators appear across the tire when the tread reaches the minimum safe depth. Replace the tire at this point.

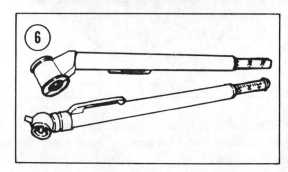

Wheels and Rims

On spoke wheels, inspect the rims for signs of damage and check for loose spokes. On models with aluminum alloy wheels, examine the wheels for cracks, bends or warpage. These wheels cannot be serviced, except for balancing. If the wheels are damaged they must be replaced.

Refer to Chapter Nine to "true" and balance spoke and alloy wheels.

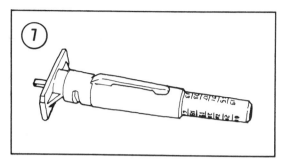

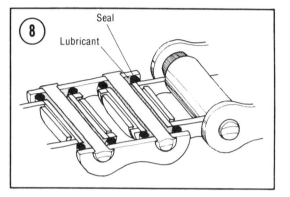

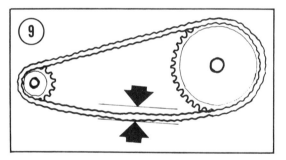

PERIODIC MAINTENANCE

The following maintenance items are summarized in **Table 1**. A good way to ensure that all necessary items are covered during a periodic service is to make a check list and use it each time you service the motorcycle. Keep an up-to-date record of all items serviced and when the service was performed; otherwise it is too easy to forget what was done and when.

Drive Chain
Adjustment and Lubrication

The drive chain should be carefully inspected at least every 600 miles (1,000 km). Lubricate and adjust the chain more frequently if necessary. The importance of proper drive chain maintenance cannot be overemphasized. Accelerated drive chain wear as a result of neglect can prove very costly. A drive chain is an expensive item to replace, and a failed chain may cause engine and/or transmission damage.

CAUTION
*Do not use a specially compounded chain oil on the drive chain unless the oil is specifically recommended for O-ring chains. The drive chain is permanently lubricated with O-ring seals around the pins as shown in **Figure 8**. The penetrants in non-approved chain lubricants may damage the O-rings or thin the permanent lubrication. If approved oil is not available, keep the outside of the chain well lubricated with heavy motor oil.*

When checking drive chain adjustment, check the slack in several places along the length of the chain by rotating the rear wheel. The chain will rarely stretch uniformly and as a result will be tighter in some places than others.

1. Measure the chain deflection (slack) halfway between both sprockets as shown in **Figure 9**. Normal deflection is 20-30 mm (13/16-1 3/16 in.).

2. If the chain requires adjustment, perform the following:

    a. Remove the cotter pin or lynch pin securing the rear axle nut (**Figure 10**) and loosen the axle nut. It may be necessary to use a phillips screwdriver shaft inserted in the axle head to keep the axle from turning.

b. Loosen the locknuts securing the axle adjusters bolts on each side (**Figure 11**).

c. Tighten or loosen the adjuster bolts until the chain deflection is 20-30 mm (13/16-1-3/16 in.). Make sure the marks on both adjusters align with the same marks on each end of the swing arm (**Figure 12**).

d. Tighten the adjuster bolt locknuts. Recheck the chain deflection and readjust if necessary.

e. Torque the axle nut to 8.5-11.5 mkg (62-83 ft.-lb.). Secure the nut with the lynch pin or a new cotter pin.

3. Lubricate the chain with an APPROVED O-ring chain lubricant according to the manufacturer's instructions. If chain lubricant is not available, perform the following:

a. Soak a clean rag in engine oil.

b. Wrap the rag around the drive chain and hold it in place.

c. Slowly turn the rear wheel to allow the chain to run through the oil soaked rag. Rotate the wheel until the chain is completely coated with a light film of oil.

4. Inspect the sprockets for signs of wear and undercutting (**Figure 13**). Refer to Chapter Four or Five for drive sprocket replacement and Chapter Ten for rear sprocket replacement.

Engine and Frame Fasteners

Constant vibration can loosen many fasteners on a motorcycle. Refer to **Table 4** and torque all the engine and frame fasteners as specified.

Engine Oil and Filter Change

Regular oil and filter service will contribute more to engine longevity than any other single factor. Change the oil and clean the oil filter at least as often as specified in **Table 1**. Change both oil and filter more often if the motorcycle is used in dusty areas or primarily on short trips.

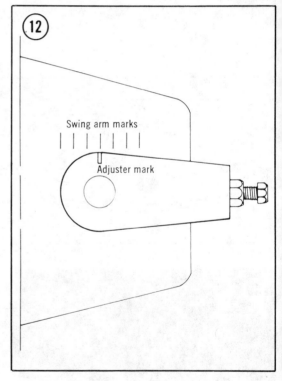

Swing arm marks

Adjuster mark

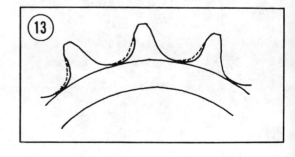

NOTE
*Never dispose of motor oil in the trash, on the ground, or down a storm drain. Many service stations accept used motor oil and waste haulers provide curbside used motor oil collection. Do not combine other fluids with motor oil to be recycled. To locate a recycler, contact the American Petroleum Institute (API) at **www.recycleoil.org**.*

1. Warm up the engine and place the motorcycle on the centerstand.

2. Remove the oil filler cap (**Figure 14**).

3. Place a drain pan under the engine. Use a 13/16 in. spark plug socket and remove the drain plug (**Figure 15**). Allow several minutes for the oil to drain completely.

4. On 1979 and earlier models, remove the 3 bolts securing the oil filter cover and remove the cover (**Figure 16**). Remove the oil filter.

5. On all TSCC engines, perform the following:

   a. Remove the nuts securing the oil pressure sensor cover (**Figure 17**).

   b. Remove the screw securing the sensor wire (**Figure 18**) and remove the wire.

   c. Remove the remaining nuts securing the oil filter cover and remove the cover (**Figure 19**). Remove the old filter.

6. Clean the filter cover and drain plug in solvent. Inspect the gasket on the drain plug and the O-ring on the filter cover (**Figure 20**). Replace the gasket or O-ring if they are not in good condition. Use a little grease to help hold the O-ring in the filter cover.

7. Install the filter (open end in) into the engine as shown in **Figure 21**.

8. Apply a thin layer of grease to the O-ring on the filter cover and install the cover.

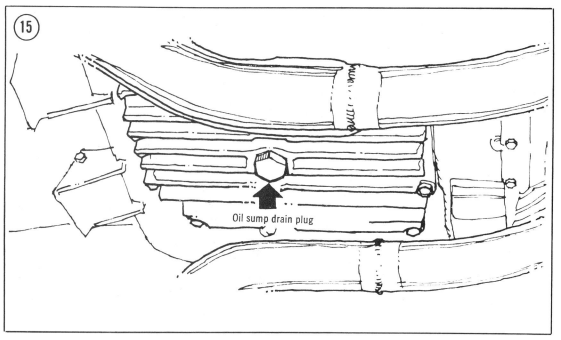

Oil sump drain plug

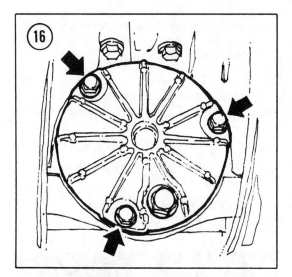

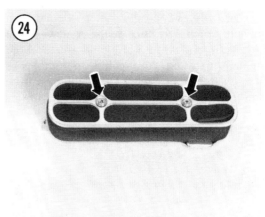

9. Hold in against the spring tension of the cover and install the washers and nuts securing the cover.

NOTE
On all TSCC engines, install the 3 flat washers on the lower studs only.

Tighten the nuts securing the filter cover fingertight.

10. On all TSCC engines, perform the following:

a. Connect the oil pressure sensor wire.

b. Install the cover over the pressure sensor and secure with the 2 nuts.

c. Ensure that the pressure sensor wire is routed through the notch in the cover as shown in **Figure 17**.

11. Tighten the nuts securing the filter cover gradually and evenly in a criss-cross manner. Take care not to overtighten the nuts. If a torque wrench is available, torque the nuts to 0.6-0.8 mkg (4.5-6.0 ft.-lb.).

12. Install the drain plug and torque to 1.0 mkg (7 ft.-lb.).

13. Add the recommended quantity and type of oil to the crankcase through the filler opening. Refer to **Table 2** and **Table 5**.

14. Start the engine and allow it to idle so the oil will circulate completely. When the engine has warmed up, shut it off, and wait at least 2 minutes. Check the oil level through the oil level window. If the level is below the "L" mark, add oil until the level is correct.

15. Check carefully for leaks around the filter cover and the drain plug.

Air Filter Service
(1979 and Earlier Models)

The foam air cleaner element should be cleaned and reoiled with every tune-up or as specified in **Table 1**. If the motorcycle is subjected to abnormally dirty conditions, the filter should be cleaned more frequently.

1. Remove the left side cover.

2. Remove the 2 screws securing the left sidecover of the air box and remove the sidecover (**Figure 22**).

3. Remove the screw securing the foam air cleaner element (**Figure 23**) and slide out the element.

4. Remove the screws securing the element frame (**Figure 24**) and separate the foam element from the frame (**Figure 25**).

5. Carefully wash the filter element in solvent, then in hot, soapy water. Rinse thoroughly in clean water and squeeze the element between your palms to remove as much water as possible. The element can be pressed between several layers of paper towels to speed up the drying process. Allow the element to dry completely.

CAUTION
Never wring or twist the foam element during the cleaning or reoiling process. The foam material can be damaged easily.

6. Carefully examine the element for any tears or splits in the foam material. Replace the element if it is damaged in any way.

7. Apply engine oil or special foam filter oil to the element and gently work the foam in your hands until the element is completely saturated with oil. Squeeze the element between your palms to remove all the excess oil.

NOTE
A good grade of special foam filter oil will adhere to the foam material better than plain engine oil and therefore provide better protection against dirt and dust.

8. Carefully install the foam element over the element frame and secure the frame with the screws (**Figure 24**).

9. Wipe out the air box with a clean rag.

10. Install the air filter element in the air box and secure with the mounting screw.

11. Install the air box sidecover and secure with 2 screws.

12. Install the left side cover.

Air Filter Service (All TSCC Models)

All machines with TSCC engines are equipped with a paper element air filter. The filter element should be cleaned every 2,000 miles (3,000 km) and replaced every 7,500 miles (12,000 km). The best way to clean the filter element is with compressed air. If the motorcycle is subjected to abnormally dirty conditions, the filter element should be checked, cleaned and replaced more frequently.

1. Remove the seat and remove the screw securing the filter cover (**Figure 26**). Remove the cover.

2. Lift up and remove the filter element (**Figure 27**).

3. Blow out the element with compressed air.

CAUTION
Only apply compressed air to the inside of the filter element. Air pressure applied to the outside will force the dirt back into the pores of the element material and destroy the filtering ability of the air cleaner.

When installing the filter element, make sure the spring inside the chamber secures the element. Install the filter cover.

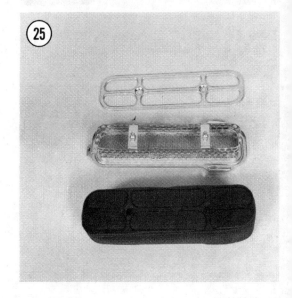

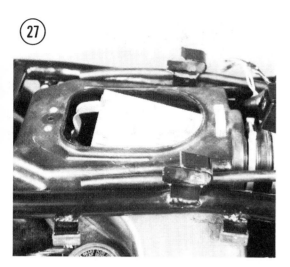

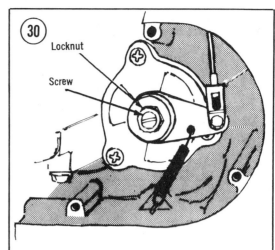

Locknut

Screw

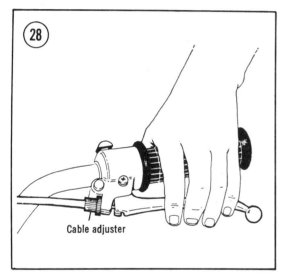

Cable adjuster

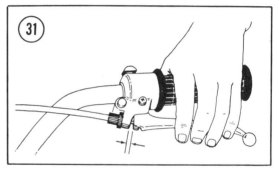

Clutch Cable Adjustment
(1979 and Earlier Models)

1. Pull back the rubber boot and loosen the large knurled locknut securing the cable adjuster on the clutch handlebar lever (**Figure 28**). Screw in the cable adjuster completely.

2. Use a hammer driven impact tool and remove the screws securing the clutch adjuster cover on the engine (**Figure 29**).

3. Refer to **Figure 30** and loosen the locknut securing the adjuster screw. Back out the locknut 2-3 turns.

4. Back out the adjuster screw 1-2 turns. Slowly screw in the adjuster screw until resistance is felt. Back out the adjuster screw 1/4 turn. Hold the adjuster screw and secure with the locknut.

5. Install the clutch adjuster cover and check the free play at the handlebar lever. Adjust the clutch lever adjuster until there is 2-3 mm (1/16-1/8 in.) of free play at the lever as shown in **Figure 31**.

Clutch Cable Adjustment
(All TSCC Models)

1. Pull back the rubber boot and loosen the locknut securing the cable adjuster (**Figure 32**).

2. Loosen the large knurled locknut and screw in the cable adjuster on the clutch handlebar lever (**Figure 28**).

3. Turn the cable adjuster on the engine until 2-3 mm (1/16-1/8 in.) of free play exists in the cable at the handlebar lever (**Figure 31**). Secure the cable adjuster with the locknut. Pull the rubber boot over the adjuster.

4. Future clutch cable adjustments can be made at the handlebar adjuster until the cable slack necessitates readjustment at the engine cable adjuster.

Brake Fluid Level

Check the brake fluid level in both master cylinder reservoirs (**Figure 33** and **Figure 34**) and maintain fluid level between upper and lower marks. To gain access to the rear master cylinder reservoir, remove the right side cover.

> *WARNING*
> *Use only glycol based brake fluid rated DOT 3 or DOT 4. Mixing silicon or petroleum based fluids into the brake system can cause brake component damage leading to brake system failure.*

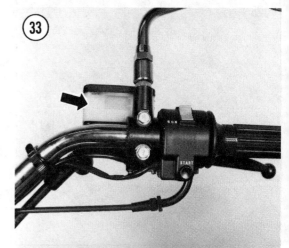

Brake Pad Inspection

Brake pad wear depends on a number of factors including riding conditions and rider habits. If most of your riding is in mountainous areas, stop-and-go traffic, or if you know you are heavy on the brakes, check them more frequently than recommended here.

Replace the front pads as a set when they are worn down to the red line as shown in **Figure 35**. The rear pad set should be replaced when the shoulder on the pads is worn as shown in **Figure 36**.

Wear on the front pads can be checked from the top edge of the caliper (**Figure 37**). All TSCC model front brake calipers are equipped with a small window to check brake wear as shown in **Figure 38**.

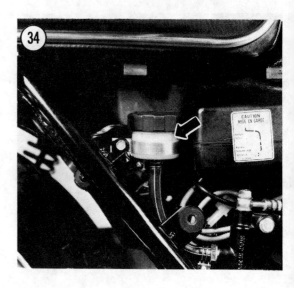

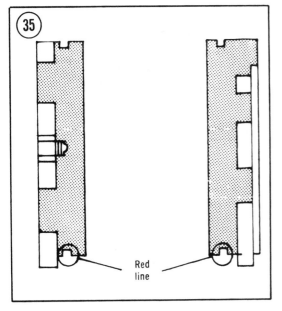

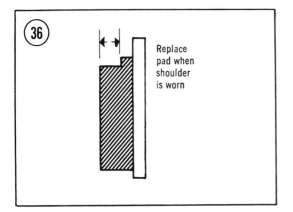

Red line

Replace pad when shoulder is worn

To gain access to the rear pads, snap off the plastic cover on the rear caliper (**Figure 39**).

Brake Pedal

Lightly oil the rear brake pedal pivot shaft. Work the oil in by moving the pedal up and down.

Brake Hoses

Check the brake hoses between both master cylinders and the front and rear calipers. If any leakage is present, tighten the connections or replace the leaking hoses. Top off the brake fluid and refer to *Bleeding* as outlined in Chapter Eleven.

Suzuki recommends that the brake fluid be changed every year and all brake hoses be replaced every 2 years. Refer to *Changing Brake Fluid* as outlined in Chapter Eleven.

Front Fork Oil

The front fork is the most adjustable component of the motorcycle. A front suspension properly set up can improve the handling characteristics of the machine as well as make it more comfortable to ride.

The front suspension requires the correct amount of damping oil in each fork leg if it is to perform correctly. Damping characteristics depend on oil viscosity therefore the handling of the motorcycle can be altered by a change from one weight oil to another. Only personal experience will enable you to find the weight of oil that is best for you and your style of riding. As a rule, the lighter oils are better suited to lighter riders and the heavier oils are usually best for heavier riders or machines that are equipped with heavy touring gear. Heavier oils might also be used if most of your riding is done with a passenger. Consult your local dealer concerning fork oils. He may be able to recommend the correct weight oil for your weight and the type of riding you will be doing. Refer to **Table 2** for the oil recommended by Suzuki.

It is impractical to add oil to a fork that has lost oil due to a leaky seal. The forks should be drained, flushed and refilled with the proper amount of oil. If seal leakage is indicated by oil oozing out around the fork wiper boots refer to Chapter Nine and replace the fork seals.

The following procedure describes how to change fork oil with the forks installed. If desired, a more efficient flushing of the forks can be achieved by removing the fork tubes as outlined in Chapter Nine.

1. Remove the 4 bolts securing the handlebars (**Figure 40**). Place a few rags on the fuel tank and carefully lay the handlebars back on the fuel tank.

2. Loosen the upper fork pinch bolt (**Figure 41**).

3. Remove the fork tube caps (**Figure 42**).

4. Place a drain pan under each fork leg and remove the fork drain screw (**Figure 43**).

Allow several minutes for the forks to drain completely. Compress the forks a few times to help force the oil out.

5. Flush each fork tube with clean solvent and allow it to drain thoroughly. Install the drain screw.

6. Refer to **Table 2** and **Table 5** and add the specified amount and type of fork oil to each fork tube. Use a graduate or a baby bottle (**Figure 44**) to ensure the oil amount is correct for each fork tube.

NOTE
Suzuki recommends that the fork oil level be measured, if possible, to ensure a more accurate filling. Proceed to Step 7 to correctly set the fork oil level.

7. Compress the forks completely and remove the springs.

8. Raise the rear of the motorcycle until the fork tubes are perfectly vertical. If it is inconvenient to raise the rear of the motorcycle, it will be necessary to remove both fork tubes. Refer to Chapter Nine.

9. Use an accurate ruler or the Suzuki oil level gauge (part No. 09943-74110) to ensure the oil level is as specified in **Table 5**.

NOTE
*An oil level measuring device can be locally fabricated as shown in **Figure 45**. Fill the fork with a few cc's more than the required amount of oil. Position the hose clamp on the top edge of the fork tube and draw out the excess oil. Oil is sucked out until the level reaches the small diameter hole. A precise oil level can be achieved with this simple device.*

10. Allow the oil to settle completely and recheck the oil level measurement. Adjust the oil level if necessary.

11. Install the fork springs with the closer coils pointing up.

12. Ensure the O-ring on the fork cap is in good condition and install the fork cap. Tighten the fork cap to 1.5-3.0 mkg (11-22 ft.-lb.). Torque the upper pinch bolt to 2.0-3.0 mkg (15-22 ft.-lb.).

13. Refer to **Figure 46** and install the handlebars. Ensure that the punch mark is properly aligned and equal clearance is present on both sides of the handlebar holders. Torque the handlebar clamp bolts to 1.2-2.0 mkg (9-14 ft.-lb.).

Steering Head Check

The steering head on all 1979 and earlier models is equipped with 36 loose ball bearings, 18 bearing balls in each of the upper and lower bearing assemblies. The steering head on all TSCC models is fitted with 2 tapered roller bearings. The steering head on all models should be checked for looseness at least as frequently as specified in **Table 1**.

Jack up the motorcycle so that the front wheel is clear of the ground. Hold onto the front fork tubes and rock the fork assembly back and forth (front to rear). If any looseness

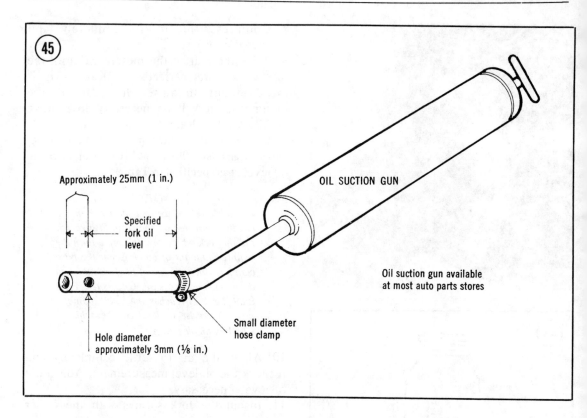

Approximately 25mm (1 in.)

Specified fork oil level

OIL SUCTION GUN

Oil suction gun available at most auto parts stores

Hole diameter approximately 3mm (⅛ in.)

Small diameter hose clamp

can be felt, refer to *Steering Head Adjustment* as outlined in Chapter Nine.

Throttle Grip

1. Loosen the screws securing the throttle grip and switch housing to the handlebar (**Figure 47**).
2. Slide the throttle grip assembly back off the handlebar.
3. Clean the end of the handlebar with a solvent-soaked rag. Dry the handlebar with a clean rag.
4. Apply a light coat of grease to the handlebar and slide the throttle grip assembly back into position.
5. Tighten the screws securing the throttle grip assembly. Check the action of the throttle. It should turn freely and snap back when released.

Swinging Arm

Use a good grade of chassis grease in a grease gun to lubricate the swinging arm. On models not equipped with a grease fitting, remove the pivot bolt. Refer to *Swinging Arm, Removal/Installation*, Chapter Ten.

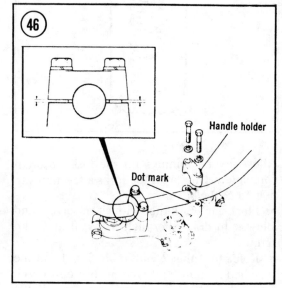

Handle holder

Dot mark

Oil Pressure Check

A special gauge is required for checking the oil pressure. Have the task performed by a dealer. Keep a record of pressure checks to determine if oil pressure decreases as engine wear increases.

All 1979 and earlier models are equipped with a high-volumne, low pressure oil pump. Normal oil pressure is 0.1 kg/cm² (1.42 psi) at 3,000 rpm.

All GS750 TSCC engines are fitted with high-pressure oil pumps. Normal oil pressure is 3.0-5.5 kg/cm² (43-78 psi) at 3,000 rpm and 60° C (140° F).

Speedometer Drive

The speedometer drive (**Figure 48**) should be removed, cleaned and greased when the front wheel bearings are serviced.

ENGINE TUNE-UP

An engine tune-up consists of several accurate and careful adjustments made in order to obtain maximum engine performance. Because different systems in an engine interact to affect overall performance, tune-ups must be carried out in the following order:

a. Valve clearance adjustment
b. Ignition adjustment and timing
c. Carburetor adjustment

Peform an engine tune-up every 3,000 miles. During every other tune-up, spark plugs and breaker points should be replaced.

Refer to **Table 6** for tune-up specifications.

NOTE
*All models **manufactured** after January 1, 1978 are engineered to meet stringent E.P.A. (Environmental Protection Agency) regulations. All tune-up specifications must be strictly adhered to whether the work is performed by the owner, dealer or an independent repair shop.*

Modifications to ignition system, exhaust system and carburetion are forbidden by law unless modifications (aftermarket exhaust systems, etc.) have received written approval from the E.P.A. Engine idle speed and carburetor synchronization adjustments are permissible. Carburetor air screw adjustments are preset and **must not** be altered.

Failure to comply with E.P.A. regulations may result in heavy fines.

Valve Clearance Adjustment (1979 and Earlier Models)

CAUTION
Valve clearance adjustments must be performed when engine is completely cold—not run for at least 12 hours. If engine is not cold, adjustments will not be accurate and engine damage may result.

Proper valve clearance is essential for engine performance and longevity. If valve clearances are too small, the valves may be burned or distorted. Excessive valve clearance will result in a noisy valve train and poor performance.

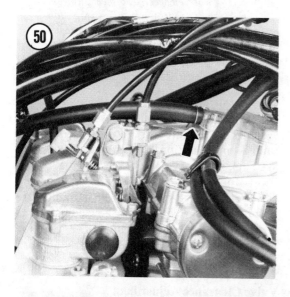

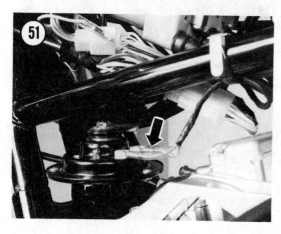

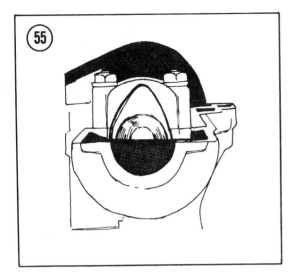

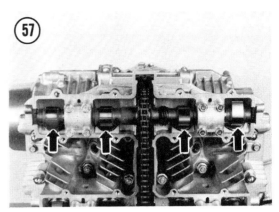

8. Remove screws securing contact breaker point cover (**Figure 53**).

9. Remove spark plug leads by grasping the spark plug caps; never pull on the plug lead itself.

10. Blow away any dirt that may have accumulated around spark plugs and remove the plugs.

11. To rotate crankshaft, use a wrench on the large hex portion of the advance governor (**Figure 54**).

CAUTION
Do not attempt to rotate crankshaft by using the small bolt that secures the advance governor or bolt may twist off.

Rotate crankshaft clockwise until one cam lobe is perpendicular to cylinder head surface (**Figure 55**).

12. Use a feeler gauge and check valve clearance (**Figure 56**). The clearance should be 0.03-0.08 mm (0.0012-0.0030 in.).

NOTE
It is recommended that Suzuki feeler gauge (part No. 09900-20803) be used to check valve clearances as it contains several small gauges not normally found in feeler gauge sets. Refer to Chapter One for tool description.

13. If valve clearance is within tolerance, repeat Steps 11 and 12 for remaining valves. If valve clearance is not as specified, the adjustment shim on the top of the tappet must be replaced.

14. Rotate tappet by hand until notch in tappet is fully exposed (**Figure 57**).

1. Remove the fuel tank; this is outlined in Chapter Seven.

2. Remove screws securing end covers to cylinder head (**Figure 49**) and remove the 4 covers.

3. Loosen clamp and remove breather hose from breather cover (**Figure 50**).

4. Disconnect horn wires (**Figure 51**).

5. Remove bolt securing horn bracket to frame and remove horn.

6. Remove bolts securing breather cover (**Figure 52**) and remove cover.

7. Remove bolts securing cam cover to cylinder head and remove cover. Note location of different length bolts.

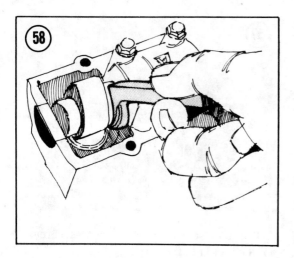

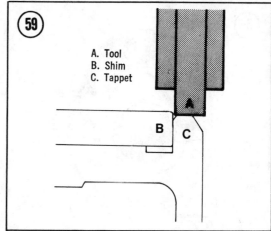

A. Tool
B. Shim
C. Tappet

15. Use a Suzuki tappet depressor (part No. 09916-64510) and press down on tappet (**Figure 58**). Make sure depressor bears on edge of tappet and not on the shim (**Figure 59**).

16. Use a small screwdriver in tappet notch to pop shim loose from tappet (**Figure 60**), otherwise the surface tension caused by the oiled parts makes the shim difficult to remove. Use tweezers and lift out shim (**Figure 61**).

> *CAUTION*
> *Never use a magnet to lift out adjustment shims. They are made of hardened steel and are easily magnetized. A magnetized part will attract and hold metal particles which will cause excessive wear. A magnetized adjustment shim could also lift out of a tappet while the engine is running and cause serious and expensive engine damage.*

17. Write down the size of the shim. Sizes are etched on each shim (**Figure 62**).

> *NOTE*
> *If etched size is not visible it will be necessary to measure shim thickness with a micrometer (**Figure 63**).*

18. Refer to **Table 7** and calculate required replacement shim as described in the following typical example:

Actual valve clearance 0.10 mm
Desired clearance (maximum) 0.08 mm
Difference (too large) 0.02 mm
Existing shim size 2.45 mm

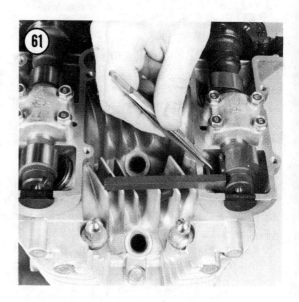

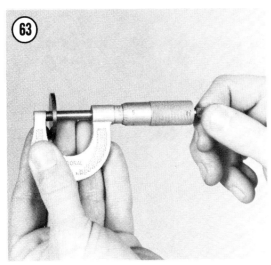

The clearance in this case is at least 0.02 mm too large. It must be reduced by at least that amount, through substitution of a thicker shim. **Table 7** indicates that the next larger shim, No. 8, is 2.50 mm. This shim will reduce the clearance by 0.05 mm. Clearance will then be 0.05 mm, well within the specified range.

19. Oil both sides of the replacement shim before installing on valve tappet. Install shim with etched number down against the tappet. Before purchasing all new shims, check to see if any shims removed from other valves may be reused. It is possible that one or several may work and save some expense.

20. After any shims have been replaced, rotate crankshaft several times to make sure shims are properly seated by the camshafts. Recheck valve clearances and readjust if necessary.

21. Check condition of cam cover gasket and replace if necessary. Install cam cover and torque bolts to 0.7-1.1 mkg (5.1-7.9 ft.-lb.) in a crisscross pattern.

22. Install breather cover, end covers, horn and fuel tank. If complete tune-up is being performed, do not install breaker point cover or spark plugs.

Valve Clearance Adjustment (All TSCC Engines)

CAUTION
Valve clearance adjustments must be performed when the engine is completely cold—not run for at least 12 hours. If the engine is not completely cold, the adjustments will not be accurate and valve damage may result.

1. Remove the screws securing the 4 end covers (**Figure 64**) and remove the covers.

2. Remove the fuel tank as outlined in Chapter Seven.

3. Spring open the clamp securing the breather hose to the breather cover (**Figure 65**) and disconnect the hose from the cover.

4. Remove the bolts securing the breather cover (**Figure 66**) and remove the cover.

5. Disconnect the wires from the horns (**Figure 67**). Remove the bolts securing the horn brackets to the frame and remove the horns.

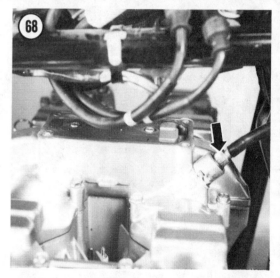

6. Disconnect the tachometer drive cable (**Figure 68**).

7. Remove each spark plug lead by pulling on the cap. Do not pull on the wire lead or it may be damaged. Tuck the spark plug leads into the upper frame to keep them clear of the engine. Blow away any dirt that may have accumulated around the spark plugs and remove the plugs. The crankshaft is easier to rotate by hand with the spark plugs removed.

8. Remove the 4 Phillips head screws from each end of the cam cover (**Figure 69**).

> NOTE
> The 4 Phillips head screws (**Figure 69**) are fitted with a special gasket that must be replaced each time the screws are removed.

9. Remove the bolts securing the cam cover and remove the cover. The left-front and right-rear cover bolts are slightly longer than the rest.

NOTE
To ease cam cover removal, tap around the sealing surface with a soft-faced mallet to help break it loose.

10. Remove the screws securing the ignition cover and remove the cover.

11. To rotate crankshaft, use a wrench on the large hex portion of the advance governor (**Figure 70**).

CAUTION
Do not attempt to rotate the crankshaft by using the small bolt that secures the advance governor or the bolt may twist off.

Use a 19 mm wrench and rotate the crankshaft until the "T" mark for cylinders 1-4 aligns with the timing pointer when viewed through the window of the signal generator unit (**Figure 71**). The signal generator unit is removed in **Figure 72** for clarity.

12. Observe the notches in the ends of each camshaft (**Figure 73**). Refer to **Table 8** to determine which valves to adjust depending on the position of the notches. The cylinders are numbered 1 through 4 from left-to-right as shown in **Figure 74**.

13. Use a feeler gauge between the valve stem and the adjuster as shown in **Figure 75** to determine the valve clearance. The correct valve clearance for all valves (intake and exhaust) is 0.09-0.13 mm (0.004-0.005 in.).

14. If the valve clearance is not as specified, perform the following:

  a. Loosen the valve adjuster locknut with a 9 mm wrench.
  b. Place the correct feeler gauge blade between the valve stem and adjuster and slowly rotate the adjuster until some resistance can be felt as the blade is inserted and withdrawn. The feeler gauge blade must move smoothy between the valve stem and the adjuster, but with noticeable resistance and no free play.

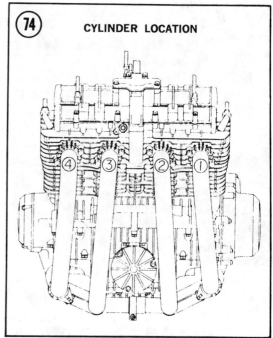

CYLINDER LOCATION

NOTE
The Suzuki adjuster tool (part No. 09917-14910) is recommended for use on the square shaft end of the valve adjusters. This small and inexpensive Suzuki tool is much easier to use around the confines of the cylinder head than a larger wrench.

c. Hold the adjuster carefully and tighten the adjuster locknut (**Figure 76**).

d. Recheck the valve clearance. Frequently the clearance will change slightly as the locknut is tightened. Readjust if necessary.

15. Rotate the crankshaft 360° until the "T" mark for cylinder 1-4 is again aligned with the timing pointer. The notches in the ends of the camshaft must now point in the opposite direction as noted in Step 12.

16. Refer to **Table 8** and check the valve clearance for the other valves. Adjust the valve clearance, if necessary, as previously described.

17. After checking and/or adjusting all the valve clearances, rotate the crankshaft several times and recheck all clearances. Readjust the valves as necessary. Make sure all adjuster locknuts are tight. If a torque wrench is available, tighten all locknuts to 0.9-1.1 mkg (6.5-8.0 ft.-lb.).

18. Install the cam cover gasket. Use a new gasket if possible. Make sure that all 4 half-moon shaped rubber end plugs (**Figure 77**) are in place.

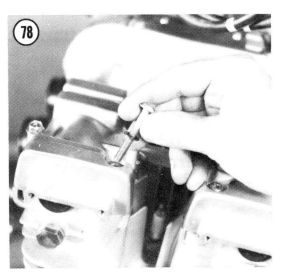

19. Carefully position the cam cover on the cylinder head so the gasket is not disturbed. Rotate the exposed end of the tachometer drive gear as the cam cover is installed to allow the drive gear to engage the camshaft.

CAUTION
The tachometer drive gear must engage the camshaft as the cam cover is installed or the gear will be damaged when the cover bolts are tightened.

20. Install the cam cover bolts. The 2 longer bolts are positioned in the left-front and right-rear positions. Tighten all the bolts gradually and evenly in a crisscross manner and torque them to 0.9-1.0 mkg (6.5-7.0 ft.-lb.).
21. Use new gaskets on the 4 Phillips head screws and install them in the ends of the cam cover (**Figure 78**).
22. Install the breather cover gasket with the opening in the gasket facing forward. Install the breather cover and secure with the 4 bolts. Torque the bolts to 0.9-1.0 mkg (6.5-7.0 ft.-lb.). Connect the breather hose to the breather cover and air box.
23. Install the 4 camshaft end covers.
24. Install the horns and connect the horn wires.
25. Connect the tachometer drive cable.
26. Install the spark plugs and connect the 4 spark plug leads. Make sure the caps fit securely over the spark plugs.

27. Install the fuel tank as outlined in Chapter Seven.

Ignition Timing (1980 and Later Models)

All 1980 and later models are equipped with a breakerless electronic ignition system. No routine service or adjustment is necessary.

Spark Plug Cleaning/Replacement

1. Grasp high-tension leads by the spark plug caps and pull them off; never pull on the lead itself.
2. Blow away any dirt that may have accumulated in spark plug wells with compressed air.

WARNING
Wear safety goggles or glasses when doing this to prevent particles from getting in your eyes.

3. Remove spark plugs with a spark plug wrench.

NOTE
If plugs are difficult to remove, apply penetrating oil around the base of the plugs and allow it to soak in for 10-20 minutes.

4. Inspect spark plugs carefully. Refer to **Figure 79**. Check for broken or cracked porcelain, excessively eroded electrodes and

SPARK PLUG CONDITION

(79)

NORMAL
- Identified by light tan or gray deposits on the firing tip.
- Can be cleaned.

GAP BRIDGED
- Identified by deposit buildup closing gap between electrodes.
- Caused by oil or carbon fouling. If deposits are not excessive, the plug can be cleaned.

OIL FOULED
- Identified by wet black deposits on the insulator shell bore and electrodes.
- Caused by excessive oil entering combustion chamber through worn rings and pistons, excessive clearance between valve guides and stems, or worn or loose bearings. Can be cleaned. If engine is not repaired, use a hotter plug.

CARBON FOULED
- Identified by black, dry fluffy carbon deposits on insulator tips, exposed shell surfaces and electrodes.
- Caused by too cold a plug, weak ignition, dirty air cleaner, too rich a fuel mixture, or excessive idling. Can be cleaned.

LEAD FOULED
- Identified by dark gray, black, yellow, or tan deposits or a fused glazed coating on the insulator tip.
- Caused by highly leaded gasoline. Can be cleaned.

WORN
- Identified by severely eroded or worn electrodes.
- Caused by normal wear. Should be replaced.

FUSED SPOT DEPOSIT
- Identified by melted or spotty deposits resembling bubbles or blisters.
- Caused by sudden acceleration. Can be cleaned.

OVERHEATING
- Identified by a white or light gray insulator with small black or gray brown spots and with bluish-burnt appearance of electrodes.
- Caused by engine overheating, wrong type of fuel, loose spark plugs, too hot a plug, or incorrect ignition timing. Replace the plug.

PREIGNITION
- Identified by melted electrodes and possibly blistered insulator. Metallic deposits on insulator indicate engine damage.
- Caused by wrong type of fuel, incorrect ignition timing or advance, too hot a plug, burned valves, or engine overheating. Replace the plug.

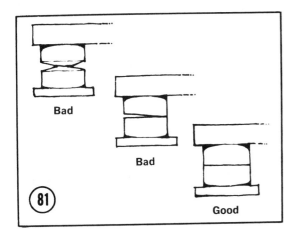

1. Always use good tools and tune-up equipment. The money saved from one or two home tune-ups will more than pay for good tools; from that point on you're money ahead. Refer to Chapter One for suitable types of tune-up/test equipment.

2. The purchase of a small set of ignition wrenches and one or two "screwholding" or magnetic screwdrivers will ease the work in replacing breaker points and help eliminate loss of small screws.

3. Always purchase quality ignition components.

4. When using a feeler gauge to set breaker points, be sure that the blade is wiped clean before inserting between the points.

5. Be sure that points are fully open when setting gap with a feeler gauge.

6. Be sure that feeler gauge is not tilted or twisted when it is inserted between the contacts. Closely observe the points and withdraw the feeler gauge slowly and carefully. A slight resistance should be felt; however, the movable contact points must *not* "spring back" even slightly when the feeler gauge blade is removed.

7. If breaker points are only slightly pitted, they can be "dressed down" lightly with a small ignition point file or Flex-Stone. *Do not* use sandpaper as it leaves a residue on the points.

8. After points have been installed, always ensure that they are properly aligned, or premature pitting or burning will result. See **Figure 81**. Bend only the *fixed* half of the points, not the movable arm.

9. When point gap has been set, clean contacts with lacquer thinner or special contact cleaner spray. Close the contacts on a clean piece of paper such as a business card and wipe contacts a few times to remove any traces of oil or grease. A small amount of oil or grease on the contact surfaces will cause the points to prematurely burn or arc.

10. When connecting a timing light or timing tester, always follow the manufacturer's instructions.

excessive carbon or oil-fouling. If deposits are light, plugs may be cleaned in solvent with a wire brush or with a special spark plug sandblast cleaner.

5. Use a round feeler gauge and gap the spark plugs to 0.6-0.7 mm (0.024-0.028 in.) by bending the side electrode (**Figure 80**). Do not file electrodes to correct the gap.

6. Install spark plugs finger-tight and tighten an additional 1/8-1/4 turn. If a torque wrench is available, torque plugs to 1.9 mkg (14 ft.-lb.).

Ignition System
Tune-up Hints

The following list of general hints will help make a tune-up easier and more successful.

Contact Breaker Point and Timing Adjustment (1979 and Earlier Models)

1. Remove breaker point cover (**Figure 82**).
2. Use a wrench on large hex portion of advance governor (**Figure 83**) and rotate crankshaft clockwise until breaker points for cylinders No. 1 and 4 are fully open.
3. Loosen 2 screws securing breaker points to the breaker plate (**Figure 84**) and set point gap to 0.3-0.4 mm (0.012-0.016 in.) with a feeler gauge (**Figure 85**). Tighten screws and recheck point gap. Readjust if necessary.

> *NOTE*
> *When installing new breaker points for cylinders 2-3, do not loosen the screws securing the half-plate (**Figure 86**). Only remove the screws securing the breaker points and install the new set. Set the breaker point gap for cylinders 2-3, as previously described for cylinders 1-4. It is not necessary to be exact at this time. The final gap is set when the timing for cylinders 2-3 is set.*

4. Rotate engine clockwise until "F" mark for cylinders No.1 and 4 is aligned with mark on timing plate as viewed through window in breaker plate. See **Figure 87**. Make sure the "1-4" mark identifying cylinders No.1 and 4 is visible.

5. Connect a timing tester or continuity device to electrical terminal (**Figure 88**) and a good ground on the engine.
6. Loosen 3 screws securing breaker plate (**Figure 89**) and rotate plate until points just begin to open (no continuity on tester). Tighten breaker plate screws. Rotate crankshaft a few turns to double check the adjustment. Readjust if necessary.
7. Rotate crankshaft clockwise until "F" mark for cylinders No. 2 and No. 3 is aligned with mark on timing plate (**Figure 90**). Make sure the "2-3" mark identifying cylinders No. 2 and No. 3 is visible.

3

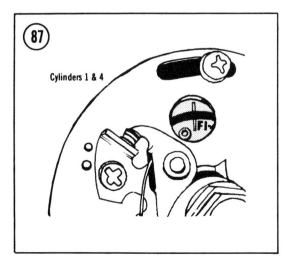

Cylinders 1 & 4

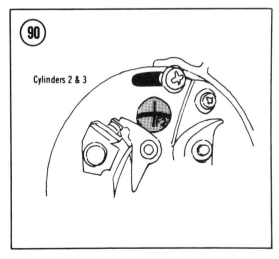

Cylinders 2 & 3

8. Connect continuity device to point terminal (**Figure 91**) and ground.

9. Loosen screws securing half-plate (**Figure 92**) and adjust plate until points just begin to open (no continuity). Tighten screws, rotate engine and double check the adjustment. Readjust if necessary.

> *NOTE*
> *This completes breaker point adjustment and static engine timing. More precise engine timing can be achieved with a timing light. If a timing light is available proceed to the next step.*

10. Connect timing light to cylinder No. 1 or 4 in accordance with the light manufacturer's instructions.

11. Start and warm up engine. Run engine below 1,500 rpm and direct timing light into window on breaker plate and observe timing marks. The "F" mark should be in perfect alignment (**Figure 87**). If timing is not correct, loosen breaker plate screws (**Figure 89**) and gradually move plate until marks are perfectly aligned. Tighten screws.

12. Increase engine speed above 2,500 rpm. Check that advance timing marks align (**Figure 93**). If timing marks are not perfectly aligned, loosen breaker plate screws and move breaker plate until marks are perfectly aligned. Tighten screws.

> *NOTE*
> *If timing mark alignment below 1,500 rpm and above 2,500 is difficult to obtain, remove the breaker plate and make sure advance governor weights move freely without binding. If advance governor weights are free and a slight variation in timing marks still exists, set the timing using the 2,500 rpm marks. This ensures timing is perfect during the engine's normal rpm range.*

13. Repeat Steps 11 and 12 for cylinders No. 2 and No. 3. To adjust timing for cylinders No. 2 and No. 3 loosen screws in the half-plate (**Figure 92**).

14. Install breaker point cover.

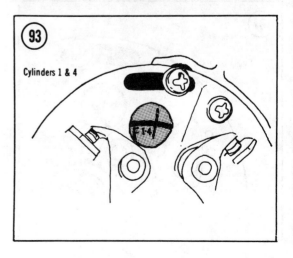

Cylinders 1 & 4

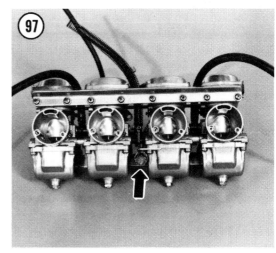

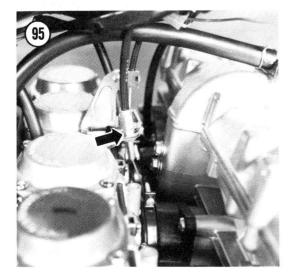

Throttle Cable Adjustment

Throttle cable free play should be 1-1.5 mm (1/32-1/16 in.). If cable adjustment is necessary, loosen locknuts on cable adjusters and turn adjusters in or out until specified free play is achieved. Tighten locknuts. Refer to **Figure 94** for models equipped with 2 cables and **Figure 95** for all single-cable models.

Carburetor Adjustments

NOTE
*Carburetors on models **manufactured** after January 1, 1978 are flow tested and preset at the factory for maximum performance within regulations set by the E.P.A. (Environmental Protection Agency). Under no circumstances should the carburetors be modified or the air screws adjusted. Heavy fines are imposed for such violations.*

All other tune-up procedures must be carried out before carburetors can be adjusted effectively.

1. Start and warm up engine. Turn throttle stop screw until engine idles between 1,000 and 1,200 rpm. See **Figure 96** for 1979 and earlier models. See **Figure 97** for later models.

2. On models manufactured *before* January 1, 1978, perform the following:

    a. Screw in air screw (**Figure 98**) on each carburetor until it bottoms out. Be careful not to overtighten and damage the screw. Back each screw out 1 1/4 turns. This is the basic setting.

b. Gradually adjust each air screw for maximum engine rpm. This should be between 1 and 2 turns open.

c. Reset idle speed to 1,000-1,200 rpm.

Carburetor Balancing (Synchronization)

Carburetor balancing, or synchronization, is essential for maximum performance. A special gauge, called a manometer, is required to do this job accurately. The one shown in **Figure 99** is marketed by Suzuki (part No. 00913-13120). There are others on the market that work equally well with virtually the same procedure.

1. Before beginning work, the gauge must be calibrated; this must be done each time the gauge is used. Unscrew the 4 mm Allen bolt from the right cylinder air intake (**Figure 100**). Screw in one balancer adapter. Connect the first hose of balancer to adapter.

2. Start engine; run it at a steady 1,200 rpm.

3. Turn air screw for the tube that is connected until steel ball lines up with center mark on tube (**Figure 99**).

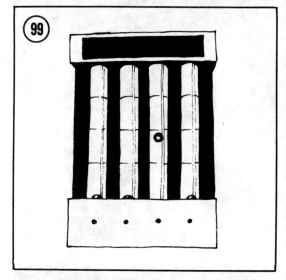

4. Remove the calibrated hose from the right cylinder and connect the other 3 hoses, one at a time, to the same cylinder adapter.

5. Turn air screw for the connected tube until steel ball lines up with center mark on tube. The 4 air tubes have now been calibrated to each other.

6. Remove 4 mm Allen bolt from the other 3 cylinders and install a balancer adapter in each air intake.

7. Connect all 4 hoses of the synchronization gauge to all 4 cylinders. Start and run the engine at a steady speed between 1,500 and 2,000 rpm.

8. On all 1979 and earlier models, if all 4 balls are positioned on the center line as shown in **Figure 99**, the carburetors are synchronized. Further adjustment is then unnecessary; proceed to Step 10. If one or more carburetors are out of sync, perform the following:

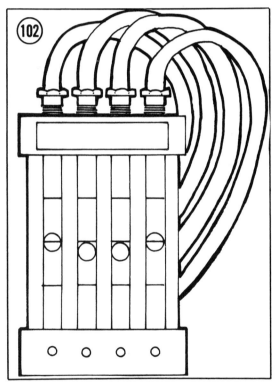

a. Refer to Chapter Seven and remove the fuel tank to gain access to the top of each carburetor. Block the vacuum hose connected to the fuel valve.

b. Remove the screws securing the cover on each carburetor that must be adjusted.

c. Loosen the locknut on the slide lifter adjusting screw (**Figure 101**).

d. Start the engine and turn the adjusting screw until the ball in the gauge is aligned as shown in **Figure 99**.

> *NOTE*
> *Suzuki throttle valve adjusting wrench (part No. 09913-14520) combines a screwdriver and wrench into one tool. This tool can greatly ease the adjustment procedure.*
> *There is usually sufficient fuel left in each carburetor to run the engine long enough to complete the adjustment procedure.*

e. Hold the adjusting screw and secure with the locknut. Replace the carburetor cover. Repeat the procedure for other carburetors as necessary.

f. Install the fuel tank.

9. On all models with CV carburetors, if all 4 balls are positioned as shown in **Figure 102**, the carburetors are synchronized. Further adjustment is then unnecessary; proceed to Step 10. If one or more carburetors are out of sync, perform the following:

a. Remove the fuel tank as outlined in Chapter Seven. Block the vacuum hose connected to the fuel valve.

b. The number 3 carburetor (right side inboard carburetor) is not equipped with a throttle valve adjustment screw, therefore all other carburetors must be synchronized to this carburetor (**Figure 103**).

c. If number 2 carburetor (left side inboard carburetor) is out of sync, loosen the locknut securing the center adjustment screw (**Figure 103**) and rotate the screw until the gauge ball (**Figure 102**) is correct. Secure the adjustment screw with the locknut.

> *NOTE*
> *A socket on a long extension and a long, thin blade screwdriver are necessary to perform this adjustment. Suzuki throttle valve adjust wrench (part No. 09913-14910), is a set of 2 long, thin tools designed to perform this adjustment*

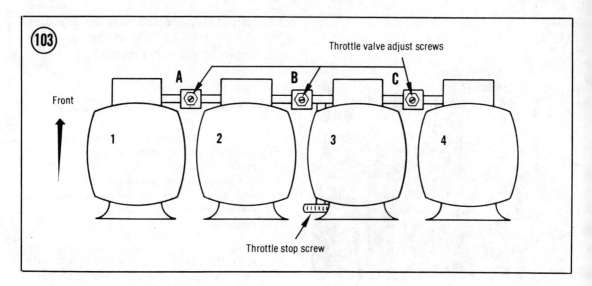

procedure. *If desired, this tool can be ordered from your Suzuki dealer.*

d. If either outboard carburetor is out of sync, loosen the locknut on the respective adjustment screw (**Figure 103**) and rotate the screw until the gauge balls are correct as shown in **Figure 102**.

e. Install the fuel tank.

10. Remove the synchronization gauge and all the balance adapters. Install the 4 mm Allen bolts. Make sure each bolt is fitted with a good washer.

11. Set the engine idle speed to 950-1,150 rpm.

Compression Test

During every tune-up, check the cylinder compression. Record the results and compare them at the next check. A running record will show trends in deterioration so that corrective action can be taken before complete failure occurs.

Both a dry test and a wet test should be carried out to isolate trouble in cylinders or valves.

1. Warm the engine to normal operating temperature.

2. Remove spark plugs.

3. Connect compression tester to one cylinder following the manufacturer's instructions.

4. Check to make sure the choke is off. With assistance, hold the throttle fully open and crank the engine until gauge needle ceases to rise. Record results and remove tester.

5. Repeat Steps 3 and 4 for the other cylinders.

When interpreting the results, actual readings are not as important as differences between readings. Cylinder compression should be 9-12 kg/cm^2 (128-171 psi). A reading below 7.0 kg/cm^2 (100 psi) indicates an engine overhaul is due. Maximum difference between cylinders is 2 kg/cm^2 (28 psi).

To determine whether the compression problem is due to valves or piston rings, perform a second compression test with approximately 15 cc (1/2 oz) of motor oil in each cylinder. If the compression reading rises significantly, piston rings and/or cylinder bore are probably worn. If the wet compression test changes little from the dry test, the valves are probably burned.

STORAGE

Several months of inactivity can cause serious problems and general deterioration of your bike. This is especially important in areas with extremely cold winters. During the winter, you should prepare your bike carefully for "hibernation."

Selecting a Storage Area

Most cyclists store their bikes in their home garage. If you do not have a garage, there are other facilities for rent or lease in most areas. When selecting an area, consider the following points.

1. The storage area must be dry; there should be no dampness or excessive humidity. A heated area is not necessary, but it should be insulated to minimize extreme temperature variations.

2. Avoid buildings with large window areas. If this is not possible, mask the window to keep direct sunlight off the bike.

3. Avoid buildings in industrial areas where factories are liable to emit corrosive fumes. Also avoid buildings near large bodies of salt water.

4. Select an area where there is minimum risk of fire, theft or vandalism. Check with your insurance agent to make sure that your insurance covers the bike where it is stored.

Preparing Bike for Storage

Careful preparation will minimize deterioration and make it easier to restore the bike to service later. Use the following procedure.

1. Wash the bike completely. Make certain you remove any road salt which may have accumulated during the first weeks of winter. Wax all painted and polished surfaces, including any chromed areas.

2. Run the engine for 20-30 minutes to stabilize oil temperature. Drain oil, regardless of mileage since last oil change. Replace the oil filter and fill engine with normal quantity of fresh oil.

3. Remove battery and coat cable terminals with petroleum jelly. If there is evidence of acid spillage in the battery box, neutralize with baking soda, wash clean and repaint the damaged area. Store the battery in a warm area and recharge it every two weeks.

4. Drain all gasoline from fuel tank, interconnecting hoses and carburetors. Leave fuel petcock in the RESERVE position. As an alternative, a fuel preservative may be added to the fuel. This preservative is available from many motorcycle shops and marine equipment suppliers.

5. Remove spark plugs and add a small quantity of oil to each cylinder. Turn the engine a few revolutions by hand to distribute the oil and install the spark plugs.

6. Check tire pressures. Move machine to storage area and store it on the centerstand.

After Storage

Before returning the motorcycle to service, thoroughly check all fasteners, suspension components and brake components. Check the oil level and top up if necessary. If possible, change the engine oil and filter. The oil may have become contaminated with condensation.

Make sure the battery is fully charged and the electrolyte level is correct before installing the battery. Fill the fuel tank with fresh gasoline.

Before starting the engine, remove the spark plugs and spin the engine over a few times to blow out the excess storage oil. Place a rag over the cylinder head to keep the oil off the engine. Install new spark plugs and connect the spark plug leads.

Tables are on the following pages.

Table 1   MAINTENANCE AND LUBRICATION SCHEDULE

Every fuel stop or every month	
	Check engine oil level
	Check tire condition and inflation
	Check battery electrolyte level
	Check wheels for damage or loose spokes
Initial 600 miles (1,000 km)	
	Check all engine, exhaust system and frame fasteners and tighten if necessary.
	Check and/or adjust valve clearance
	Check and/or adjust contact breaker points and ignition timing (1979 and earlier models)
	Change engine oil and oil filter
	Adjust engine idle speed
	Adjust clutch
	Check brake fluid level
	Check brake pad wear
	Clean, lubricate and adjust drive chain
	Check and/or adjust steering stem
	Adjust throttle and choke cables (see Note 1)
	Perform compression check
Every 2,000 miles (3,000 km, see Note 2)	
	Change engine oil (1979 and earlier models)
	Clean paper air cleaner element (all TSCC models)
Every 3,000 miles (5,000 km)	
	Lubricate throttle, clutch and choke cables with oil or special cable lubricant
	Lubricate brake pedal shaft
Every 4,000 miles (6,000 km, see Note 3)	
	Perform all maintenance items specified under initial 600 miles (1,000 km) plus the following:
	Change engine oil and filter (all TSCC models)
	Clean spark plugs and adjust gap
	Clean and reoil foam air cleaner element (1979 and earlier models)
	Inspect battery electrolyte level; check specific gravity of electrolyte with hydrometer
	Check oil pressure
	Change fork oil
Every 7,500 miles (12,000 km, see Note 4)	
	Perform all maintenance items specified under initial 600 miles (1,000 km) and 4,000 mile (6,000 km) service plus the following:
	Replace spark plugs
	Replace paper air cleaner element (all TSCC models)
	Lubricate throttle grip with grease
	Lubricate speedometer and tachometer cables with grease

(continued)

Table 1   MAINTENANCE AND LUBRICATION SCHEDULE (continued)

Every year	
	Bleed and change brake fluid
Every 2 years, 15,000 miles (24,000 km)	
	Replace fuel line Replace brake hoses Lubricate steering stem bearings and swing arm bearings with grease

NOTES:
1. 1978 and earlier models are not equipped with choke cables.
2. For all 1978 and earlier models, 1,500 miles (2,500 km).
3. For all 1978 and earlier models, 3,000 miles (5,000 km).
4. For all 1978 and earlier models, 6,000 miles (10,000 km).

Table 2   RECOMMENDED FUEL AND LUBRICANTS

Fuel	Unleaded or low-lead; 85-95 octane
Engine/transmission oil	SAE 10W/40 SE or SD rated
Fork oil	SAE 10 or 20 fork oil or A.T.F. (automatic transmission fluid) mixed 1:1 with SAE 10W/30
Brake fluid	Rated DOT 3 or DOT 4

WARNING
   Use only glycol based brake fluid rated DOT 3 or DOT 4. Mixing silicon or petroleum based fluids can cause brake component damage leading to brake system failure.

Table 3   TIRE PRESSURE

	Cold Inflation Pressure			
	Solo Riding		Dual Riding	
	PSI	KG/CM^2	PSI	KG/CM^2
Front Normal riding	25	1.75	25	1.75
Continuous high speed riding	28	2.00	28	2.00
Rear Normal riding	28	2.00	32	2.25
Continuous high speed riding	32	2.25	40	2.80

3

Table 4   TORQUE SPECIFICATIONS

ENGINE			
Item	**Bolt Diameter (mm)**	**Mkg**	**Ft.-lb.**
Clutch sleeve hub nut	24	4.0-6.0	29.0-43.4
Drive sprocket nut		4.0-6.0	29.0-43.4
Drive sprocket nut (1979 and earlier models)		**4.0-6.0**	**29.0-43.4**
(TSCC models)		**9.0-10.0**	**65.0-72.5**
Starter clutch bolt	8	1.5-2.0	10.8-14.5
Contact breaker cam bolt	8	1.8-2.8	13.0-20.3
Cam chain tensioner locknut	6	1.0-1.2	7.2-8.7
Camshaft sprocket bolt	6	1.0	7.2
Cylinder head bolt	6	0.7-1.1	5.1-8.0
Cylinder head nut	8	3.5-4.0	25.3-29.0
Cylinder head cover bolt	6	0.7-1.1	5.1-8.0
Camshaft holder bolt	6	0.8-1.2	5.8-8.7
Oil filter cover nut	6	0.6-0.8	4.3-5.8
Oil pan bolt	6	1.0	7.2
Crankcase bolt	6	1.0	7.2
Crankcase bolt	8	2.0	14.5
Engine mounting bolt	10	4.0	29.0
Engine mounting bolt	8	2.0	14.5
Alternator rotor bolt	12	6.0-7.0	43.4-50.6
Spark plug	14	1.9	14.0

CHASSIS			
Item	**Bolt Diameter (mm)**	**Mkg**	**Ft.-lb.**
Front axle holder nut	8	1.5-2.5	10.8-18.1
Front axle nut	12	3.6-5.2	26.0-37.6
Front fork tube upper pinch nut (right and left)	10	2.0-3.0	14.5-21.7
Front fork tube lower pinch bolt (right and left)	10	2.0-3.0	14.5-21.7
Steering stem pinch nut	8	1.5-2.5	10.8-18.1
Steering stem bolt	12	3.6-5.2	26.0-37.6
Handlebar clamp bolt	8	1.2-2.0	8.7-14.5
Brake hose union bolt	10		
Brake caliper air bleeder	8	0.6-0.9	4.3-6.5
Front brake caliper mounting bolt	10	2.5-4.0	18.1-29.0
Rear brake caliper mounting bolt	10	2.0-3.0	14.5-21.7
Front master cylinder mounting bolt	6	0.6-1.0	4.3-7.2
Rear master cylinder mounting bolt	8	1.5-2.5	10.8-18.1
Chain adjuster support bolt	8	1.5-2.0	10.8-14.5
Brake hose coupler	10	1.3-1.8	9.4-13.0
Rear swing arm pivot shaft nut	14	5.0-8.0	36.2-57.8
Rear shock absorber nut (upper and lower)	10	2.0-3.0	14.5-21.7
Rear axle nut	16	8.5-11.5	62.0-83.0
Rear brake torque link nut (front and rear)	10	2.0-3.0	14.5-21.7
Front footrest bolt	10	2.7-4.3	19.5-31.1

Table 5   CAPACITIES

Fuel tank			
"L" models	13 liters	3.4 U.S. gal.	2.9 Imp. gal.
All others	18 liters	4.8 U.S. gal.	4.0 Imp. gal.
Engine/transmission oil			
Without filter change			
TSCC engines	3.2 liters	3.4 U.S. qt.	2.8 Imp. qt.
All others	3.4 liters	3.6 U.S. qt.	3.0 Imp. qt.
With filter change			
(All models)	3.8 liters	4.0 U.S. qt.	3.3 Imp. qt.
After overhaul			
TSCC engines	4.0 liters	4.2 U.S. qt.	3.5 Imp. qt.
All others	4.2 liters	4.4 U.S. qt.	3.7 Imp. qt.
Front fork oil			
"LN" Models	280 cc	9.5 U.S. oz.	9.9 Imp. oz.
All "TSCC" Models	237 cc	8.0 U.S. oz.	8.3 Imp. oz.
All other models	180 cc	6.0 U.S. oz.	6.3 Imp. oz.
Fork oil level (See note)			
"LN" Models	202 mm (8.0 in.)		
All "TSCC" Models	229 mm (9.0 in.)		
All other models	206 mm (8.1 in.)		

NOTE: Remove spring and measure oil level from top of fork leg with fork leg held vertical and fully compressed.

Table 6   TUNE-UP SPECIFICATIONS

Recommended spark plugs	
All TSCC engines	NGK D8EA or ND X24ES-U
All other models	NGK B8ES or ND W24ES
Spark plug gap	0.6-0.7 mm (0.024-0.028 in.)
Breaker point gap	0.3-0.4 mm (0.012-0.016 in.)
Ignition timing	
All TSCC engines (preset—non-adjustable)	15 degrees B.T.D.C. below 1,500 rpm
	35 degrees B.T.D.C. above 2,350 rpm
All other models	17 degrees B.T.D.C. below 1,500 rpm
	37 degrees B.T.D.C. above 2,500 rpm
Valve clearance	
All TSCC engines	0.09-0.13 mm (0.004-0.005 in.)
All other models	0.03-0.08 mm (0.0012-0.0031 in.)
Idle speed	950-1,150 rpm
Carburetor air screw	
All models manufactured after Janurary 1978	Preset (non-adjustable)
All earlier models	2 turns open

Table 7   TAPPET SHIM SIZES

No.	Thickness (mm)	Part No.	No.	Thickness	Part No.
1	2.15	12892-45000	11	2.65	12892-45010
2	2.20	12892-45001	12	2.70	12892-45011
3	2.25	12892-45002	13	2.75	12892-45012
4	2.30	12892-45003	14	2.80	12892-45013
5	2.35	12892-45004	15	2.85	12892-45014
6	2.40	12892-45005	16	2.90	12892-45015
7	2.45	12892-45006	17	2.95	12892-45016
8	2.50	12892-45007	18	3.00	12892-45017
9	2.55	12892-45008	19	3.05	12892-45018
10	2.60	12892-45009	20	3.10	12892-45019

Table 8   VALVE ADJUSTMENT ORDER (All TSCC Engines)

Camshaft notch position	Valves to adjust
Intake and exhaust notches point out	No. 1 intake No. 1 exhaust No. 3 intake No. 2 exhaust
Intake and exhaust notches point in	No. 4 intake No. 4 exhaust No. 2 intake No. 3 exhaust

4

ENGINE (1979 AND EARLIER)

The GS750 engine is an air-cooled, 4-cylinder, 4-cycle model equipped with dual overhead camshafts (DOHC). The crankshaft is supported by six main (ball and roller) bearings in a horizontally split crankcase.

The camshafts are chain driven from the crankshaft. Cam chain tension is controlled automatically by a spring-loaded slipper tensioner which bears against the rear vertical run of the chain.

The engine and transmission are lubricated from a common wet-sump oil supply. The clutch is a wet-plate type located inside the right engine cover.

This chapter provides complete service and overhaul procedures for the 1979 and earlier GS750 engines. Refer to Chapter Six for transmission and clutch procedures.

All engine upper end repair, including camshafts, cylinder head, and cylinder block, can be performed with the engine installed in the motorcycle. Engine removal is necessary to perform repair of the crankshaft, transmission, and certain components of the gearshift and kickstarter mechanisms.

CAMSHAFTS

Removal

1. Perform *Carburetor Removal* as outlined in Chapter Seven.
2. Remove screws securing end covers to cylinder head (**Figure 1**) and remove 4 covers.
3. Loosen clamp and remove breather hose from breather cover (**Figure 2**).
4. Disconnect horn wires (**Figure 3**).
5. Remove bolt securing horn bracket to frame and remove horn.
6. Remove bolts securing breather cover (**Figure 4**) and remove cover.
7. Remove bolts securing cam cover to cylinder head and remove cover. Note the location of different length bolts, and that

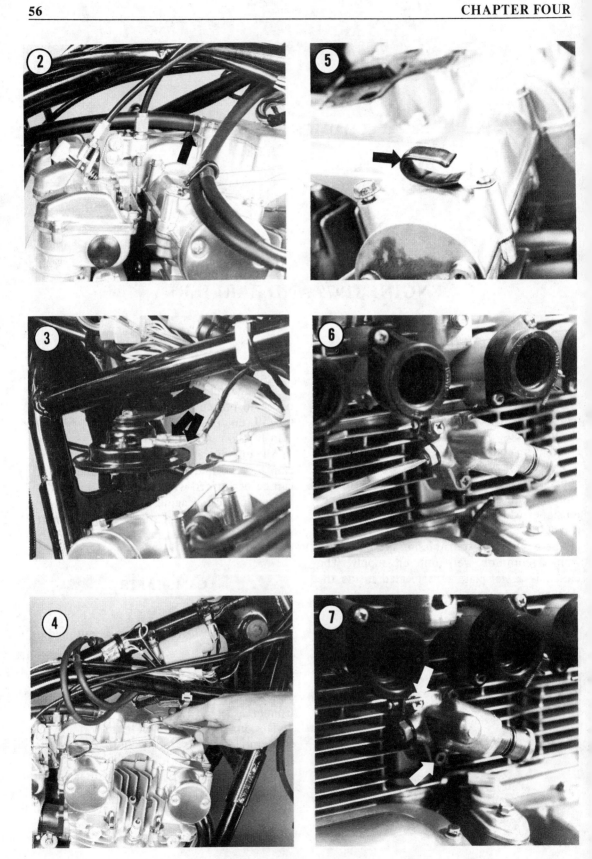

spark plug lead clips are on outboard rear bolts (**Figure 5**).

NOTE
To ease cam cover removal, tap cover around sealing surface with a soft mallet to break it loose.

8. Loosen locknut on cam chain tensioner and turn slotted lockscrew clockwise to lock tensioner pushrod (**Figure 6**).
9. Remove 3 bolts (**Figure 7**) and remove cam chain tensioner. See **Figure 8**.
10. Gradually loosen, then remove, 4 bolts securing cam chain idler (**Figure 9**). Lift off idler assembly taking care that the cushions and spacers do not fall into cam chain opening.

NOTE
If idler cushion and spacer are accidently dropped down the cam chain opening, they can be removed by a strong magnetic tool retriever.

11. Gradually and evenly loosen bolts securing cam bearing caps (**Figure 10**), and remove caps.

NOTE
*Cam bearing caps are marked "A," "B," "C," and "D" with corresponding marks on the cylinder head (**Figure 11**).*

12. Lift up on cam chain and lift out intake (rear) camshaft (**Figure 12**).
13. Tie a piece of wire or cord to cam chain to prevent chain from falling into engine. If the engine is still installed in the motorcycle, attach the wire or cord to the frame to hold the chain.
14. Disengage chain and remove exhaust cam.
15. Perform *Inspection* procedure.

Inspection

1. Carefully examine both camshafts for evidence of excessive or abnormal wear on lobes and journals.
2. Inspect each cam sprocket for signs of wear. Excessive wear is unlikely except in engines with high mileage or misaligned sprockets. If sprockets are worn, they must be replaced in pairs and and a new cam chain must be installed.

When installing sprockets, ensure that they are positioned on cams correctly. Refer to **Figure 13** for correct positioning of marks in relation to notches on ends of cams. Use Loctite Lock N' Seal on Allen head bolts and torque them to 1.0 mkg (7.2 ft.-lb.).
3. Use a micrometer and measure height of each camshaft lobe (**Figure 14**). Refer to **Table 1** for wear specifications.
4. Measure bearing journal wear with Plastigage as follows:
   a. Wipe off all oil from bearing journal and camshaft bearing surface, and place camshaft on cylinder head.
   b. Place a small strip of Plastigage on each cam surface as shown in **Figure 15**.
   c. Install bearing caps and gradually torque bolts to 0.8-1.2 mkg (5.8-8.6 ft.-lb.). Make sure camshaft does not shift or rotate.
   d. Remove bearing caps and measure thickness of Plastigage with Plastigage wrapper (**Figure 16**). Plastigage may adhere to cam or bearing cap; either location will provide a correct indication. Refer to **Table 2** for wear specifications. Replace camshaft if wear is excessive.

Installation and Timing

1. Remove 3 screws (**Figure 17**) and remove breaker point cover.
2. Using large hex shoulder of advance governor (**Figure 18**), rotate engine until timing mark "T" for cylinders 1-4 aligns with mark on timing plate (**Figure 19**). This positions pistons 1 and 4 at TDC (top dead center).

NOTE
*The timing mark is viewed through the window in the breaker point plate. Due to small window size and recessed location of timing marks, it is recommended that the breaker plate be removed to allow a better view for a more precise alignment of marks. Remove 3 screws securing breaker plate (**Figure 20**), gently spread points, and slide off breaker plate. Reinstall timing plate and secure with 3 screws.*

3. Lubricate camshaft lobes and bearing surfaces with molybdenum disulfide lubricant.

4

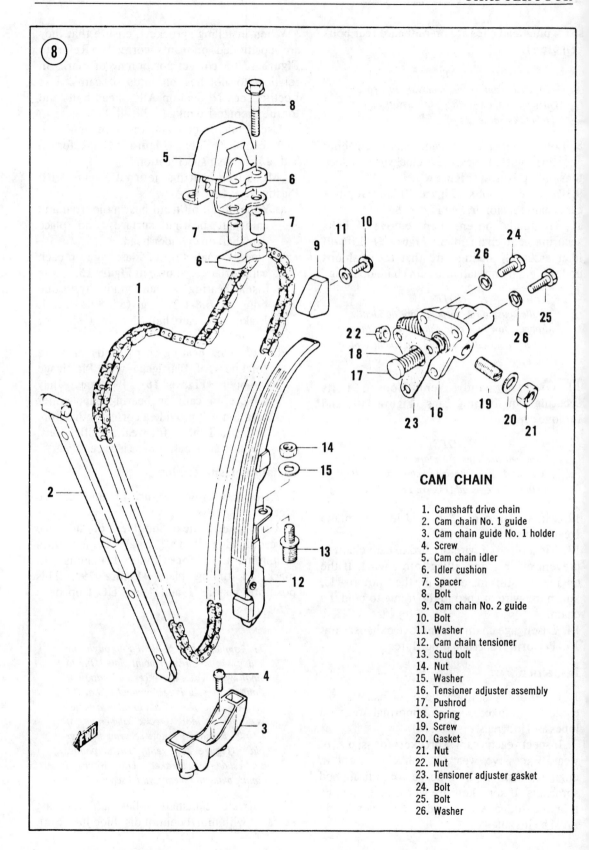

CAM CHAIN

1. Camshaft drive chain
2. Cam chain No. 1 guide
3. Cam chain guide No. 1 holder
4. Screw
5. Cam chain idler
6. Idler cushion
7. Spacer
8. Bolt
9. Cam chain No. 2 guide
10. Bolt
11. Washer
12. Cam chain tensioner
13. Stud bolt
14. Nut
15. Washer
16. Tensioner adjuster assembly
17. Pushrod
18. Spring
19. Screw
20. Gasket
21. Nut
22. Nut
23. Tensioner adjuster gasket
24. Bolt
25. Bolt
26. Washer

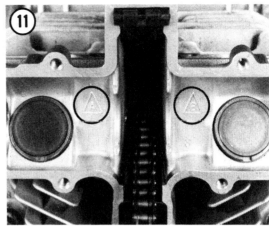

4

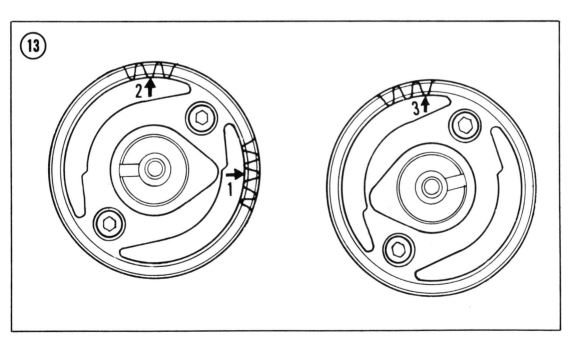

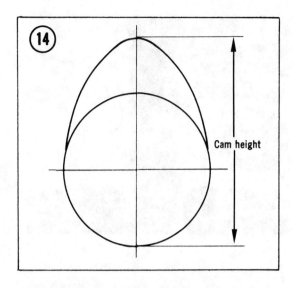

Cam height

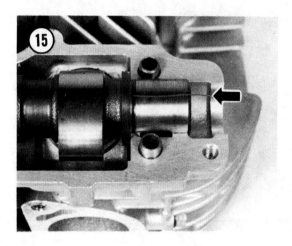

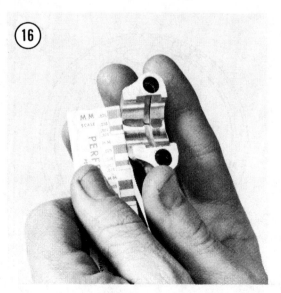

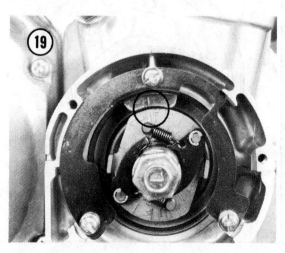

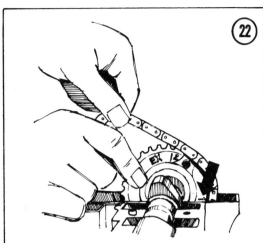

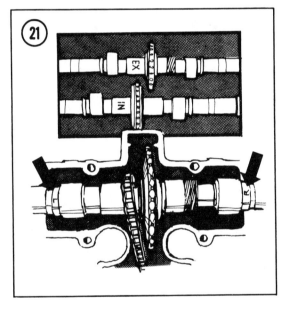

that TDC mark is still correctly positioned and no slack exists in the front of the chain.

5. Check that TDC timing mark "T" is correctly positioned.

6. Install camshaft bearing caps. Make sure cast letters on caps correspond to cast letters on cylinder head as shown in **Figure 23**. Tighten bolts securing bearing caps gradually and evenly.

CAUTION
Bearing cap bolts are specially hardened and are identified by a "9" cast on bolt head. Use of any other type of bolt could cause serious engine damage.

NOTE
It is necessary to hold cam chain in position on sprocket while tightening bearing caps. Valve spring tension against cam lobe will cause cam to rotate slightly as bearing caps are tightened. If chain is not held in place, it will jump off alignment by 1 or 2 teeth and the procedure will have to be started over from the beginning.

When bearing cap bolts are tight, recheck timing mark alignment and readjust if necessary. If alignment is correct, engine can be rotated slightly to relieve valve spring load on cam lobe and lessen chance of chain slipping.

7. Lubricate and install intake camshaft (marked IN, **Figure 21**) carefully through cam

Spread lubricant evenly without leaving any dry spots. Lubricate bearing journals in cylinder head with engine oil.

4. Install exhaust cam through cam chain and position cam in bearing journals. The exhaust cam is marked EX as shown in **Figure 21**. Ensure that the end of the cam is correctly positioned: "R" to the right and "L" to the left as shown in **Figure 21**. Pull up on cam chain to remove all slack and install chain over cam sprocket so No. 1 arrow (**Figure 22**) points directly toward or slightly below (1-2 mm) gasket surface on cylinder head. Ensure

chain, and position cam into bearing journals. Make sure right and left ends are in correct locations.

8. Position cam chain on intake cam sprocket so there are exactly 20 chain pins between arrow 2 on exhaust cam and arrow 3 on intake cam (**Figure 24**).

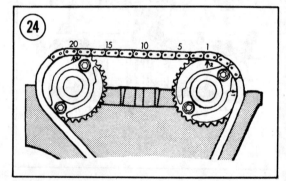

9. Install camshaft bearing caps. Make sure cast letters on caps correspond to cast letters on cylinder head as shown in **Figure 23**. Torque bolts securing caps gradually and evenly to 0.8 mkg (5.8 ft.-lb.). See **Figure 25**.

10. Install cam chain idler assembly and gradually tighten 4 bolts securing idler (**Figure 26**). Torque bolts to 0.6-1.0 mkg (4.4-7.2 ft.-lb.).

11. Loosen locknut and lockscrew on cam chain tensioner. Push in on spring-loaded plunger while rotating large knurled nut counterclockwise (**Figure 27**). When plunger is pushed in as far as it will go, secure it with the lockscrew.

12. Make sure gasket is in place and install cam chain tensioner (**Figure 28**).

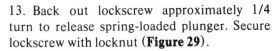

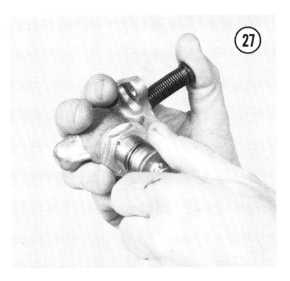

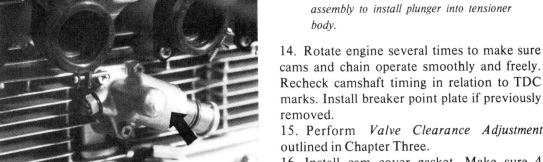

13. Back out lockscrew approximately 1/4 turn to release spring-loaded plunger. Secure lockscrew with locknut (**Figure 29**).

NOTE
Do not back out lockscrew more than 1/2 turn or plunger will become disengaged from tensioner body. If this should occur it will be necessary to remove tensioner assembly to install plunger into tensioner body.

14. Rotate engine several times to make sure cams and chain operate smoothly and freely. Recheck camshaft timing in relation to TDC marks. Install breaker point plate if previously removed.
15. Perform *Valve Clearance Adjustment* outlined in Chapter Three.
16. Install cam cover gasket. Make sure 4 half-moon shaped rubber end plugs are in place (**Figure 30**).

17. Install cam cover and tighten bolts gradually and evenly in a crisscross pattern. Torque bolts to 0.7-1.1 mkg (5.1-7.9 ft.-lb.).
18. Install breather cover and connect breather hose.
19. Install camshaft end covers.
20. Install horn and connect horn wires.
21. Install the carburetors as outlined in Chapter Seven.

CYLINDER HEAD

The cylinder head can be removed while engine is installed in the motorcycle.

Removal

1. Perform *Camshaft Removal.*
2. Perform *Exhaust System Removal* as outlined in Chapter Seven.
3. Remove the spark plugs if not previously removed. Disconnect the tachometer drive cable.
4. Use a small screwdriver and gently pry up on the end of No. 1 cam chain guide until the end is free from the head (**Figure 31**). Pull out the cam chain guide.
5. Remove two 6 mm bolts, one from each end of the head (**Figure 32**).

NOTE
On engines serial No. 77026 and subsequent, remove the 6 mm bolt located on the front of the engine between the 2 inboard exhaust ports.

6. Remove 8 head nuts gradually and evenly in descending order (**Figure 33**). Numbers denoting sequence are cast in head close to each head nut (**Figure 34**). Note that copper washers are used with dome nuts.

NOTE
A magnetic tool can be used to lift out head nuts in center recesses.

7. Carefully lift cylinder head off cylinder block.

8. Remove and discard rectangular O-ring (**Figure 35**) and head gasket.

Inspection

1. Lift out tappets complete with adjusting shims (**Figure 36**). Note the location of each tappet.

> *CAUTION*
> *Never use a magnet to lift out valve tappets or adjustment shims. They are made of hardened steel and are easily magnetized. A magnetized part will attract and hold metal particles which will cause excessive wear. A magnetized adjustment shim could also lift out of a tappet while the engine is running and cause serious and expensive damage.*

2. Remove all traces of gasket from head and from sealing surface of cylinder block.

3. Without removing valves, remove all carbon deposits from combustion chambers with a wire brush and solvent. Stubborn deposits can be removed with a blunt scraper made of soft aluminum or hardwood. Steel scrapers and screwdrivers tend to damage combustion chamber surfaces. After all carbon has been removed from combustion chambers and exhaust ports, clean entire head in solvent.

4. Check combustion chambers and ports for cracks. While it is possible to repair such damage with heliarc welding, the service is usually very costly and requires machining of the sealing surface to true it. It is best to replace a cracked cylinder head with a new one.

4

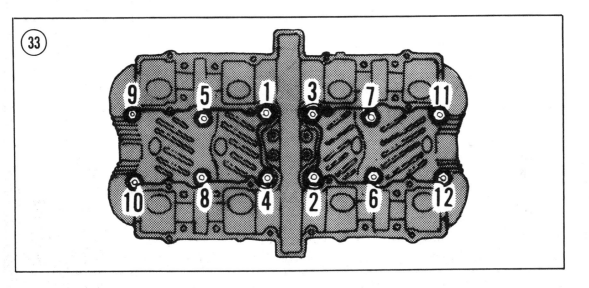

Installation

1. Install a new head gasket on the cylinder block. The word "TOP" must face up as shown in **Figure 37**.

2. Install the rectangular O-ring on the cylinder block. Apply a film of Suzuki Bond No. 1211 (or equivalent) to the O-ring to prevent oil leaks. Do not use Bond No. 4 as it will not withstand the high temperatures in this part of the engine.

3. Pull the cam chain up through the opening in the head and carefully lower the head down over the cylinder studs. Make sure the alignment dowels are engaged, then press the head down against the gasket.

4. Install 4 dome nuts with copper washers on the exposed studs and plain nuts with steel washers on the recessed studs. Tighten the nuts gradually in the sequence shown in **Figure 33**. Torque the nuts to 3.5-4.0 mkg (25-29 ft.-lb.).

5. Install the two 6 mm bolts in each end of the head. On models so equipped, install the 6 mm bolt in the front of the engine between the inboard exhaust ports. Torque the bolts to 0.7-1.1 mkg (5-8 ft.-lb.).

6. Install the tappets and shims if removed during inspection.

7. Perform *Camshaft Installation* and install the spark plugs.

8. Install the exhaust system as outlined in Chapter Seven.

9. Connect the tachometer drive cable.

VALVES

Valve servicing requires the use of a valve spring compressor tool to remove the valves from the head. Suitable valve spring compressors can often be rented from motorcycle dealers or rental agencies.

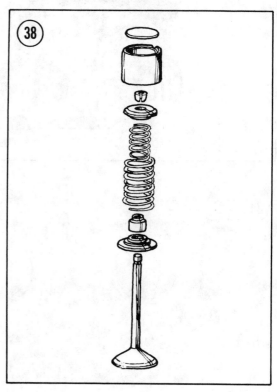

Removal

Refer to **Figure 38** for this procedure.

> *CAUTION*
> *All component parts of each valve assembly must be kept together. Do not mix with like components from other valves or excessive wear may result.*

1. Do *Cylinder Head, Removal/Inspection*.

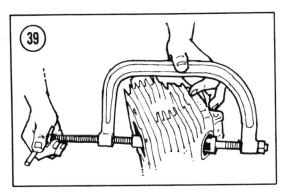

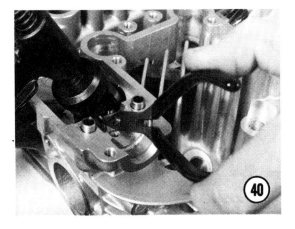

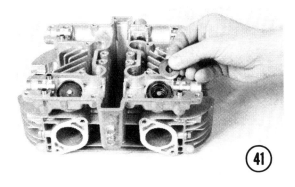

2. Install valve spring compressor squarely over valve retainer with other end of tool placed against valve head (**Figure 39**).

3. Tighten valve spring compressor until split valve keeper separates. Lift out split keeper with needle nose pliers (**Figure 40**).

4. Gradually loosen valve spring compressor and remove from head. Lift off valve retainer (**Figure 41**).

5. Remove outer and inner valve springs (**Figure 42**). Keep springs together, as they are a matched pair.

6. Tip up head and remove valve (**Figure 43**).

7. Use needle nose pliers and remove old valve guide oil seal (**Figure 44**). Discard old seal; oil seals are destroyed when removed.

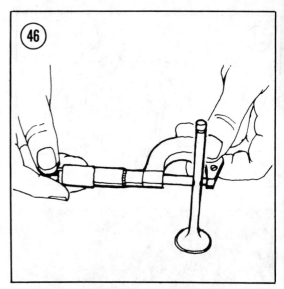

8. Remove lower spring seat (**Figure 45**).
9. Repeat procedure and remove remaining valves.

Inspection

1. Clean valves with a wire brush and solvent. Discard valves that are burned, warped, or cracked.
2. Measure valve stem with a micrometer (**Figure 46**). Replace if not within specified tolerance (**Table 3**).
3. Remove all carbon and varnish from valve guides with a stiff spiral wire brush.
4. Insert each valve in its guide. Hold valve just slightly off its seat and rock it sideways. If it rocks more than slightly, guide is worn and must be replaced. Refer to *Guide Replacement*.
5. Measure valve spring heights (**Figure 47**). All should be of length specified in **Table 4** with no bends or other distortions. Replace defective springs in pairs.
6. Check valve spring retainers and valve keepers. If they are in good condition, they may be reused.
7. Inspect valve seats. If worn or burned, they must be reconditioned. This should be performed by your dealer or local machine shop. Seats and valves in near-perfect condition can be reconditioned by lapping. Refer to *Valve Lapping*, this chapter.

Installation

1. Install lower spring seat over valve guide (**Figure 45**).

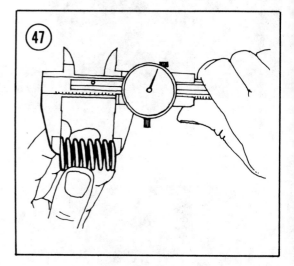

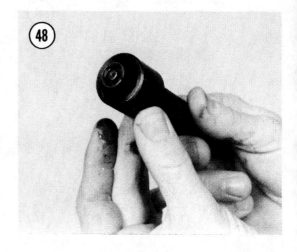

2. Lubricate lip on new valve guide seal with molybdenum disulfide and install seal over valve guide. If using special seal installation tool, position seal into tool (**Figure 48**), then tap seal into place. If special tool is not available, use a 10 mm socket (**Figure 49**) and tap seal into place. Ensure seal is seated squarely over valve guide and is locked into place (**Figure 50**).

3. Install inner and outer valve springs. Spring coils are closer together on bottom (cylinder head) end of springs (**Figure 51**). Ensure that springs are installed correctly.

4. Lubricate valve stems with molybdenum disulfide lubricant and install valves in cylinder head.

5. Place upper spring retainer over valve spring. Install valve spring compressor and tighten until end of valve is exposed enough to install split keepers.

6. Apply a little grease to keeper half and stick keeper to a small screwdriver to aid installation. Install split keepers onto valve stem (**Figure 52**).

7. Remove valve spring compressor. Use a soft drift and hammer and tap end of each valve to seat valve keepers.

8. Perform *Cylinder Head, Installation.*

Valve Lapping

Valve lapping should only be performed on heads whose valves and seats are in good condition. Lapping should be considered a

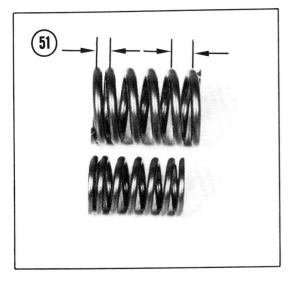

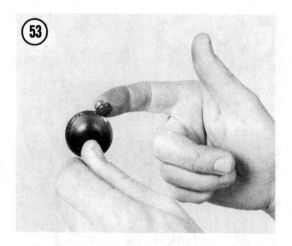

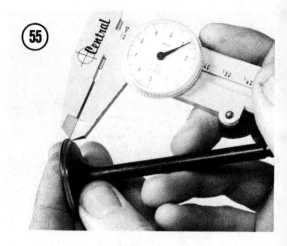

"touch up" operation, not a cure for burned or damaged valves and/or seats.

1. Perform *Valves, Removal/Inspection.*
2. Smear a light coating of fine grade valve lapping compound on seating surface of valve (**Figure 53**).
3. Install valve into head and use "suction cup" type lapping tool to lap valves. Spin tool between palms while lifting and moving valve around seat 1/4 turn at a time.
4. Wipe off valve and seat frequently to check progress of lapping. Lap only enough to achieve a precise seating "ring" around valve head (**Figure 54**). Measure width of seat as shown in **Figure 55**. If seat width is not within tolerance in **Table 5**, valve seat in cylinder head must be resurfaced.

NOTE
Valves are specially hardened material and cannot be ground.

5. Closely examine valve seat in cylinder head. It should be smooth and even with a smooth, polished seating "ring" (**Figure 56**).
6. Use solvent and clean off all traces of grinding compound from valves and seats.
7. Perform *Valves, Installation.*

Valve Guide Replacement

When guides are worn so that there is excessive stem-to-guide clearance or valve tipping, they must be replaced. Replace all, even if only one is worn. This job should only be done by a dealer as special tools are required.

Valve Seat Reconditioning

This job is best left to your dealer or local machine shop. They have the special equipment and knowledge for this exacting job. You can still save considerable money by

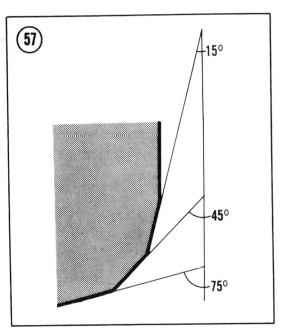

4

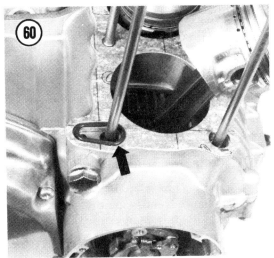

removing the cylinder head and taking just the head to the shop. The following procedure is provided in the event that you are not near a dealer and the local machine shop is not familiar with the GS750.

1. With a 15° valve seat cutter, remove just enough metal to make bottom of seat concentric. See **Figure 57**.

2. With a 75° valve seat cutter, remove just enough metal from top of seat to make it concentric.

3. With a 45° valve seat cutter, cut a seat that measures 1.0-1.2 mm (0.039-0.047 in.) wide.

CYLINDER BLOCK AND PISTONS

Cylinder block and piston repair work can be performed with the engine installed in the motorcycle.

Removal

1. Perform *Cylinder Head, Removal.*

2. Gently lift up and remove cylinder block from engine (**Figure 58**). Note that arrows on pistons point forward (**Figure 59**).

3. Remove and discard cylinder base gasket and triangular O-rings (**Figure 60**).

4. Stuff clean rags into crankcase opening around connecting rods to prevent dirt, moisture, and piston snap rings from entering engine.

5. Use a small screwdriver and pry out snap ring through notch in piston (**Figure 61**). Partially cover opening in piston with your thumb to prevent snap ring from flying out. Discard old snap ring.

6. Using a suitably sized wooden dowel or socket extension, push out piston pin and remove piston (**Figure 62**).

> *CAUTION*
> *On high mileage engines, piston pin may be difficult to remove. Do not attempt to drive out pin or connecting rod damage may result.*
>
> *If pins cannot be pushed or gently tapped out, use a piston pin extractor tool (**Figure 63**). If such a tool is not available, have the task performed by your dealer. It is a quick and inexpensive job with the right tools, and will prevent expensive engine damage.*

Mark inside of piston with a felt pen or metal scribe to identify location. Repeat procedure for other pistons.

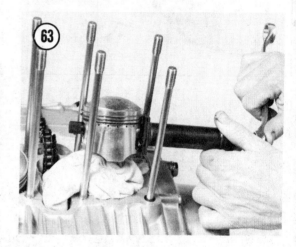

7. Perform *Cylinder Block Inspection* and *Piston and Ring Inspection.*

Cylinder Block Inspection

The following procedure requires the use of highly specialized and expensive measuring instruments. If such equipment is not readily available, have measurements performed by a dealer or machine shop.

1. Use an inside micrometer or cylinder gauge and measure each cylinder bore (**Figure 64**).

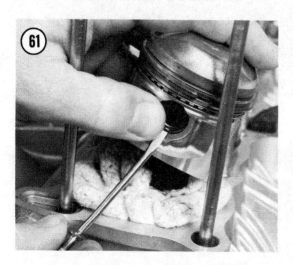

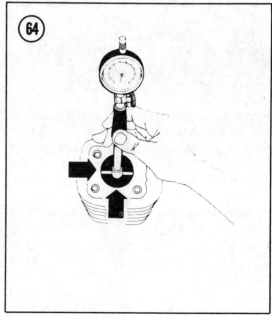

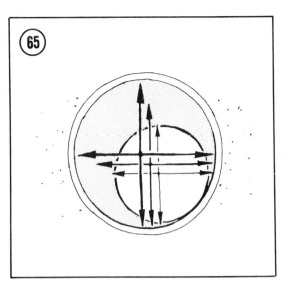

Measure bore at 3 locations as shown in **Figure 65** and in 2 planes, 90° apart. Compare measurements with specifications in **Table 6** and rebore cylinders if necessary.

2. Examine condition of each cylinder bore. The cylinders should be rebored if surface is scored or abraded. Pistons are available in oversize increases of both 0.5 mm (0.0197 in.) and 1.0 mm (0.0394 in.). Purchase pistons before cylinders are bored so pistons can be measured and cylinders bored accordingly to maintain correct piston-to-cylinder clearance.

Piston and Ring Inspection

NOTE
The inspection steps are designed to determine overall condition of the upper end; they should not be used to isolate one or two out-of-spec parts, such as one piston or a couple of rings. While some of the parts may be within service limits it is best that all like parts be replaced at the same time as long as the out-of-spec condition is caused by normal wear.

1. Measure piston at point shown in **Figure 66**. If any piston is not within specified tolerance (**Table 6**) replace all 4 pistons as a set. It may not be necessary to replace pistons if cylinder bores are within service limits. Refer to *Cylinder Block Inspection.*

2. Clean the piston crown with a soft metal scraper to remove carbon (**Figure 67**). Use a piece of old piston ring to clean ring grooves (**Figure 68**).

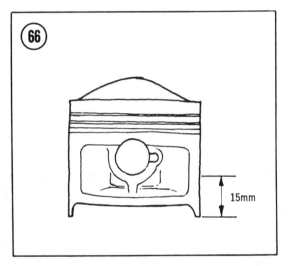

15mm

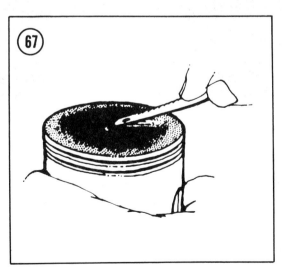

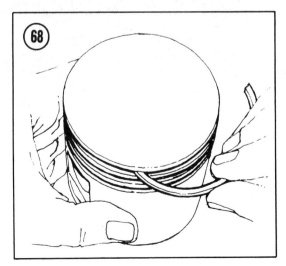

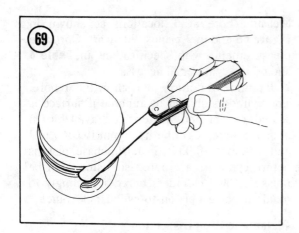

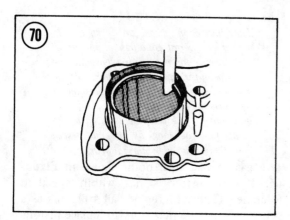

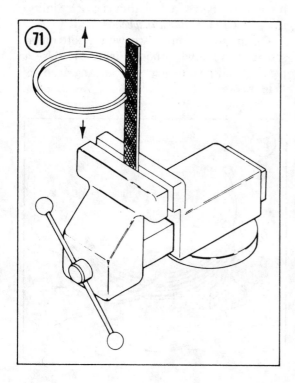

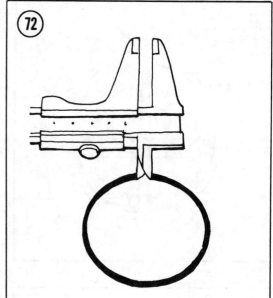

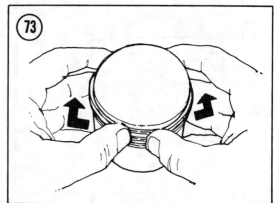

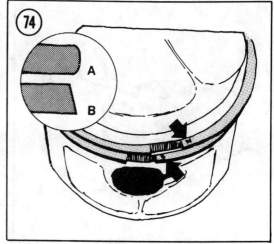

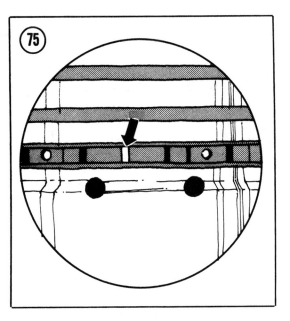

3. With a feeler gauge, check side clearance of rings in grooves (**Figure 69**). If clearance is greater than that shown in **Table 7**, measure ring thickness, then groove width, to determine which is worn. All pieces that are worn beyond their respective service limits should be replaced. Ring thickness and groove width standards and service limits are also shown in **Table 7**.

4. Place 2 top piston rings, one at a time, into cylinder bore and measure end gap (**Figure 70**). Use piston to push ring squarely into cylinder bore approximately 1 in. This is required for new rings as well as old ones. Compare actual gap to **Table 7** and replace old rings if their gap is greater than service limit. For new rings, it is more likely that the gap will be less than minimum. If such is the case, clamp a fine, small file in a vise and file ring ends as shown in **Figure 71**.

5. Measure free-state ring gap with a caliper as shown in **Figure 72**. If in-cylinder gap is correct, but free-state gap is less than service limit (**Table 7**), ring will not seal well and should be replaced.

6. Carefully examine piston around area of skirt, pin, and ring grooves for signs of cracks, stress, or metal fatigue. Replace all 4 pistons if any one is defective.

Installation

1. Spread piston rings with your thumbs (**Figure 73**) and install rings in appropriate grooves (**Figure 74**). Identifying letters on rings face toward top piston. Top ring is plated and is shinier and lighter in color than 2nd ring. Check that some clearance exists between ends of oil ring spacer (**Figure 75**) or that ends butt together; they must not overlap.

2. Install a new snap ring on inner piston pin groove. Lightly oil piston, piston pin, and connecting rod, and install piston on connecting rod (**Figure 76**). Ensure that arrow on piston points toward front of engine.

CAUTION
Never use STP or similar products as assembly lubricant. Even a small amount will combine with engine oil and destroy the friction properties of the clutch, necessitating a complete flushing of the engine's lubrication system and installation of new clutch plates.

3. Partially hold new snap ring in position with your thumb and install snap ring in piston groove (**Figure 77**). Make sure snap ring locks into groove. Rotate snap ring so that a solid portion of the snap ring is exposed in the piston notch (**Figure 78**).

4. Install new cylinder base gasket and triangular O-rings. Make sure O-rings are properly positioned in grooves (**Figure 79**). Remove old O-rings from base of each

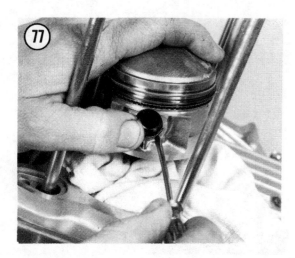

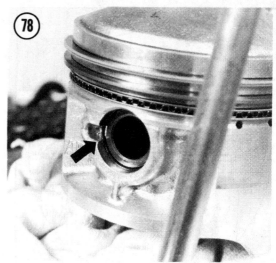

cylinder bore (**Figure 80**) and replace with new ones.

5. Stagger end gaps on all piston rings as shown in **Figure 81**.

6. Oil the pistons and the cylinder bores with engine oil.

7. Feed cam chain up through cylinder block and start block down over studs. Compress rings with a ring compressor or your fingers and gradually slide block over pistons.

NOTE
*Large hose clamps make an effective inexpensive ring compressor. See **Figure 82**.*

8. Remove ring compressor and push cylinder block down fully.

9. Perform *Cylinder Head, Installation.*

ENGINE
REMOVAL/INSTALLATION

Engine must be removed from motorcycle to perform repair on crankshaft and transmission. If you are performing repair work without assistance, it may be easier to first remove cylinder head and cylinder block. Head and block removal will greatly reduce bulk and weight of engine, making engine removal much more manageable for one person. Refer to *Cylinder Head Removal* and *Cylinder Block and Pistons, Removal.*

If only transmission repair is to be performed it is not necessary to remove cylinder head and block.

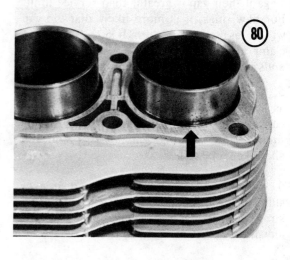

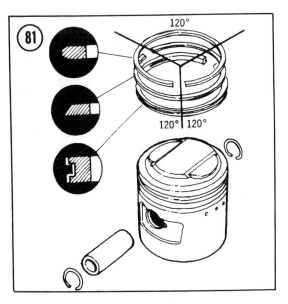

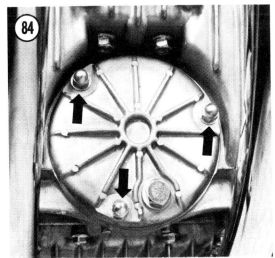

4

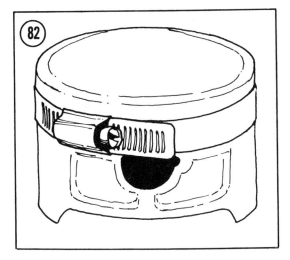

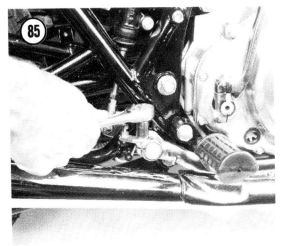

1. Place motorcycle on centerstand and remove any accessories such as fairing or safety bars.

2. Remove drain plug (**Figure 83**) and drain engine oil. Remove bolts securing oil filter cover and remove oil filter (**Figure 84**).

3. Remove pinch bolt securing footbrake pedal (**Figure 85**). Disengage return spring and slide brake pedal off shaft. Note that punch mark on shaft is aligned with punch mark or split opening on brake pedal (**Figure 86**).

4. Remove bolts securing right footrest (**Figure 87**) and remove footrest.

5. Remove gearshift lever pinch bolt (**Figure 88**). Bolt must be removed completely, not just loosened. Remove shift lever.

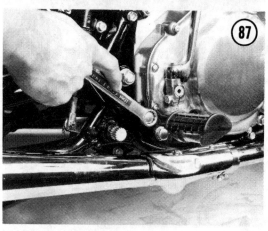

6. Remove bolts securing left footrest and remove the footrest.

7. Remove 3 screws securing clutch adjustment cover and remove cover (**Figure 89**).

8. Use a hammer driven impact tool and loosen screws securing sprocket cover. Do not overlook the 2 screws inside the clutch adjuster cavity (**Figure 90**). Remove screws and swing cover up out of the way with clutch cable still attached.

9. Use a chisel and fold back tab lockwasher securing engine sprocket nut (**Figure 91**).

10. Temporarily install gearshift lever and shift transmission into gear. Hold rear brake on and remove engine sprocket nut. Note that recess in nut (**Figure 92**) is installed toward sprocket. Slide sprocket off shaft and disengage from drive chain. Remove spacer located behind sprocket.

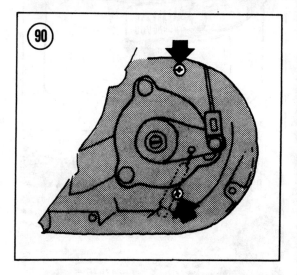

11. Lift up seat and remove plastic tool tray to gain access to battery leads. Disconnect leads—negative first, then positive.

12. Remove left side cover and open rubber boot to gain access to alternator wires (**Figure 93**). Disconnect yellow, white/green, and white/blue alternator wires.

13. Pull back rubber boot and remove starter lead from starter solenoid (**Figure 94**).

14. Remove bolt securing rear of fuel tank to frame (**Figure 95**).

15. Turn fuel valve to OFF. Disconnect 2 rubber hoses from fuel valve.

16. Lift up on rear of tank and slide back to disengage from rubber mounting pads (**Figure 96**). Make sure rubber washers on mounting bolt are not lost (**Figure 97**).

17. Disconnect wire connector for gearshift indicator and blue neutral indicator wire (**Figure 98**). Unfasten clamps securing wires to frame.

18. Unscrew tachometer drive cable from cylinder head (**Figure 99**).

19. Remove bolts from exhaust pipe flanges (**Figure 100**) and slide flanges down exhaust pipe.

20. Remove bolt securing each muffler to frame (**Figure 101**).

21. Slide exhaust pipes out of cylinder head and remove pipes and muffler together (**Figure 102**).

22. Loosen locknuts securing throttle cable adjusters (**Figure 103**) and slacken throttle cables. Disconnect cable ends from carburetor throttle shaft.

23. Loosen 4 clamp screws securing carburetors to the airbox (**Figure 104**).

24. Remove 2 bolts securing airbox to the frame and remove the airbox (**Figure 105**).

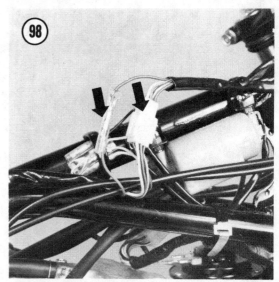

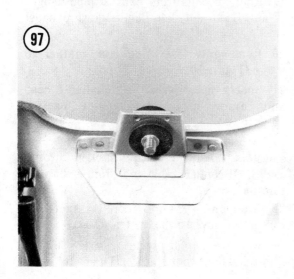

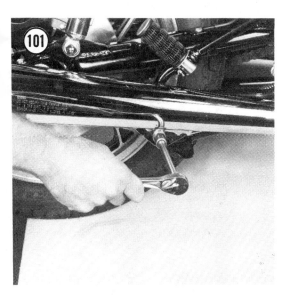

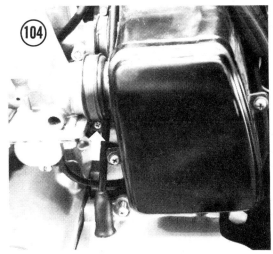

4

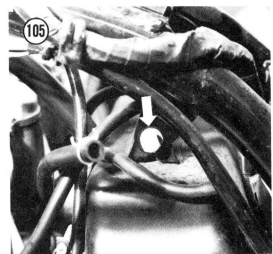

25. Loosen 4 clamp screws securing carburetors to intake flanges (**Figure 106**).

26. Unclamp carburetor vent and overflow hoses from the frame. Slide carburetors back out of intake flange and remove as an assembly.

27. Pull back rubber boot and disconnect 2 breaker point leads (white and black wires). See **Figure 107**. Unclamp breaker point lead wires from the frame.

28. Disconnect wire from oil pressure sending unit.

29. Remove engine mount bolts and nuts (**Figure 108**). Note that lower engine mount bolts are secured by nut plates on bottom of engine (**Figure 109**). Lift out engine from right side of motorcycle.

30. Engine installation is the reverse of these steps. Keep the following points in mind:

    a. Install 3 long engine mount bolts from left side of motorcycle.

    b. Route oil drain pipe from airbox between engine crankcase and swing arm.

    c. Torque 8 mm engine mount bolts to 2.0

mkg (14.5 ft.-lb.), and 10 mm bolts to 4.0 mkg (29.0 ft.-lb.).

    d. Clamp carburetor overflow tubes and breaker point lead wires to the frame.

    e. Install spacer and engine sprocket and torque sprocket nut to 4.0-6.0 mkg (29.0-43.2 ft.-lb.). Secure nut with folding lockwasher.

f. Lightly lubricate fuel tank mounting pads with rubber lubricant or WD-40 to aid tank installation.

31. Refer to Chapter Three and perform the following procedures:

    a. Install oil filter and add engine oil.

    b. Perform *Engine Tune-up.*

    c. Perform *Clutch Adjustment.*

    d. Perform *Drive Chain Adjustment.*

LOWER END

Disassembly

It is necessary to split the crankcase apart to gain access to the crankshaft, transmission, kickstarter, and some components of the gearshift mechanism.

If less than full engine disassembly is required for a specific repair task, perform only the steps necessary to accomplish the desired repair.

1. Perform *Engine Removal.*

> *NOTE*
> *If crankshaft is to be removed, perform* **Cylinder Head Removal** *and* **Cylinder Block Removal***. Leave pistons installed at this time; they can be used to help disassemble engine.*

2. Remove screws securing starter motor cover, and remove cover.

3. Remove bolts from starter assembly and slide out starter motor (**Figure 110**).

4. Fold back locking tabs and remove bolts securing seal retainer on left side of engine (**Figure 111**). Remove seal retainer.

5. Remove screws securing gear shift indicator switch (**Figure 112**) and remove

switch. Note how wiring is routed. Make sure spring-loaded plunger in end of shift cam is not lost (**Figure 113**). Remove O-ring.

6. Use a hammer driven impact tool and loosen screws on left engine cover. Remove screws, cover, and gasket (**Figure 114**). Note the location of different length screws. Keep a few rags handy as some oil is bound to run out when cover is removed.

> *CAUTION*
> *Do not pry cover loose with screwdriver or cover and/or crankcase damage may result. Cover is held tight by magnetic attraction of alternator rotor. A strong pull is required to overcome magnetic field.*

7. Remove outside washer from starter idler gear shaft (**Figure 115**). If washer is not on shaft it may be stuck to inside of left engine cover.

8. Hold gear in place and withdraw idler gear shaft enough to disengage shaft end from the engine.

9. Remove idler gear and shaft (**Figure 116**). Note washer on shaft between gear and engine.

> *NOTE*
> *It is not necessary to remove starter clutch assembly to remove crankshaft. If starter clutch removal is desired, perform Steps 10 and 11. If not required, proceed to Step 12.*

10. To remove starter clutch assembly it is necessary to use a slide hammer. If such a tool

is not available, take engine to your local dealer and have him perform the task. If slide hammer is available, perform the following:

a. Place 2 small blocks of wood under one piston to hold crankshaft from turning.

b. Remove bolt securing starter clutch assembly.

c. Install slide hammer on starter clutch assembly and pull clutch assembly from tapered end of crankshaft.

NOTE

*Clutch assembly contains 3 rollers and 3 spring-loaded plungers (**Figure 117**). Take care no parts are lost as some rollers often fall out when clutch is removed. Roller installation is described under* **Lower End, Assembly**.

11. Remove large starter gear then slide off 2 bearings and brass thrust washer (**Figure 118**). Note chamber on washer (**Figure 119**) faces toward engine.

12. Remove 3 screws securing magneto cover and remove cover.

13. Remove 3 screws securing breaker plate (**Figure 120**) and remove plate. Remove breaker point wire from retainer clips secured to oil pan.

4

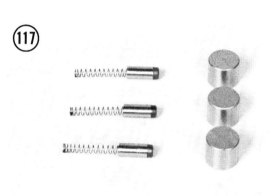

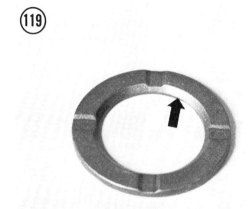

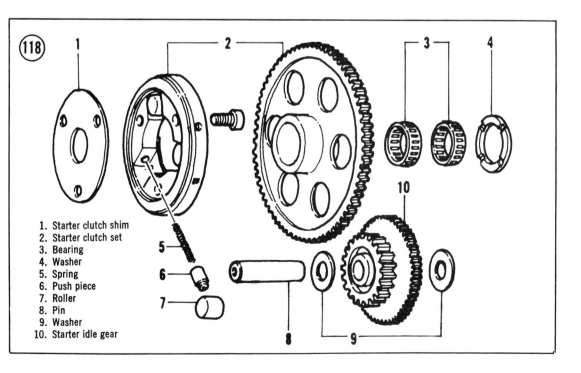

1. Starter clutch shim
2. Starter clutch set
3. Bearing
4. Washer
5. Spring
6. Push piece
7. Roller
8. Pin
9. Washer
10. Starter idle gear

14. Refer to Chapter Six and remove clutch and gearshift components.

15. Remove bearing and seal retainers shown in **Figure 121**.

16. Double nut the upper stud on the oil filter cavity (**Figure 122**). Back out stud to gain access to the crankcase bolt above it.

17. Remove bolts securing top half of crankcase in descending order of numbers in **Figure 123**.

> *NOTE*
> *Before removing crankcase bolts, cut a cardboard template. Punch holes in template for each bolt location. Place bolts in template holes as they are removed. This procedure will greatly speed up assembly time by eliminating the search for the correct bolt.*

18. Turn engine over to gain access to bottom crankcase bolts.

> *NOTE*
> *Have plenty of rags ready. Approximately one pint of oil is trapped in engine and will run out when engine is turned over.*
> *Gradually and evenly loosen, then remove, 13 bolts securing the oil pan (**Figure 124**) and lift off oil pan.*

19. Gradually loosen, then remove, 6 mm and 8 mm bolts securing lower crankcase half to upper half. Loosen the 8 mm bolts in descending order of the numbers cast in the crankcase (**Figure 125**).

20. Gently tap all around bottom crankcase half with a rubber mallet to break it loose then lift off crankcase.

> *CAUTION*
> *Never attempt to pry crankcase apart with a screwdriver or similar tool, or serious damage may result to crankcase sealing surfaces.*

21. Carefully lift out crankshaft assembly.

22. Remove 3 screws and remove oil pump pickup screen. Remove O-ring from oil passage.

23. Use solvent and clean all oil and sludge deposits from both crankcase halves.

Inspection

Except for preliminary checks, crankshaft service should be entrusted to a dealer. The crankshaft is pressed together and requires a press to separate it and assemble it as well as considerable expertise to correctly align it.

1. Carefully examine condition of crankshaft bearings. Bearings must spin freely without excessive play or roughness. If in doubt as to bearing condition, have them examined and/or replaced by a dealer.

2. Measure big end side clearance on connecting rod with a feeler gauge (**Figure 126**). Clearance should be 0.10-0.65 mm (0.0039-0.0256 in.) with a service limit of 1.0 mm (0.04 in.). If side clearance is out of tolerance, refer crankshaft assembly to a dealer for repair.

4

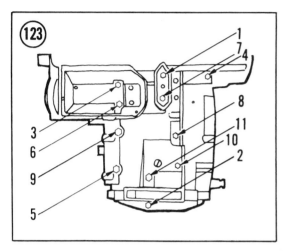

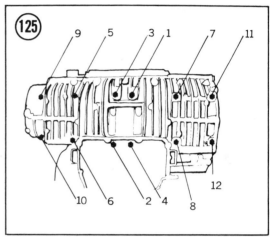

Assembly

CAUTION
Never use STP or similar products as assembly lubricant. Even a small amount will combine with engine oil and destroy the friction properties of the clutch, necessitating a complete flushing of the engine's lubrication system and installation of new clutch plates.

Use a thread locking compound such as Loctite Lock N' Seal No. 2114 on all fasteners during engine assembly. A small bolt or screw working loose inside the engine could have disastrous and expensive consequences.

1. Make sure all engine parts are clean and all fasteners are in good condition. Replace all bolts, nuts, and screws with damaged heads or stripped threads.
2. Install oil pump pickup screen in bottom crankcase half.
3. Make sure bearing retainer C-ring is properly positioned in crankcase (**Figure 127**).
4. Carefully install crankshaft assembly in crankcase.

NOTE
On engines undergoing a complete rebuild, it is recommended that cam chain be replaced prior to crankshaft installation.

Make sure groove on crankshaft bearing engages C-ring. Outer bearing races on other 5 crankshaft bearings have a small indentation that must engage dowels (**Figure 128**) installed in the crankcase half. Slowly rotate bearing races until you can feel the indentation engage the dowels. Small punch marks on bearing races should be nearly perpendicular to case sealing surface when bearing races are in proper position (**Figure 129**). Rotate race on outside bearing until locating pin engages notch in crankcase (**Figure 130**).

5. If transmission or gearshift components were removed from crankcase for repair, install them at this time. Refer to Chapter Six for applicable installation procedures.
6. Carefully apply a non-hardening sealant compound to sealing surface of bottom crankcase half. Use Suzuki Bond No. 4 or Permatex Forma Gasket Non-hardening Sealant No. 2B. Do not use a silicone sealant. Use just enough sealant to cover sealing surfaces. Do not apply a thick layer or allow sealant to run inside crankcase. Wipe off any sealant that may have gotten on bearing surfaces. Use lacquer thinner to clean off any excess sealant.

7. Install a new O-ring in crankcase (**Figure 131**).

8. Check that all bearing locating pins are properly engaged in crankcase notches. Check that sealing surface of upper crankcase half is clean and all sealant has been removed. Carefully install lower crankcase half over upper half. Gently tap crankcase together with rubber mallet or block of wood.

(130)   (131)

9. Install bolts in bottom crankcase and
tighten the 8 mm bolts gradually and evenly in
the order shown in **Figure 125**. Gradually
tighten all 6 mm bolts. Tighten 8 mm bolts to
2 mkg (14.5 ft.-lb.) and 6 mm bolts to 1.0 mkg
(7.2 ft.-lb.).
10. Turn engine over and install upper
crankcase bolts in order shown in **Figure 123**.
Tighten all bolts gradually and evenly. Torque
8 mm bolts to 2.0 mkg (4.5 ft.-lb.) and 6 mm
bolts to 1.0 mkg (7.2 ft.-lb.).

CAUTION
*Hold slack out of cam chain and rotate
crankshaft several times. Crankshaft and
transmission shafts should rotate freely
and easily with no binding or stiff spots. If
something does not feel right, investigate
and correct the problem now. An engine
that feels rough when rotated by hand will
not "wear in," and such an engine will
likely cause expensive damage if run.*

11. Install bearing and seal retainers as shown
in **Figure 132**.
12. Install clutch and gearshift components as
outlined in Chapter Six.
13. Install the clutch pushrod seal retainer
and secure bolts by bending locking tabs over
bolt heads (**Figure 133**).

NOTE
*If starter clutch assembly was removed
during engine disassembly, perform Steps
14 and 15. If starter clutch assembly was
not removed, proceed to Step 16.*

14. Install brass thrust washer and 2 bearings.
Ensure that chamfer on thrust washer faces
toward engine. Slide on large starter gear.
15. Wipe tapered end of crankshaft clean with
solvent or lacquer thinner and install starter

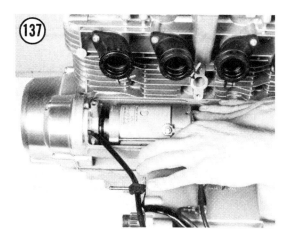

clutch. Tighten clutch bolt to 4.0-6.0 mkg (29.0-43.4 ft.-lb.). If rollers fell out of clutch assembly during removal, refer to **Figure 118** and perform the following:

a. Place assembly on a clean surface and install spring and plunger (push piece). Hold plunger in position with a small drill bit inserted through hole in assembly body (**Figure 134**).

b. Slide roller in assembly and gently withdraw drill bit so spring tension holds roller in place (**Figure 135**). Repeat for other rollers.

CAUTION
Carefully examine magnets in alternator rotor. Remove all foreign objects, metal filings, etc., that may have been picked up by the magnets. A small washer or nut stuck to the magnets could cause serious alternator damage.

16. Install starter idler gear as follows:
a. Lightly grease inner washer to hold it in place on engine.
b. Hold idler gear in place and align shaft hole.
c. Insert idler gear shaft through gear into engine. Install washer on outside of gear.

17. Use a new gasket and install left engine cover. Ensure that rubber grommet around alternator wires is correctly located in engine cover. Route wires as shown in **Figure 136**.

18. Install large O-ring and spring-loaded plunger in gearshift cam. Install gearshift indicator switch. Secure switch and route wires as shown in **Figure 136**.

19. Carefully install starter motor (**Figure 137**) and secure with 2 bolts. Route wires from alternator assembly and starter as shown in **Figure 138**.

20. Make sure gasket is correctly positioned and install cover over starter motor.

21. Install upper stud on the oil filter cavity.

22. Install breaker plate. Route wire as shown in **Figure 139**.

23. Install cylinder block and head if removed, and install engine.

OIL PUMP

The GS750 uses a high volume, low pressure oil pump. The pump is not repairable and should be replaced if engine is undergoing a complete rebuild.

If low pressure is suspected, have pressure checked by a dealer as a special gauge is required to perform the task.

Removal/Installation

1. To gain access to oil pump, perform *Clutch Removal* as outlined in Chapter Six.

2. Use snap ring pliers and remove snap ring securing oil pump driven gear (**Figure 140**). Remove driven gear.

3. Remove drive pin from pump shaft (**Figure 141**).

4. Remove 3 screws securing oil pump and remove pump (**Figure 142**).

5. Remove and discard 2 O-rings from oil pump passages (**Figure 143**).

6. Installation is the reverse of these steps. Use new O-rings in oil passages. Make sure drive gear engages drive pin on pump shaft.

Inspection

The following procedure is provided to determine overall wear of the oil pump. The pump is not repairable and must be replaced if any tolerance is greater than specified.

1. Drive out pins that hold oil pump halves together and separate them (**Figure 144**).

2. Measure clearance between inner and outer rotors (**Figure 145**). It should measure 0.2mm (0.008in.).

3. Measure clearance between outer rotor and body (**Figure 146**). It should measure 0.25mm (0.0098in.).

4. With a straightedge, measure rotor side clearance (**Figure 147**). It should be 0.15mm (0.0059in.).

CAM CHAIN TENSIONER

Removal/Installation

NOTE
If engine is still installed in motorcycle, it is necessary to remove carburetors to gain access to the tensioner. Perform **Carburetor Removal** *as outlined in Chapter Seven.*

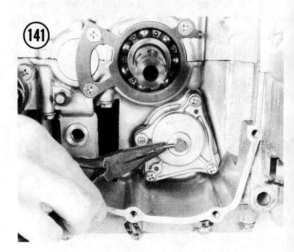

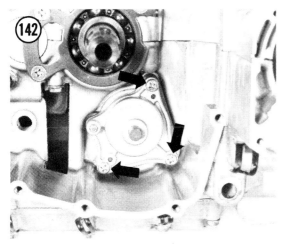

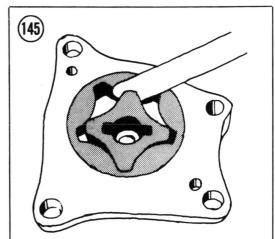

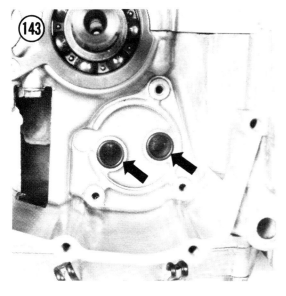

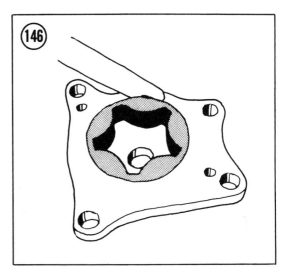

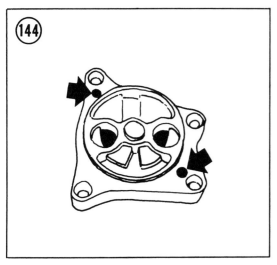

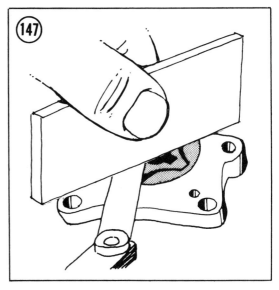

4

1. Loosen locknut securing lockscrew and tighten lockscrew to hold tensioner pushrod (**Figure 148**).

2. Remove 3 bolts securing tensioner assembly (**Figure 149**) and remove tensioner.

3. Installation is the reverse of these steps. Make sure gasket is properly positioned on engine. Loosen locknut and back out lockscrew 1/4 turn to release plunger. Tighten locknut.

NOTE
Do not back out lockscrew more than 1/2 turn or plunger will become disengaged from tensioner body. If this should occur it will be necessary to remove tensioner assembly to install plunger into tensioner body.

Disassembly/Assembly

1. Loosen locknut and back out lockscrew until pushrod is fully released.

2. Remove pushrod and spring.

3. Clean all parts in solvent and inspect assembly for excessive wear or damage (**Figure 150**).

4. Lightly grease pushrod and opening in tensioner body.

5. Rotate large knurled nut fully counterclockwise and install pushrod and spring. Make sure that flat spot on pushrod coincides with position of lockscrew. Move pushrod in and out several times to make sure it moves freely without sticking or binding.

6. Fully install pushrod and secure with lockscrew. Secure lockscrew with locknut.

Table 1
CAMSHAFT LOBE HEIGHT SPECIFICATIONS

	Standard	Service Limit
Intake	36.265-36.295mm (1.4278-1.4289 in.)	36.150mm (1.4232 in.)
Exhaust	35.735-35.765mm (1.4069-1.4081 in.)	35.600mm (1.4016 in.)

Table 2   CAMSHAFT JOURNAL WEAR SPECIFICATIONS

Standard	Service Limit
0.020-0.054mm (0.0008-0.0021 in.)	0.15mm (0.0059 in.)

Table 3   VALVE STEM SPECIFICATIONS

Valve	Standard	Service limit
Intake valves	6.965-6.980mm (0.2742-0.2748 in.)	6.90mm (0.2716 in.)
Exhaust valves	6.955-6.970mm (0.2738-0.2744 in.)	6.805mm (0.2679 in.)

Table 4   VALVE SPRING SPECIFICATIONS

Spring	Standard	Limit
Inner	35.3-37.0mm (1.39-1.46 in.)	33.8mm (1.33 in.)
Outer	43.0-43.25mm (1.69-1.703 in.)	41.5mm (1.63 in.)

Table 5   VALVE SEAT WIDTH SPECIFICATION

Standard	Wear Limit
1.0-1.2mm (0.04-0.05 in.)	1.5mm (0.06 in.)

Table 6
CYLINDER AND PISTON SPECIFICATIONS

Cylinder inner diameter New	65.000-65.015mm (2.5591-2.5596 in.)
Wear limit	65.100mm (2.5629 in.)
Piston diameter Standard	64.945-64.960mm (2.5569-2.5575 in.)
Wear limit	64.800mm (2.5512 in.)
Piston to cylinder clearance	0.050-0.060mm (0.0020-0.0024 in.)

Table 7   PISTON RING SPECIFICATIONS

	Standard	Limit
Ring-to-groove clearance		
Top	0.020-0.055mm (0.0008-0.0022 in.)	0.18mm (0.007 in.)
Middle	0.020-0.060mm (0.0008-0.0024 in.)	0.18mm (0.007 in.)
Oil		0.15mm (0.006 in.)
Ring thickness		
Top	1.175-1.190mm (0.0463-0.0469 in.)	1.10mm (0.043 in.)
Middle	1.170-1.190mm (0.0460-0.0469 in.)	1.10mm (0.043 in.)
Ring groove width		
Top	1.21-1.23mm (0.0476-0.0484 in.)	1.30mm (0.051 in.)
Middle	1.21-1.23mm (0.0476-0.0484 in.)	1.30mm (0.051 in.)
Bottom	2.51-2.53mm (0.0988-0.0996 in.)	2.60mm (0.102 in.)
Ring gap		
Top and middle	0.1-0.3mm (0.004-0.012 in.)	0.6mm (0.024 in.)
Free-state ring gap		
Top and middle	8mm (0.31 in.)	6mm (0.24 in.)

NOTE: If you own a 1981 and later model, first check the Supplement at the back of the book for any new service information.

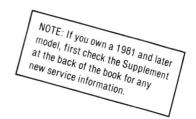

CHAPTER FIVE

5

TSCC ENGINE

The GS750 TSCC engine is an air-cooled 4-cylinder, 4-cycle model equipped with dual overhead camshafts (DOHC). The TSCC (Twin Swirl Combustion Chamber) cylinder head is equipped with 4 valves per cylinder. This patented design (**Figure 1**) combustion chamber provides smoother and more efficient combustion of the fuel/air mixture. Valve operation is by rocker arms directly actuated by the camshafts.

The one-piece forged crankshaft is supported by 6 main bearings. Both the main and connecting rod bearings are automotive-style "plain" insert bearings.

The camshafts are chain-driven from the crankshaft. The cam chain tension is controlled by a spring-loaded slipper tensioner which bears against the rear vertical run of the chain. The cam chain tensioner is automatic and does not require routine adjustment.

The engine and transmission are lubricated from a common wet-sump oil supply. The oil is pumped throughout the engine by a high-pressure pump driven by the clutch. The clutch is a wet-plate type located inside the right engine cover.

This chapter provides complete service and overhaul procedures for the GS750 TSCC engine. Refer to Chapter Six for transmission and clutch repair procedures.

All engine upper end repair, including camshafts, cylinder head and cylinder block, can be performed with the engine installed in the motorcycle. Engine removal is necessary to perform repair on the crankshaft, transmission and certain components of the gearshift and mechanism.

Refer to **Table 1** for all engine torque specifications. **Tables 1-10** are at the end of the chapter.

CAMSHAFTS

Removal/Installation

1. Remove the screws securing the 4 end covers (**Figure 2**) and remove the covers.
2. Refer to Chapter Seven and remove the carburetors.
3. Spring open the clamp securing the breather hose to the breather cover (**Figure 3**) and disconnect the hose from the cover.
4. Remove the bolts securing the breather cover (**Figure 4**) and remove the cover.
5. Disconnect the wires from the horns (**Figure 5**). Remove the bolts securing the horn brackets to the frame and remove the horns.
6. Disconnect the tachometer drive cable (**Figure 6**).
7. Remove each spark plug lead by pulling on the cap. Do not pull on the wire lead or it may

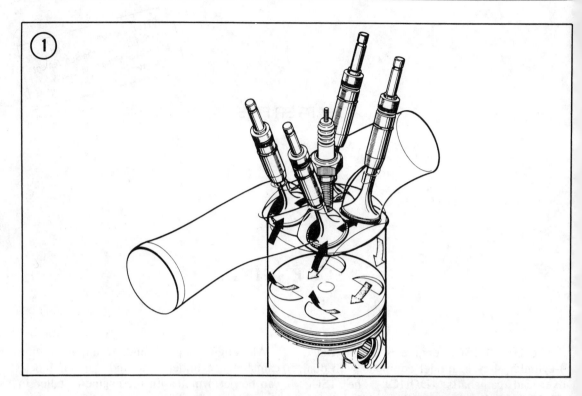

be damaged. Tuck the spark plug leads into the upper frame to keep them clear of the engine.

8. Remove the 4 Phillips head screws from each end of the cam cover (**Figure 7**).

> *NOTE*
> *The 4 Phillips head screws (**Figure 7**) are fitted with a special gasket that must be replaced each time the screws are removed.*

9. Remove the bolts securing the cam cover and remove the cover. The left-front and right-rear cover bolts are slightly longer than the rest.

> *NOTE*
> *To ease cam cover removal, tap around the sealing surface with a soft-faced mallet to help break it loose.*

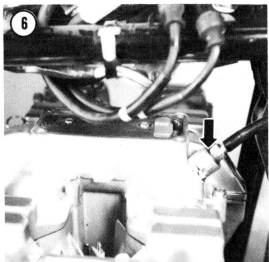

10. Loosen the locknut on the cam chain tensioner and turn the slotted screw clockwise to lock the tensioner pushrod (**Figure 8**).

11. Remove the bolts securing the tensioner assembly to the engine and remove the assembly (**Figure 9**).

12. Gradually loosen then remove the bolts securing the end bearing caps (**Figure 10**) and remove the caps.

NOTE
*The bearing caps are marked with "A", "B", "C" and "D" with corresponding marks on the cylinder head (**Figure 11**).*

The "triangle" enclosing the mark points forward.

13. Gradually and in a crisscross pattern loosen the bolts securing the 4 main camshaft bearing caps and remove the caps (**Figure 10**).

14. Lift up the cam chain and remove the intake (rear) camshaft (**Figure 12**).

15. Tie a piece of wire or cord to the cam chain and secure it to the frame to prevent the chain from falling into the engine.

16. Disengage the cam chain and carefully lift out the exhaust camshaft.

17. Perform the *Inspection* procedure.

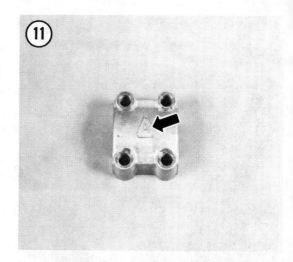

Inspection

NOTE
This procedure describes how to use Plastigage to measure camshaft bearing journal wear. Plastigage can be purchased from most auto supply stores and is available in several sizes. Make sure you purchase Plastigage small enough to measure the camshaft bearing clearance as specified in **Table 2**.

1. Carefully examine both camshafts for evidence of excessive or abnormal wear on the lobes or bearing journals.
2. Inspect each cam sprocket for signs of wear. Excessive wear is unlikely except in engines with high mileage or misaligned sprockets. If sprockets are worn, they must be

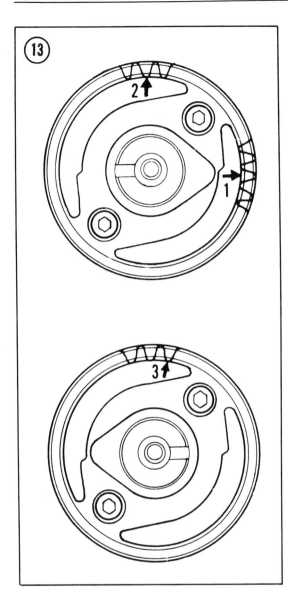

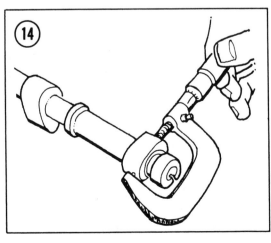

replaced in pairs and a new cam chain must be installed.

NOTE
*The cam chain is a one-piece unit. To replace the chain it is necessary to remove the crankshaft. Refer to **Lower End Disassembly**.*

3. If sprockets are replaced, ensure that they are positioned on the camshafts correctly. Refer to **Figure 13** for the correct positioning of the marks in relation to the notches on the ends of the camshafts. Apply a couple of drops of blue Loctite (Lock N' Seal No. 2114) to the sprocket Allen head bolts and torque them to 0.9-1.2 mkg (6.5-8.5 ft.-lb.).

4. Use a micrometer and measure the height of each camshaft lobe as shown in **Figure 14**. Refer to **Table 2** for wear specifications.

5. Measure bearing journal wear with Plastigage as follows:

  a. Wipe off all oil from the bearing journal and camshaft bearing surfaces and place the camshaft on the cylinder head.

  b. Place a small strip of Plastigage on each bearing surface.

  c. Install the inside, then outside bearing caps. Tighten the bolts gradually and evenly in a crisscross pattern. Torque the bolts to 0.8-1.2 mkg (6.0-8.5 ft.-lb.).

NOTE
It is not necessary to install the cam chain over the camshafts to check the bearing clearance with Plastigage. Do not allow the camshaft to turn while tightening the bearing cap bolts. If the camshaft is allowed to turn, the Plastigage will be damaged and the whole procedure must be repeated.

6. Remove the bearing caps as outlined under *Camshaft Removal*. Measure the thickness of the Plastigage with the wrapper as shown in **Figure 15**. The Plastigage may adhere to the camshaft or the bearing cap; either location will provide a correct indication. The service limit for bearing journal clearance is 0.15 mm (0.0059 in.). If the clearance exceeds the service limit, determine the defective component as follows:

a. Measure the camshaft bearing journals with a micrometer (**Figure 16**). If the camshaft journals are not within tolerances specified in **Table 2**, the camshafts must be replaced.

b. Install the camshaft bearing caps on the cylinder head without the camshafts. Tighten the bolts gradually and evenly in a crisscross pattern, then torque to 0.8-1.2 mkg (6.0-8.5 ft.-lb.). Use an inside micrometer and measure the inside diameter of each bearing journal on the cylinder head. If the inside diameter exceeds the tolerances specified in **Table 2** the cylinder head must be replaced.

7. Place each camshaft in V-blocks and use a dial indicator to measure the camshaft runout (**Figure 17**). Replace either camshaft if runout exceeds 0.1 mm (0.004 in.).

Installation and Timing

1. Remove the 3 screws securing the ignition cover and remove the cover.

2. Use a 19 mm wrench on the large hex shoulder (**Figure 18**) and rotate the crankshaft clockwise until the timing mark "T" for cylinders 1 and 4 aligns with the pointer on the engine. This positions pistons 1 and 4 at TDC (top dead center).

NOTE
The pointer is visible through the window in the ignition signal generator assembly (Figure 19). Due to the small window size and recessed location of the pointer, it is recommended that the signal generator

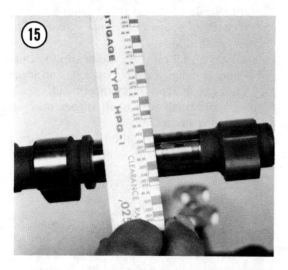

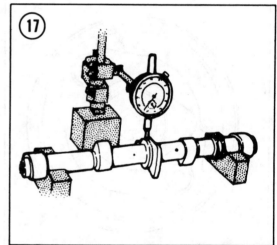

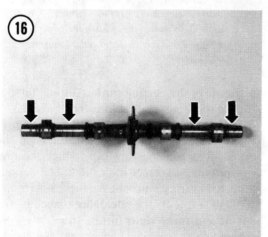

assembly be removed to allow a better view for a more precise alignment of marks. Remove the 3 screws securing the assembly and carefully slide the assembly off the end of the crankshaft.

3. Lubricate the camshaft lobes and bearing journals with molybdenum disulfide lubricant such as Bel-Ray Moly Lube. Spread the lubricant evenly without leaving any dry spots. Lubricate the bearing journals in the cylinder head with engine oil.

4. Lift up the cam chain and install the exhaust camshaft in the cylinder head. The exhaust cam is marked "EX" as shown in **Figure 20**. The notch in the end of the camshaft is positioned on the *right* side of the engine.

5. Check that the TDC timing mark "T" is correctly aligned as shown in **Figure 21**. Pull up on the front of the cam chain to remove all the slack and install the chain over the camshaft sprocket so the No. 1 arrow (**Figure 22**) is directly opposite the gasket surface of the cylinder head. Ensure that the TDC mark is still correctly aligned and no slack exists in the front of the cam chain.

6. Install the inside and outside bearing caps. Make sure that the cast letters on the caps correspond to the cast letters on the cylinder head. The "triangle" enclosing the cast letters must point forward.

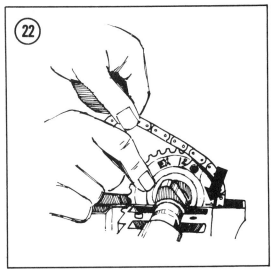

NOTE
The letters on the bearing caps are positioned in a left-to-right order. Letter "A" is located in the left-front of the engine, letter "B" in the right-front, letter "C" in the left-rear and letter "D" in the right-rear.

7. Tighten the bearing cap bolts gradually and evenly in a crisscross pattern. Tighten the bolts on the inside bearing caps first, then the outside bolts.

CAUTION
The bearing cap bolts are specially hardened and are identified by a "9" cast on the bolt head. Use of any other type of bolt could lead to failure and subsequent serious engine damage.

NOTE
It is necessary to hold the cam chain in position on the front sprocket while tightening the bearing cap bolts. As the cap bolts are tightened, the valve spring tension against the rocker arms and the camshaft lobes may cause the camshaft to rotate slightly, causing the chain to jump off alignment by 1 or 2 sprocket teeth. If this should occur, the whole camshaft timing procedure will have to be started over from the beginning.

8. Torque the bearing cap bolts to 0.8-1.2 mkg (6.0-8.5 ft.-lb). Recheck the timing mark alignment and readjust if necessary. If the alignment is correct, the crankshaft can be rotated slightly to relieve the valve spring load on the camshaft and lessen the chance of the chain slipping.

9. Lubricate and install the intake camshaft through the cam chain. The intake camshaft is marked "IN" as shown in **Figure 23**. Make sure the notch in the end of the camshaft is on the right side of the cylinder head.

10. Position the cam chain on the intake cam sprocket so there are exactly 20 chain pins between arrow "2" on the exhaust camshaft and arrow "3" on the intake camshaft as shown in **Figure 24**.

11. Install the bearing caps. Make sure the cast letters on the caps correspond to the cast letters in the cylinder head and that the "triangles" enclosing the marks point

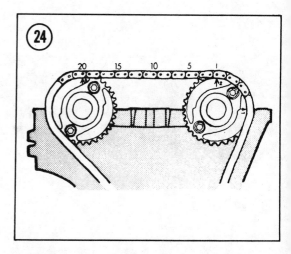

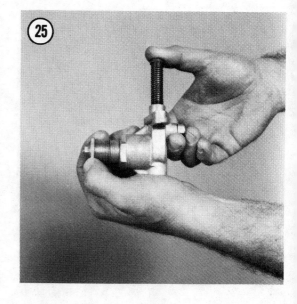

forward. Tighten the bearing cap bolts gradually and evenly in a crisscross pattern. Tighten the bolts on the inside bearing caps first, then the outside caps. Torque the bolts to 0.8-1.2 mkg (6.0-8.5 ft.-lb.).

12. Loosen the locknut and lockscrew on the cam chain tensioner assembly. Push in on the spring-loaded plunger while rotating the large knurled nut counterclockwise (**Figure 25**). When the plunger is pushed in as far as possible, secure it with the lockscrew.

13. Make sure the gasket is in place and install the chain tensioner assembly (**Figure 26**).

14. Back out the lockscrew approximately 1/4 turn to release the spring-loaded plunger. Secure the lockscrew with the locknut (**Figure 27**).

NOTE
Do not back out the lockscrew more than 1/2 turn or the plunger may become disengaged from the tensioner body. If this should occur it will be necessary to remove the tensioner assembly to install the plunger into the tensioner body.

15. Use a 19 mm wrench on the end of the crankshaft and rotate the crankshaft several turns to make sure the camshafts and chain operate smoothly and freely. Recheck the camshaft timing in relation to the TDC marks.

NOTE
Rotate the large knurled nut on the cam chain tensioner counterclockwise while slowly rotating the crankshaft counterclockwise. This rotation will cause the cam chain to push back against the tensioner plunger. Release the knurled nut and slowly rotate the crankshaft clockwise (normal rotation). The knurled nut should rotate clockwise as the plunger takes up the slack in the cam chain. If the knurled nut does not respond as described, the plunger lockscrew may be too tight or the plunger may be sticking. If necessary, refer to **Cam Chain Tensioner** *as outlined in this chapter to disassemble the tensioner assembly.*

16. Install the signal generator assembly if it was removed.

17. Perform *Valve Clearance Adjustment* as outlined in Chapter Three.

18. Use approximately 50 cc's (2 oz.) of engine oil and pour the oil over each camshaft bearing and the tachometer drive gear.

19. Install the cam cover gasket. Use a new gasket if possible. Make sure that all 4 half-moon shaped rubber end plugs (**Figure 28**) are in place.

20. Carefully position the cam cover on the cylinder head so the gasket is not disturbed. Rotate the exposed end of the tachometer drive gear as the cam cover is installed so that the drive gear will engage the camshaft.

CAUTION
The tachometer drive gear must engage the camshaft as the cam cover is installed or the gear will be damaged when the cover bolts are tightened.

5

21. Install the cam cover bolts. The 2 longer bolts are positioned in the left-front and right-rear positions. Tighten all the bolts gradually and evenly in a crisscross pattern and torque them to 0.9-1.0 mkg (6.5-7.0 ft.-lb.).

22. Use new gaskets on the 4 Phillips head screws and install them in the ends of the cam cover (**Figure 29**).

23. Install the breather cover gasket with the opening in the gasket facing forward. Install the breather cover and secure with the 4 bolts. Torque the bolts to 0.9-1.0 mkg (6.5-7.0 ft.-lb.). Connect the breather hose to the breather cover and air box.

24. Install the 4 camshaft end covers.

25. Install the horns and connect the horn wires.

26. Install the carburetors as outlined in Chapter Seven.

27. Connect the tachometer drive cable.

28. Connect the 4 spark plug leads. Make sure the caps fit securely over the spark plugs.

ROCKER ARMS AND ROCKER SHAFTS

The rocker arms and rocker arm shafts are installed in the cylinder head. Each rocker arm bears directly against 2 valves and is actuated by one camshaft lobe.

Removal/Installation

> *NOTE*
> *It is not necessary to remove the rocker arms to remove the valves from the cylinder head.*

1. Perform *Camshaft Removal* as outlined in this chapter.

2. Remove the rocker shaft end cap from the cylinder head (**Figure 30**).

3. Remove the rocker shaft stopper bolt (**Figure 31**).

> *CAUTION*
> *All component parts of each rocker assembly must be kept together in the proper order as they are removed. Do not mix any parts with like components from other rocker assemblies. Wear patterns have developed on these moving parts and*

damage or rapid and excessive wear may result if the parts are intermixed. An egg carton makes an excellent storage unit to keep the rocker components in order.

4. Screw a 6 mm bolt, such as a cam cover bolt, into the end of the rocker shaft as shown in **Figure 32**.

5. Carefully slide out the rocker shaft. Collect each rocker arm and spring as the shaft is removed (**Figure 33**).

NOTE
*All exhaust rocker arms can be identified by the oil groove machined in the surface as shown in **Figure 34**.*

6. Perform the *Inspection* procedure.

7. Installation is the reverse of these steps. Keep the following points in mind:

   a. Ensure that the rocker arm springs are positioned on the outside of each rocker arm.

   b. Use an awl or small Phillips screwdriver to locate the hole for the shaft stopper bolt as shown in **Figure 35**.

   c. Torque the rocker shaft stopper bolt to 0.8-1.0 mkg (6.0-7.0 ft.-lb.).

   d. Make sure the gasket on each rocker shaft end cap is in good condition and install the cap in the cylinder head.

Inspection

1. Carefully examine each rocker arm shaft (**Figure 36**) for signs of galling, scoring or excessive wear. Replace the shaft if necessary.

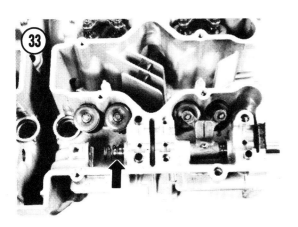

2. Inspect the machined surface of each rocker arm (**Figure 37**) for signs of excessive wear or damage. Replace all defective rocker arms. Make sure the oil hole is completely clear of any sludge or particles.

3. Carefully inspect the end of each valve adjuster where it contacts the end of the valve (**Figure 38**). Excessive or uneven wear can cause improper valve adjustment, leading to more serious damage. All worn adjusters should be replaced.

4. Slide the rocker arms and springs on the rocker shaft in the proper order. Check that the rocker arms move freely on the shaft without excessive play.

5. Use an inside micrometer and measure the inside diameter of each rocker arm. Replace any rocker arm not within the tolerances specified in **Table 3**.

6. Use a micrometer and measure the outside diameter of the rocker arm shafts at each rocker arm pivot location. Replace any rocker arm shaft not within the tolerances specified in **Table 3**.

CYLINDER HEAD

The cylinder head can be removed while the engine is installed in the motorcycle frame.

Removal

1. Perform *Camshaft Removal* as outlined in this chapter.

2. Perform *Exhaust System Removal* as outlined in Chapter Seven.

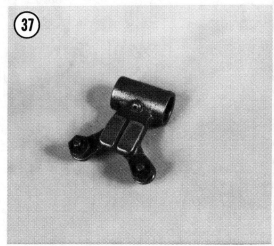

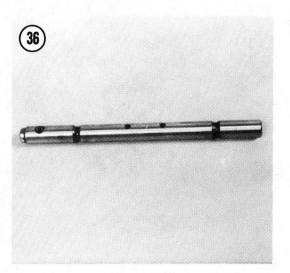

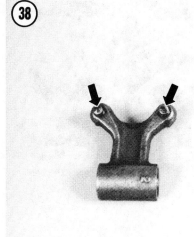

3. Gently pry up on the end of the forward chain guide until the end is free from the head (**Figure 39**). Pull the chain guide straight up and out of the engine. If the engine is still installed in the frame, it will be necessary to pull the chain guide up between the upper frame tubes in order to clear the engine with the lower end of the guide.

4. Remove the two 6 mm bolts from each end of the cylinder head (**Figure 40**).

5. Remove the 6 mm bolt from the front of the engine between the center exhaust ports (**Figure 41**).

6. Refer to **Figure 42** and gradually and evenly remove the 12 head nuts in descending order. Numbers denoting sequence are cast in the head close to each head nut. A magnetic tool retriever can be used to lift the head nuts out of the center recesses.

NOTE
Four different types of nuts and 2 types of washers are used to secure the head. The 4 corner studs use 4 long nuts with copper washers. The 2 center-rear studs use chrome acorn nuts with copper washers. The 2 center-front studs use special machined nuts with O-rings and no washers. The remaining 4 shouldered nuts are used with steel washers.

7. Tap around the base of the cylinder head with a plastic or rubber mallet to break the head loose from the cylinder and lift off the head.

5

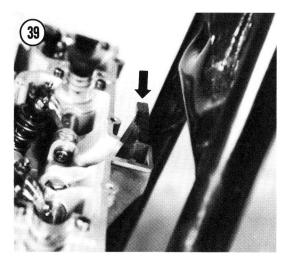

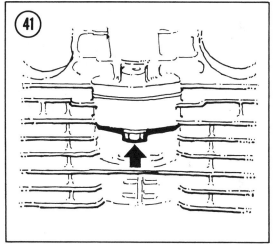

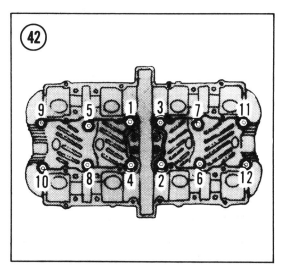

CAUTION
The cooling fins on the cylinder head are fragile. Tap the cylinder head carefully to avoid damaging the fins. Never use a metal hammer.

8. Remove and discard the old head gasket (**Figure 43**).

9. Perform *Inspection.*

Inspection

1. Carefully clean all traces of gasket and sealant residue from the combustion chamber side and camshaft side of the cylinder head.

2. Without removing the valves, remove all carbon deposits from the combustion chambers with a wire brush and solvent. Stubborn deposits can be removed with a blunt scraper made of hardwood or a piece of aluminum that has been rounded and smoothed on one end as shown in **Figure 44**. Never use a hard metal scraper. Small burrs resulting from gouges in the combustion chamber will create hot spots which can cause preignition and heat erosion of the head and piston. After all carbon has been removed from the combustion chamber and exhaust ports, clean the entire head in solvent.

NOTE
*If valve inspection and/or repair is desired, refer to **Valves** as outlined in this chapter.*

3. Carefully examine the combustion chambers and ports for cracks or damage. Some types of cracks and/or damage can be repaired with heliarc welding. Refer such work to an authorized dealer or welding shop experienced with cylinder head repair.

4. Use a straightedge and check the gasket surface of the head in several places as shown in **Figure 45**. Such an inspection might be best performed by a dealer or machine shop. Replace the head if the gasket surface is warped beyond the service limit of 0.2 mm (0.008 in.).

Installation

1. Ensure that the gasket surface on the cylinder is clean and free of old gasket residue.

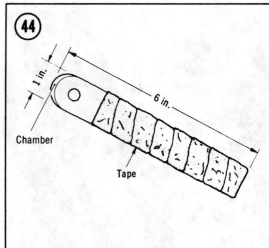

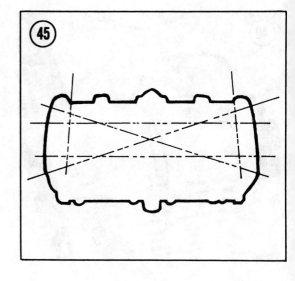

2. Clean all the carbon from the pistons. Wipe out each cylinder carefully to remove all debris.

3. Install a new head gasket over the studs on the cylinder. Make sure the wider portion of the metal ring around the combustion chamber is positioned toward the front of the cylinder (**Figure 46**).

4. Pull the cam chain up through the opening in the head and carefully lower the head down over the cylinder studs. Make sure the alignment dowels are engaged, then press the head down against the gasket.

5. Install new O-rings on the machined head nuts (**Figure 47**). Lubricate the O-rings with motor oil and install the nuts on the 2 center-front studs *without washers*.

NOTE
Stuff rags into the cam chain tunnel before attempting to install the washers over the head studs. A copper washer accidentally dropped into the chain tunnel obviously cannot be removed with a magnetic tool retriever. Dropping a washer into the engine could easily cause a lot of extra work and aggravation.

6. Install the 4 long head nuts on the 4 corner studs with copper washers. Use a screwdriver as shown in **Figure 48** to help route the washers over the studs.

7. Install copper washers and the chrome acorn nuts on the 2 center-rear studs.

8. Use steel washers with the remaining 4 shouldered head nuts. Remove the rags from the cam chain tunnel.

9. Tighten the head nuts gradually and evenly in the sequence shown in **Figure 49**. Torque the nuts to 3.5-4.0 mkg (26-29 ft.-lb.).

10. Install the two 6 mm bolts in each end of the head and the one 6 mm bolt between the center exhaust ports. See **Figure 50** and **Figure 51**. Torque the bolts to 0.7-1.1 mkg (5.8 ft.-lb.)

11. Install the forward chain guide. The lower end of the guide must "slip into place" and feel secure in the bottom of the engine. If the bottom of the guide is correctly installed, it will be necessary to slightly spring back the upper portion of the chain guide in order to

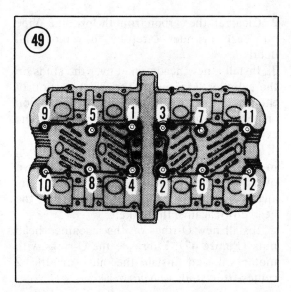

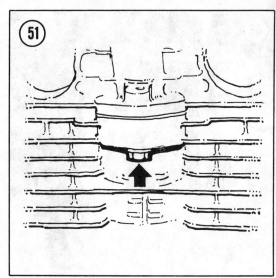

Make sure that the upper end of the guide fits securely in the groove as shown in **Figure 52**.

12. Refer to Chapter Seven and install the exhaust system.

13. Perform *Camshaft, Installation and Timing* as outlined in this chapter.

14. Refer to Chapter Three and perform *Valve Adjustment*.

VALVES

Valve servicing requires the use of a valve spring compressor tool to remove the valves from the head. Suitable valve spring compressors can be rented from most rental shops; however, it may be less expensive to have a dealer or other motorcycle repair shop remove the valves from the head. This is especially true on the TSCC engine. The valves are smaller than on many motorcycles or small automobiles. It may be necessary to take the head to a dealer who is equipped with the proper spring compressor.

Removal

Refer to **Figure 53** for this procedure.

1. Perform *Cylinder Head, Removal* as outlined in this chapter.

2. Install one end of the valve spring compressor against one valve head. Place the

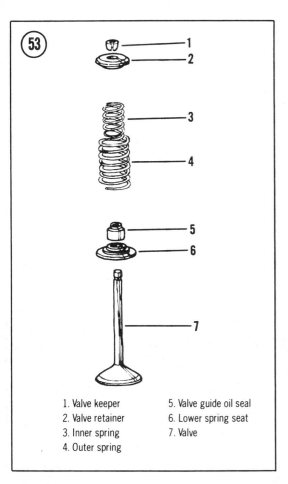

1. Valve keeper
2. Valve retainer
3. Inner spring
4. Outer spring
5. Valve guide oil seal
6. Lower spring seat
7. Valve

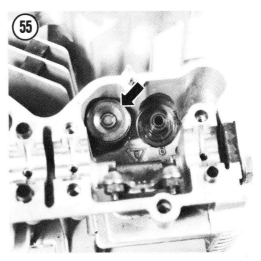

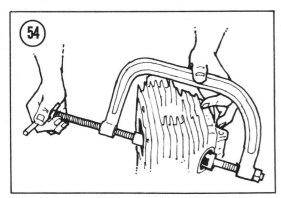

other end of the tool squarely over the valve retainer (**Figure 54**).

CAUTION
All component parts of each valve assembly must be kept together in the proper order as they are removed. Do not mix any parts with like components from other valve assemblies. Wear patterns

have developed on these moving parts and damage or rapid and excessive wear may result if the parts are intermixed. An egg carton makes an excellent storage unit to keep the valve components in order.

3. Tighten the valve spring compressor until the split valve keeper separates. Lift out both split keepers with needlenose pliers.
4. Gradually loosen the compressor tool and remove it from the cylinder head. Lift off the upper valve retainer (**Figure 55**).
5. Remove the inner and outer valve springs. Keep the springs together as they are a matched pair.
6. Tip up the head and remove the valve.
7. Use needlenose pliers and remove the valve guide oil seal (**Figure 56**). Discard the

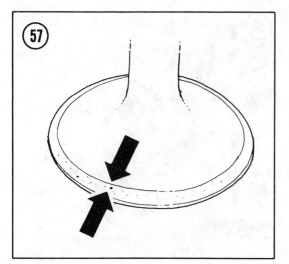

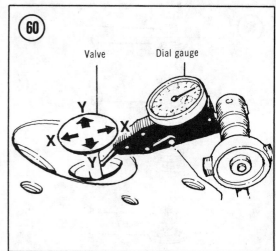

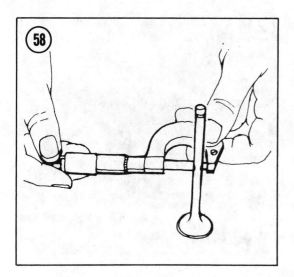

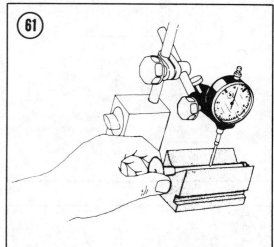

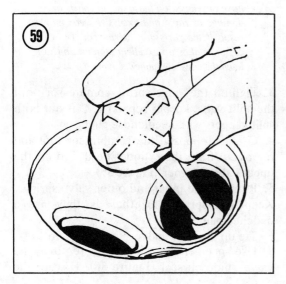

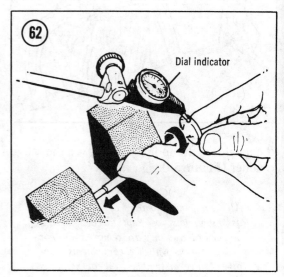

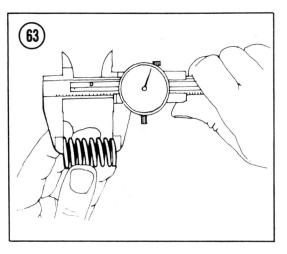

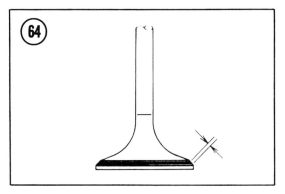

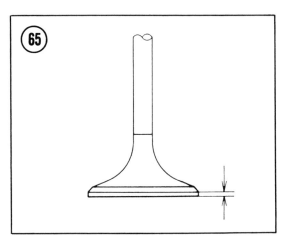

old seal as it will be destroyed when it is removed.

NOTE
Valve guide oil seals should be routinely replaced whenever the valves are removed. Failure to replace the seals may result in excessive oil consumption.

8. Lift out the lower valve seat.
9. Repeat the procedure for the other valves.
10. Perform *Inspection.*

Inspection

1. Clean the valves with a wire brush and solvent.
2. Inspect the contact surface of each valve for burning or pitting (**Figure 57**). Replace any valve that is burned, pitted, warped or cracked. The valves are made from a specially hardened material and should not be ground or refaced.
3. Measure the valve stem with a micrometer as shown in **Figure 58**. Replace the valve if not within limits specified in **Table 4**.
4. Remove all carbon and varnish from the valve guides with a stiff spiral wire brush.
5. Insert each valve in its guide. Hold the valve just slightly off its seat and rock it sideways in 2 directions as shown in **Figure 59**. If it rocks more than slightly, the guide is worn and must be replaced. If a dial indicator is available, a more accurate measurement can be made as shown in **Figure 60**. Replace any guides that exceed the valve-to-guide clearance specified in **Table 4**. If guides must be replaced, refer the task to an authorized dealer or machine shop.
6. Use a dial indicator and V-blocks as shown in **Figure 61** and measure the valve stem deflection or runout. Replace valves if the stem deflection exceeds 0.05 mm (0.002 in.).
7. Use a dial indicator and one V-block as shown in **Figure 62** and measure the runout or deflection of the valve head. Replace valves if the head deflection exceeds 0.03 mm (0.001 in.).
8. Measure valve springs heights as shown in **Figure 63**. All springs should be as specified in **Table 4**, with no bends or distortions. Replace defective springs in pairs.
9. Measure valve seat width (**Figure 64**). If valve seat width exceeds the dimension specified in **Table 4** valve seat reconditioning is necessary. Refer to *Valve Seat Reconditioning.*
10. Measure the face (margin) on each valve with a caliper (**Figure 65**). The valve face decreases as the valve seat wears. If valve face

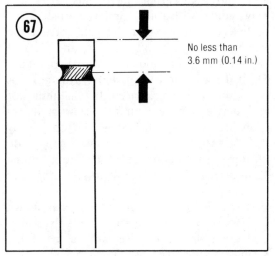

No less than
3.6 mm (0.14 in.)

is not as specified in **Table 4**, the valve must be replaced.

11. Inspect the valve seats in the cylinder head (**Figure 66**). If the seats are burned or damaged they must be reconditioned. This should be performed by an authorized dealer or local machine shop.

12. The ends of the valve stems can be refaced if necessary; however, the end of the valve must not be less than 3.6 mm (0.14 in.) as shown in **Figure 67**.

Installation

1. Install the lower spring seat over the valve guide.

2. Lubricate the lip on the new valve guide seal with engine oil. Use a 7 or 8 mm socket as a seal installing tool and position the seal over the end of the valve guide. Gently tap the seal into place. Ensure that the seal is seated squarely over the valve guide and is locked into place (**Figure 68**).

3. Install the inner and outer valve springs. Note that the coils are closer together on the bottom end (toward cylinder head) of the springs (**Figure 69**). Ensure that the springs are installed correctly.

4. Lubricate the valve stems with Bel-Ray Moly Lube or equivalent and install the valves in the head.

5. Place the upper spring retainer over the valve springs. Install the spring compressor tool and tighten the compressor until the end of the valve is exposed enough to install the split keepers.

6. Apply a small amount of grease to each keeper half and stick the keeper to a small screwdriver to aid installation. Install the split keepers on the valve stem and back off the spring compressor until the split keepers secure the valve mechanism.

7. Remove the valve spring compressor. Use a soft drift or a soft-faced hammer and tap the end of each valve to make sure the keepers are properly seated.

8. Perform *Cylinder Head, Installation.*

Valve Seat and Seal Inspection

1. Use a caliper and measure the width of the seat on the valve. If the seat width is not within the tolerance specified in **Table 4**, the valve seat in the cylinder head must be reconditioned.

2. The most accurate method for checking the seal of the valve is to use Prussian Blue or machinist's dye, available from auto part stores or machine shops. If Prussian Blue or dye is available, perform the following:

  a. Thoroughly clean the valve and valve seat with solvent or detergent.

  b. Spread a thin layer of Prussian Blue or machinist's dye evenly on the valve face.

  c. Moisten the end of a "suction cup" valve tool (**Figure 70**) and attach it to the valve. Insert the valve into the guide.

  d. Tap the valve up and down in the head. Do not rotate the valve or a false indication will result.

  e. Remove the valve and examine the impression left by the Prussian Blue or dye. If the impression left in the dye (on the valve or in the head) is not even and continuous and the valve seat width (**Figure 71**) is not within specified tolerance (**Table 4**) the seat in the cylinder head must be reconditioned. Refer to *Valve Seat Reconditioning.*

3. Closely examine the valve seat in the cylinder head. It should be smooth and even with a polished seating surface.

4. Perform *Valves, Installation.*

Valve Guide Replacement

Perform *Valves, Inspection* to determine the condition of the valve guides. The valve guides must be replaced if there is excessive stem-to-guide clearance or valve tipping. Guide replacement requires special tools as well as considerable expertise. If guide replacement is required, refer the task to an authorized dealer or machine shop.

Valve Seat Reconditioning

Special valve cutter tools and considerable expertise is required to properly recondition the valve seats in the cylinder head. You can save considerable money by removing the cylinder head and taking just the head to a dealer or machine shop. The following procedure is provided in the event that you are not near a dealer and the local machine shop is not familiar with the cutting process

used on GS750 TSCC engines. Refer to
Figure 72 for the following procedure.
1. Use a 45° cutter and descale and clean the
valve seat with one or two turns.
2. Measure the valve seat. The seat should be
0.9-1.1 mm (0.035-0.043 in.). If the seat is
burned or pitted additional turns with the 45°
cutter are required.

> *NOTE*
> *Measure the valve seat contact area after
> each cut to make sure the contact area is
> correct and to prevent removing too much
> material.*

3. If the seat contact area is too low, the 15°
cutter must be used to raise and narrow the
contact area.
4. If the seat contact area is too high, the 45°
cutter must be used to lower and narrow the
contact area.
5. Recheck the seat width and recut the seat
with the 45° cutter if necessary.
6. Check that the finished valve seat has a
smooth and velvety surface. Do not lap the
finished seat. The final seating of the valve
will take place when the engine is first run.
7. Thoroughly clean all valve components
and the cylinder head in solvent or detergent
and hot water. Install the valves and fill the
ports with solvent to check for leaks. If any
leaks are present the valve seats must be
inspected for foreign material or burrs that can
prevent a proper seal.

CYLINDER BLOCK AND PISTONS

Cylinder block and piston repair work can
be performed with the engine installed in the
motorcycle.

Removal

1. Perform *Cylinder Head, Removal* as
outlined in this chapter.
2. Tap around the base of the cylinder with a
rubber mallet or plastic hammer to break the
cylinder loose from the crankcase.
3. Gently lift up and remove the cylinder
block from the engine (**Figure 73**). Note that
the arrows on all the pistons point forward
(**Figure 74**).

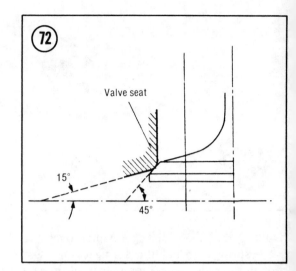
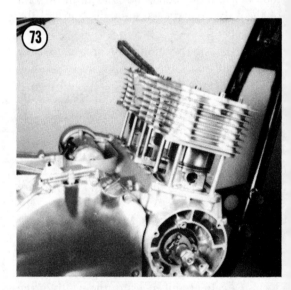
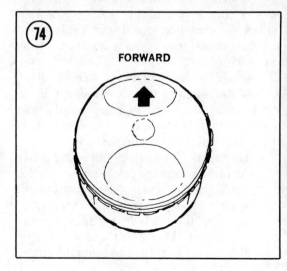

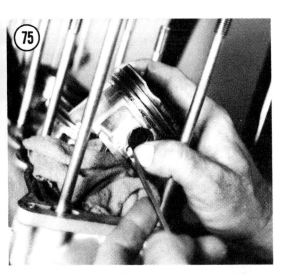

4. Remove and discard the cylinder base gasket.

5. Stuff clean rags into the crankcase openings around each connecting rod to prevent dirt and piston pin snap rings from falling into the engine.

6. Use a small screwdriver or awl and carefully pry out the snap ring through the notch in the piston (**Figure 75**). Partially cover the opening in the piston with your thumb to prevent the snap ring from flying out. Discard the old snap ring.

7. Use a wooden dowel or socket extension and push out the piston pin (**Figure 76**). Remove the pin and lift off the piston.

> *CAUTION*
> *On some engines (particularly those with high mileage) the piston pin may be difficult to remove. Do not attempt to drive out the pin or connecting rod damage may result. If the piston pin cannot be pushed or gently tapped out, use a piston pin extractor tool. Refer to **Figure 77** for an example of a locally fabricated type. If such a tool is not available, have a dealer remove the piston pin. It is a quick and inexpensive job with the right tools and will prevent expensive engine damage.*

8. Mark the inside of the piston with a felt pen or scribe to identify its location. Repeat the removal procedure for the other pistons.

> *NOTE*
> *If the engine is to be completely disassembled, it may be desirable to leave one piston temporarily installed. An installed piston can be used with a piston holding fixture to prevent the crankshaft from turning. This may be required if the magneto rotor or ignition advance governor must be removed. Refer to **Lower End Disassembly.***

9. Perform *Cylinder Block Inspection* and *Piston and Ring Inspection*.

Cylinder Block Inspection

The following procedure requires the use of highly specialized and expensive measuring equipment. If such equipment is not available,

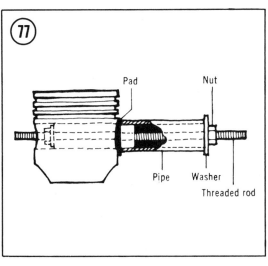

Pad   Nut

Pipe   Washer

Threaded rod

have a dealer or machine shop perform the following measurements.

1. Use an inside micrometer or cylinder bore gauge and measure the cylinder bore (**Figure 78**). Measure the bore at 3 locations as shown in **Figure 79** and in 2 positions, 90° apart. Compare the measurements with the specifications in **Table 5** and rebore the cylinder if necessary.

2. Examine the condition of the cylinder bore. The cylinder should be rebored if the surface is scored or abraded. Pistons are available in oversize increases of 0.5 mm and 1.0 mm. Purchase the oversize pistons before having the cylinder bored. The pistons must first be measured and the cylinder bored to match them in order to maintain the specified piston-to-cylinder clearance. All pistons should be replaced as a set.

Piston and Ring Inspection

1. Measure the pistons at the point shown in **Figure 80**. If any piston is not within the tolerance specified in **Table 5** replace all pistons as a set.

2. Use a bore gauge or a snap gauge and micrometer and measure the piston pin bore in each piston (**Figure 81**). Use a micrometer and measure each piston pin in the center and at both ends. Subtract the piston pin dimension from the inside piston pin bore dimension to obtain the piston pin-pin bore clearance. If the bore clearance dimension exceeds the service limit of 0.12 mm (0.0047 in.), replace the piston and pin as a set.

3. Clean the top of the pistons with a soft metal scaper to remove carbon (**Figure 82**). Use a piece of old piston ring to clean the ring grooves (**Figure 83**). Thoroughly clean the pistons in solvent or detergent and hot water.

4. Use a feeler gauge and check the side clearance of the rings in the piston grooves (**Figure 84**). If the clearance is greater than that specified in **Table 6**, measure the ring thickness, then the groove width to determine which part is worn. All parts worn beyond their respective service limits must be replaced. Ring thickness and groove width specifications are shown in **Table 6**.

5. Place the 2 top piston rings, one at a time, into the cylinder bore and measure the ring

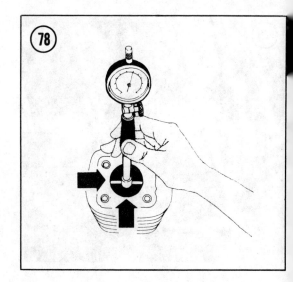

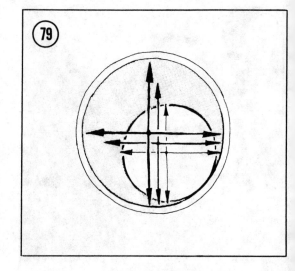

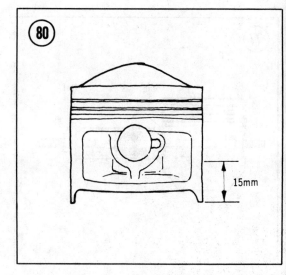

15mm

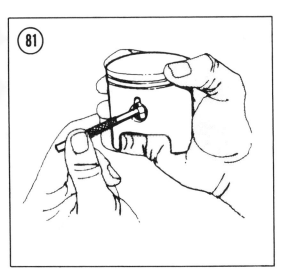

end gap (**Figure 85**). Use the piston to push the ring squarely into the cylinder bore approximately 25 mm (1 in.). This measurement is required for new rings as well as old ones. Compare the actual ring gap to **Table 6** and replace the old rings if their gap is greater than the specified service limit. For new rings it is more likely that the gap will be less than minimum. If such is the case, clamp a fine file in a vise and carefully file the ring ends as shown in **Figure 86**.

6. Measure the free-state ring gap as shown in **Figure 87**. If the free-state ring gap is less than specified, the ring does not have sufficient spring tension to seat well. Such a ring should be replaced.

5

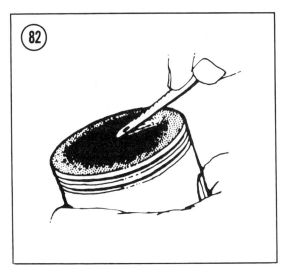

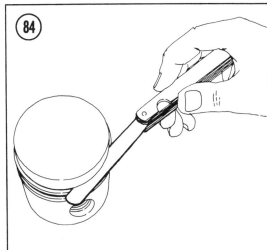

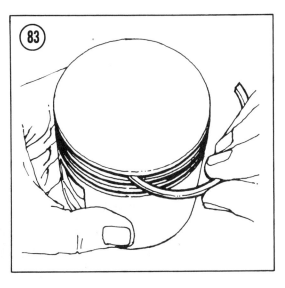

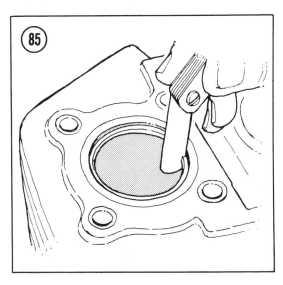

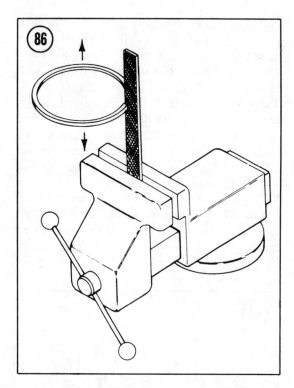

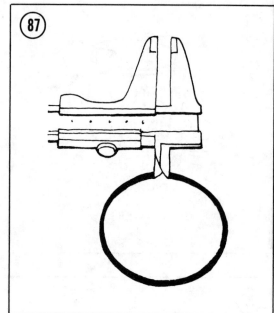

7. Existing rings that are oversize can be identified in the following manner:

   a. The top 2 rings are stamped with code numbers next to the letter on the ring end. A 0.5 mm oversized ring is stamped with the number "50" while a 1.0 mm oversized ring is stamped with the number "100."

   b. An oversized oil ring spacer is identified by color codes. A 0.5 mm oversized spacer is painted red while a 1.0 mm oversize spacer is painted yellow.

   c. Oversized oil ring side rails must be measured with a caliper to determine their size in relation to standard size side-rails. Oversized oil ring side rails are 0.5 mm or 1.0 mm larger than the standard bore size.

8. Carefully examine each piston around the area of the skirt, pin and ring grooves for signs of cracks, stress or metal fatigue. Replace all the pistons as a set if any signs of abnormal wear are present on any piston.

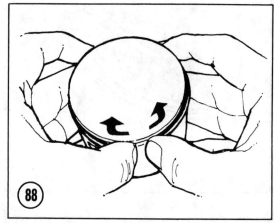

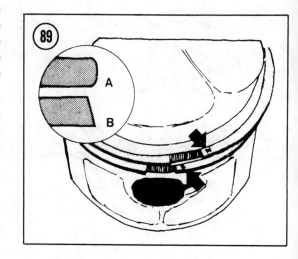

Installation

1. Carefully spread the piston rings with your thumbs as shown in **Figure 88** and install the rings in the appropriate grooves (**Figure 89**).

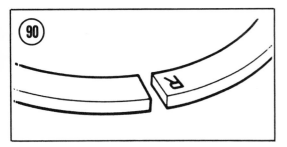

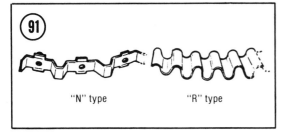

"N" type   "R" type

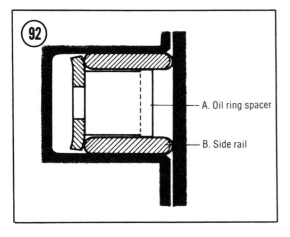

A. Oil ring spacer

B. Side rail

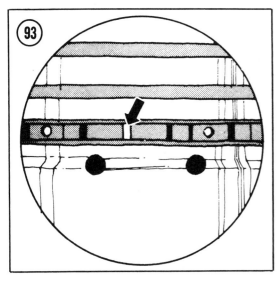

5

The 2 top rings are stamped with either a letter "R" or "N" as shown in **Figure 90**. The identifying letters on the ring ends always face toward the top of the piston.

2. Two types of oil ring spacers are used (**Figure 91**). The "R" type spacer must always be installed with "R" type upper rings and "N" type spacer with "N" type upper rings. The side rails on the oil rings are not marked and can be used with either type of oil ring spacer.

3. Install the oil ring spacer first. The 2 side rails can then be installed. There is no top or bottom designation for the side rails. Ensure that the side rails fit around the spacer as shown in **Figure 92**. Some clearance may be present between the ends of the oil ring spacer (**Figure 93**) or the ends may butt together. Do not allow the ends of the oil spacer to overlap.

4. Install one new snap ring into the piston pin groove.

CAUTION
If possible, always use new snap rings to secure the piston pin. An old snap ring could work out and cause serious and expensive engine damage.

5. Lubricate the piston, piston pin and connecting rod with assembly oil or engine oil and install the piston on the connecting rod (**Figure 94**). Make sure that the arrow on the piston points forward toward the front of the engine.

CAUTION
Never use STP or similar friction-reducing products as assembly lubricant. Even a

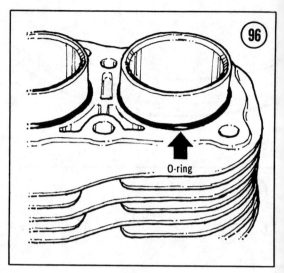

O-ring

small amount will combine with the engine oil and destroy the friction properties of the clutch. If this should occur, the engine's entire lubrication system must be flushed and new clutch plates installed.

CAUTION
If it is necessary to tap the piston pin into the connecting rod, do so with a soft-faced hammer. Make sure you support the piston to prevent the lateral shock from being transmitted to the lower connecting rod bearing.

6. Partially hold a new snap ring in position with your thumb and install the snap ring into the piston groove. Make sure the snap ring locks into the groove. Rotate the snap ring so that a solid portion of the snap ring is opposite the notch in the piston (**Figure 95**).
7. Make sure that the engine base and the bottom of the cylinder block are clean and free of old gasket residue. Install a new base gasket on the crankcase.
8. Remove the old O-rings from the base of each cylinder liner and replace with new ones (**Figure 96**).
9. Stagger the rings on each piston so that the end gaps are approximately 120° from each other (**Figure 97**).
10. Install a piston holding fixture under one of the inboard pistons (**Figure 98**) to hold the pistons in position while installing the cylinder block. Carefully rotate the crankshaft until the piston is firmly against the holding fixture.

NOTE
*A simple homemade holding fixture can be made of wood. Refer to **Figure 99** for approximate dimensions.*

11. Oil each piston and cylinder bore with assembly oil or engine oil. Feed the cam chain up through the chain tunnel and start the cylinder block down over the studs (**Figure 100**). Compress the rings on the 2 inboard pistons with your fingers or a ring compressor and carefully slide the cylinder block over the pistons until the cylinder block contacts the 2 outboard pistons.

NOTE
*A large hose clamp (**Figure 101**) can be used for an effective and inexpensive ring compressor.*

12. Using your fingers or a ring compressor, carefully compress the outboard piston rings while pushing down on the cylinder block until all 3 rings on each piston are fully installed into the cylinder bores.
13. Remove the ring compressors and piston holding fixture. Push the cylinder down completely against the gasket.
14. Perform *Cylinder Head, Installation.*

ENGINE

Engine Removal and External Disassembly

The engine must be removed from the motorcycle to perform repair on the

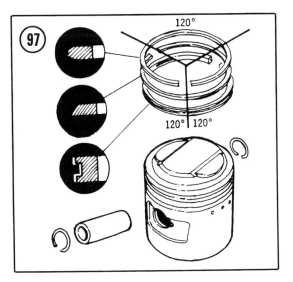

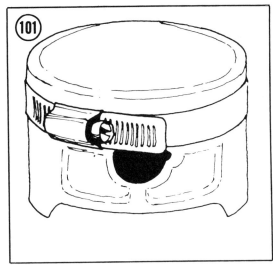

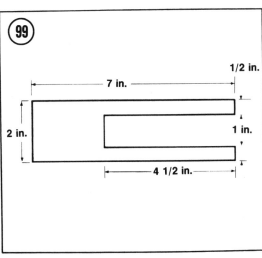

crankshaft, transmission and most of the gearshifting mechanism. If you are performing the repair work without assistance, it may be easier to first remove the cylinder head and cylinder block. Head and block removal will greatly reduce the bulk and weight of the engine, making engine removal much more manageable for one person. Refer to *Cylinder Head Removal* and *Cylinder Block and Pistons, Removal* as outlined in the chapter.

NOTE
The following procedure contains several steps that are only necessary if complete

engine disassembly is desired. Certain components on the engine are more easily removed while the engine is still mounted in the frame as the frame makes an excellent holding device for the engine. Perform the full procedure if disassembly is desired.

1. Thoroughly clean the motorcycle at a coin-operated car wash or with detergent and a hose. Make sure the engine and all nuts and bolts are as clean as possible. A clean motorcycle is not only more pleasant to work on, it helps prevent contamination of vital moving parts.

2. Remove any accessories such as a fairing or safety bars that may interfere with the engine removal.

3. Place the motorcycle on the centerstand and position a drain pan under the engine. Use a 13/16 in. spark plug socket and remove the oil sump drain plug (**Figure 102**). Allow several minutes for the oil to drain completely.

4. Remove the 2 acorn nuts securing the chrome cover over the oil pressure sensor (**Figure 103**). Unscrew the small bolt securing the oil pressure sensor wire and remove the wire (**Figure 104**).

5. Position the drain pan under the oil filter housing and remove the remaining 3 acorn nuts securing the oil filter cover. Remove the cover (**Figure 105**) and the oil filter.

NOTE
Flat washers are only used with the 3 lower acorn nuts.

6. Remove the bolts securing the right footrest (**Figure 106**) and remove the footrest.

7. Remove the pinch bolt securing the footbrake pedal (**Figure 107**). Disengage the return spring and slide the pedal off the shaft. Note that the punch mark on the shaft is aligned with the split opening on the brake pedal (**Figure 108**).

NOTE
When removing the brake pedal and gearshift lever, it may be necessary to slightly pry open the split opening in the pedal or lever with a screwdriver to ease the removal from the shaft.

8. Remove the bolts securing the left footrest (**Figure 109**) and remove the footrest.

9. Remove the pinch bolt securing the gearshift lever (**Figure 110**). The bolt must be removed completely, not just loosened. Slide off the shift lever.

10. Remove the seat and remove the bolt securing the fuel tank to the frame (**Figure 111**).

11. Disconnect the fuel line and vacuum line from the fuel valve.

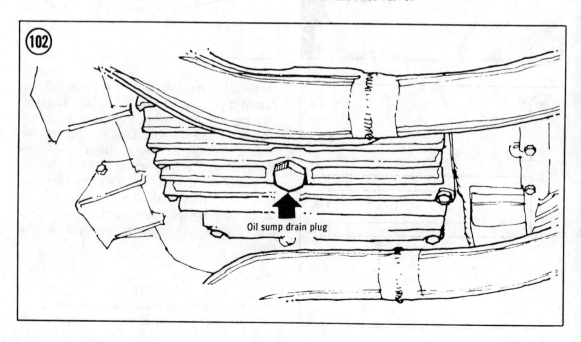

Oil sump drain plug

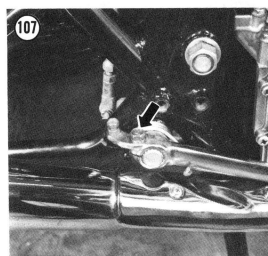

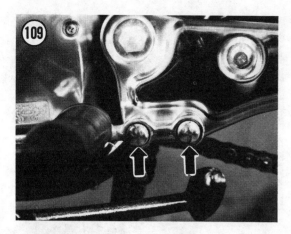

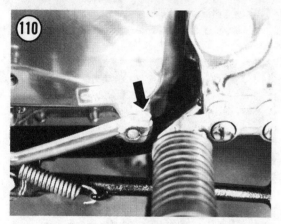

12. Disconnect the black/white and yellow/black fuel gauge wires near the left rear corner of the air filter chamber (**Figure 112**).

13. Lift up on the rear of the tank and slide the tank back enough to disengage the front rubber mounting pads (**Figure 113**). Make sure the rubber washers on the mounting bolt are not lost.

14. Loosen the clamp securing the front of the air filter chamber (**Figure 114**). Remove the bolt securing the rear of the air filter chamber (**Figure 115**).

15. Remove the right side cover and loosen the clamp bolt securing the rear master cylinder reservoir enough to allow the reservoir to be moved slightly. Lift out and remove the air filter chamber.

16. Disconnect the battery leads, negative first, then positive (**Figure 116**).

17. Open the rubber wire boots and disconnect the following (**Figure 117**):

a. White/green, white blue and yellow alternator wires

b. Yellow/green starter motor wire

18. Disconnect the following from behind the rear master cylinder (**Figure 118**):

a. Signal generator wire connector (green and blue wires)

b. Green/yellow oil pressure sensor wire

19. Disconnect the following connectors near the upper frame tube (**Figure 119**):

a. Blue neutral indicator wire

b. Gear position indicator connector

20. Pull back the rubber boot and disconnect the main starter lead from the starter relay (**Figure 120**).

21. Loosen the clamp bolts securing the inner exhaust pipes to the mufflers.

22. Loosen the bolts on each side that secure the mufflers and rear footrests to the frame. Do not remove the bolts at this time.

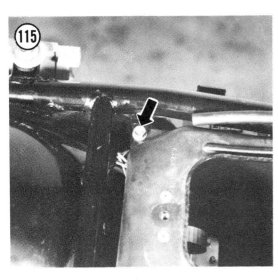

23. Remove the bolts securing each exhaust pipe flange to the engine (**Figure 121**).

24. Support the weight of the exhaust system and remove the rear mounting bolts completely. Spread the mufflers apart slightly while pulling the whole exhaust system forward enough to disengage the exhaust pipes from the engine. Note that 2-piece rings are used around each inboard exhaust pipe where they are installed in the cylinder head. Remove the exhaust system.

25. Remove the bolt securing the clutch release arm (**Figure 122**) and remove the release arm from the shaft.

NOTE
It may be necessary to slightly pry open the slot in the release arm with a screwdriver to ease release arm removal.

26. Loosen the locknut securing the clutch cable adjuster (**Figure 123**). Unscrew the cable adjuster completely to free the cable from the crankcase.

27. Remove the bolt securing the choke cable to the carburetor bracket (**Figure 124**).

28. Refer to **Figure 125** and loosen the locknuts securing the throttle cable. Slide the outer cable end out of the carburetor bracket and disconnect the inner cable end from the throttle shaft.

29. Spring open the clamps securing the breather hose to the engine and air box (**Figure 126**) and remove the breather hose.

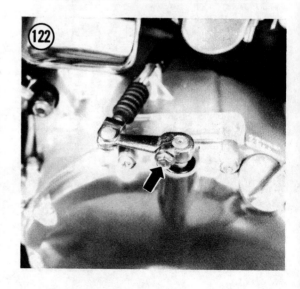

30. Loosen the clamp screws securing the carburetors to the engine flanges and the air box (**Figure 127**).

31. Remove the 2 bolts (**Figure 128**) securing the air box to the frame. Pull the air box back as far as possible and remove the air box flanges from the carburetor throats.

32. Pull the carburetors back out of the engine flanges. Lower the carburetors enough so that the choke cable bracket clears the wires and the upper frame tube and remove the carburetors. Note that the 2 large carburetor vent tubes are routed back through the seat mounting bracket.

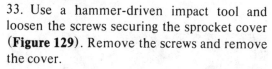

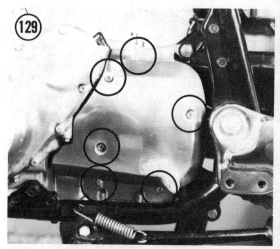

33. Use a hammer-driven impact tool and loosen the screws securing the sprocket cover (**Figure 129**). Remove the screws and remove the cover.

34A. On all except "L" models, use a chisel or screwdriver and bend back the fold on the locking washer (**Figure 130**).

34B. On "L" models, remove the retaining bolt and washer from the end of the engine drive shaft.

35. Temporarily install the gearshift lever and the brake pedal. Shift the transmission into gear and hold the rear brake on. Remove the engine sprocket nut and lockwasher (**Figure 131**).

36. Remove the drive chain from the sprocket and slide the sprocket off the drive shaft (**Figure 132**). Note that on "L" models, the countersunk screw heads on the sprocket face in toward the engine. On all other models, the screw heads face out. On "L" models, remove the washer behind the sprocket next to the drive shaft spacer. It may be necessary to loosen the drive chain to provide sufficient slack to remove the sprocket. Refer to *Drive Chain Adjustment and Lubrication* in Chapter Three.

NOTE
If engine disassembly is desired, perform Steps 37 through 45. If engine removal without disassembly is desired, proceed to Step 46.

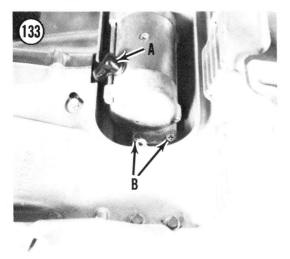

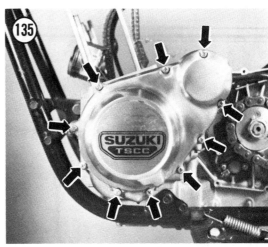

37. Remove the camshafts, cylinder head, cylinder block and pistons as outlined in this chapter.

38. Remove the screws securing the starter motor cover and remove the cover.

39. Pull back the rubber boot and remove the lead from the starter motor (A, **Figure 133**). Remove the 2 bolts securing the starter motor (B, **Figure 133**). Lift up on the rear of the motor and slide the motor out of the engine (**Figure 134**).

40. Use a hammer-driven impact tool and remove the screws securing the alternator cover (**Figure 135**). Note the location of different length screws. Carefully remove the alternator cover and the old gasket. Have a few rags handy as some oil is bound to run out when the cover is removed. Note how the alternator wires are routed in the cover and through the crankcase.

CAUTION
Do not pry the alternator cover loose with a screwdriver or similar tool or damage may result to the cover and/or the crankcase. The cover is held tight by the magnetic attraction of the alternator rotor. A strong pull is required to overcome the magnetic field.

41. Remove the thrust washer from the idler gear shaft (**Figure 136**). If the washer is not on the shaft, it may be stuck to the inside of the alternator cover.

42. Hold the gear in place and withdraw the idler gear shaft enough to disengage the shaft

end from the engine (**Figure 137**). Remove the idler gear and shaft.

43. If alternator rotor/starter clutch assembly removal is desired, a slide hammer and a special threaded adapter (Suzuki part No. 09930-33710) are necessary. If these tools are not available, remove the engine and have an authorized dealer perform the task. If the tools are available, perform the following:

> *NOTE*
> *It is not necessary to remove the alternator rotor/starter clutch assembly to remove the crankshaft or to disassemble the engine. Starter clutch removal is only required if the crankshaft or the alternator rotor/starter clutch must be replaced.*

a. Install a piston holding fixture under one piston as shown in **Figure 138** to keep the crankshaft from turning.
b. Remove the bolt securing the alternator rotor/starter clutch assembly.
c. Install the slide hammer on the end of the rotor. Operate the slide hammer and remove the rotor/clutch assembly from the end of the crankshaft.

> *NOTE*
> *The starter clutch assembly contains 3 rollers and 3 spring-loaded plungers (**Figure 139**). Take care that no parts are lost as some rollers often fall out when the clutch is removed. Roller installation is described under **Installation and External Assembly**.*

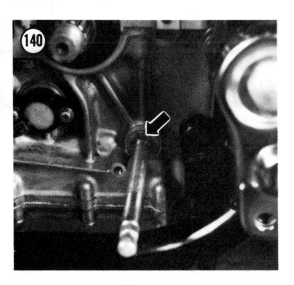

d. Remove the large starter gear.

44. Remove the retaining clip and washer securing the gearshift shaft (**Figure 140**).

45. Refer to Chapter Six and remove the clutch and external gearshift components.

46. Remove the 2 screws securing the gearshift indicator switch and remove the switch (**Figure 141**). Note how switch wiring is routed around the crankcase.

47. Remove the O-ring and spring-loaded plunger from the end of the gearshifting cam (**Figure 142**).

48. If the camshafts or cylinder head have not been previously removed, perform the following:

    a. Unscrew the tachometer cable from the cylinder head (**Figure 143**).

    b. Disconnect the horn wires (**Figure 144**). Remove the bolt securing the horn bracket to the frame and remove the horn.

c. Remove the 4 bolts securing the breather cover (**Figure 145**) and remove the cover.

NOTE
Carefully check that the engine is free of all cables, wires, hoses and accessories that may interfere with engine removal.

49. Place a jack or block under the engine to support the engine weight while removing the mounting bolts. Refer to **Figure 146** and remove the engine mounting bolts as indicated. It is not necessary to remove the upper-left, rear mounting bracket from the frame. Note that the lower mounting bolts are secured by nut plates (**Figure 147**). Carefully lift the engine out from the right side of the motorcycle. Do not lose the spacer used on the upper-rear mounting bolt.

Engine Installation and External Assembly

NOTE
*During engine installation and assembly of external components, frequently refer to **Figure 148** and **Figure 149** to ensure that all wires and cables are correctly routed.*

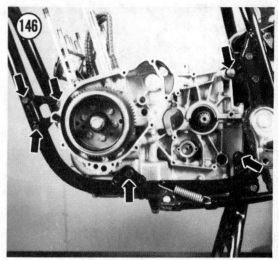

1. Tape some rags to the frame tubes to prevent scratches in the frame paint.

2. Install the engine from the right side of the motorcycle.

3. Temporarily secure the mounting brackets to the frame before installing the long mounting bolts. Do not install the lower-right engine mounting bracket until the ignition and oil pressure sensor wires have been routed along the engine. These wires must route behind the lower-right mounting bracket.

4. Insert the long engine mount bolts from the left side. Make sure the spacer is installed on the upper-rear mounting bolt.

5. Torque the 8 mm mounting bolts to 2.0-3.0 mkg (15-22 ft.-lb.) and the 10 mm mounting bolts to 3.0-3.7 mkg (22-27 ft.-lb.). Torque

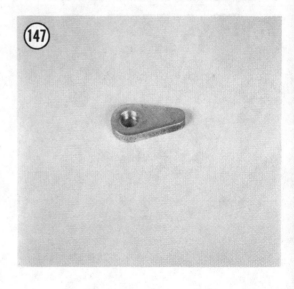

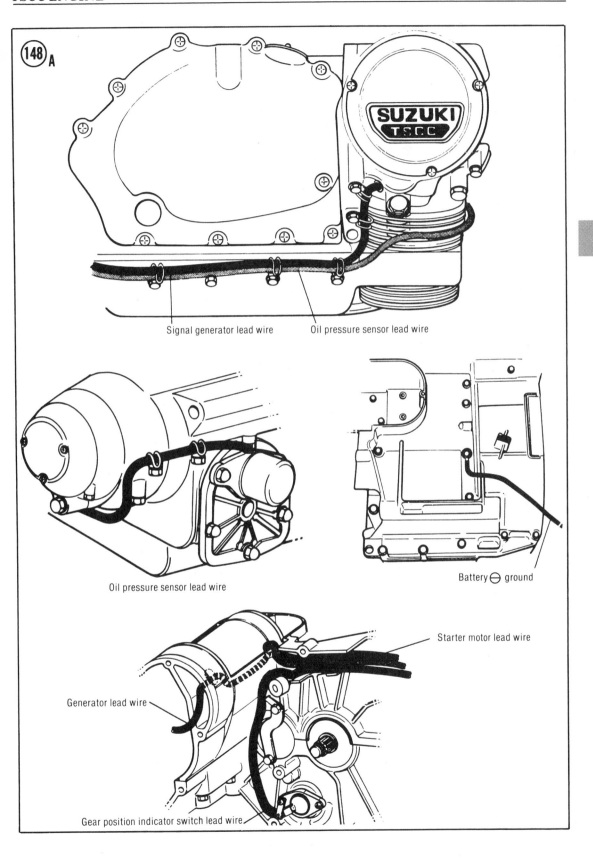

5

Signal generator lead wire   Oil pressure sensor lead wire

Oil pressure sensor lead wire

Battery ⊖ ground

Starter motor lead wire

Generator lead wire

Gear position indicator switch lead wire

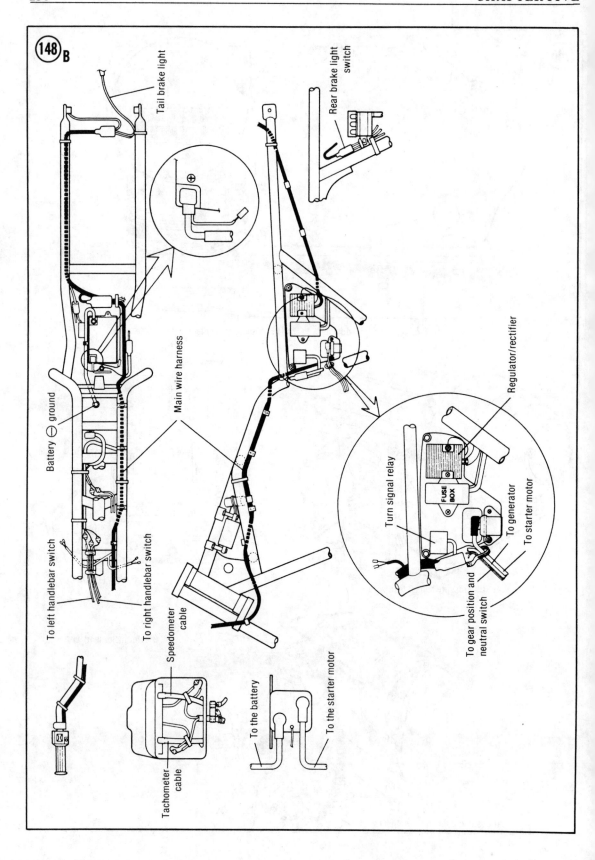

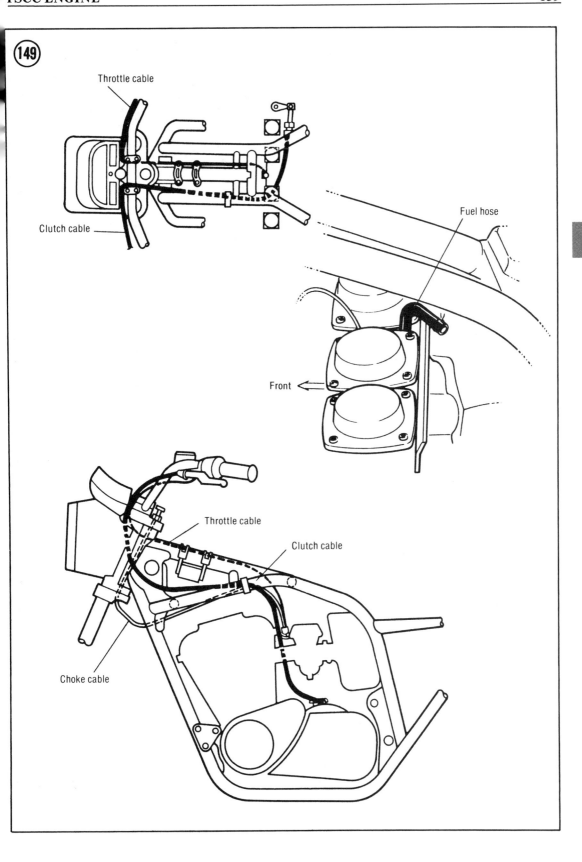

(149)

Throttle cable

Clutch cable

Fuel hose

Front

Throttle cable

Clutch cable

Choke cable

the main forward mounting bolt (**Figure 150**) to 4.5-5.5 mkg (33-40 ft.-lb.).

6. Install the O-ring and spring-loaded plunger in the end of the gearshifting cam (**Figure 151**).

7. Install the gear position indicator switch (**Figure 152**) and secure with 2 screws. Route the switch wires around the crankcase and under the folded tab on the bearing retainer as shown in **Figure 153**.

> *NOTE*
> *If the engine was disassembled, perform Steps 8 through 18 to complete external engine assembly. If the engine was not disassembled, proceed to Step 19.*

8. If the alternator rotor/starter clutch was removed, wipe the end of the crankshaft clean with lacquer thinner or contact spray. Install the starter clutch on the crankshaft. Secure the crankshaft from turning with a piston holding fixture as described during the removal procedure. Apply a few drops of red Loctite (Stud N' Bearing Mount No. 2214) to the alternator rotor bolt and install the bolt (**Figure 154**). Torque the bolt to 6.0-7.0 mkg (44-51 ft.-lb.). If any rollers fell out when the starter clutch assembly was removed, refer to **Figure 155** and perform the following:

   a. Place the assembly on a clean surface and install a spring and plunger (push piece). Hold the plunger in position with a small wire or drill bit inserted through the hole in the assembly body (**Figure 156**).

   b. Slide a roller into place and carefully withdraw the wire or drill bit so the

5

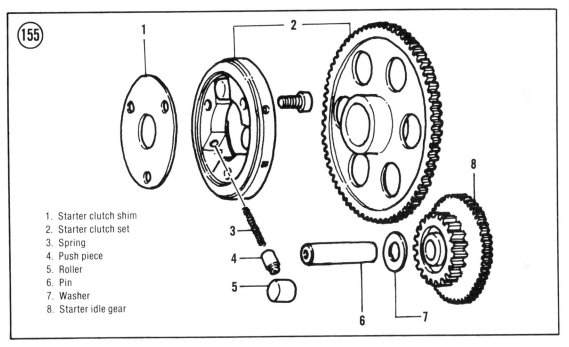

1. Starter clutch shim
2. Starter clutch set
3. Spring
4. Push piece
5. Roller
6. Pin
7. Washer
8. Starter idle gear

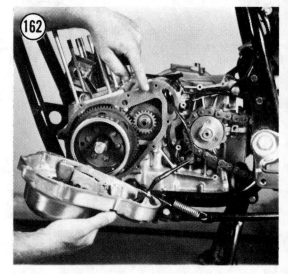

spring tension holds the roller in place (**Figure 157**). Repeat for other rollers, if necessary.

CAUTION
Carefully examine the magnets in the alternator rotor. Remove all foreign objects, metal fillings, washers, etc., that may have been picked up by the magnets. A small washer or nut stuck to the magnets could cause serious damage to the alternator stator assembly.

9. Hold the starter idler gear in place and install the idler gear shaft as shown in **Figure 158**.

10. Install the thrust washer on the idler gear shaft (**Figure 159**).

11. Apply a thin layer of Bond No. 4 approximately 1 in. on each side of the crankcase seam behind the alternator cover (**Figure 160**).

12. Make sure the alternator wires are correctly routed in the alternator cover and the grommet is installed in the notch as shown in **Figure 161**.

13. Install a new cover gasket and route the alternator wires into the crankcase opening. Hold the gasket in place and install the alternator cover (**Figure 162**).

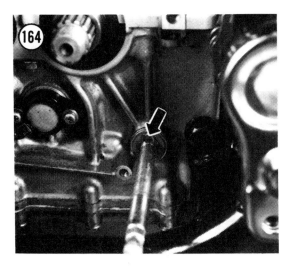

14. Install the starter motor as shown in **Figure 163**. Apply a couple of drops of blue Loctite (Lock N' Seal No. 2114) to the bolts securing the starter motor and torque the bolts to 0.4-0.7 mkg (3.0-5.0 ft.-lb.). Connect the starter wire to the starter motor. Make sure that the wires are routed correctly as shown in **Figure 148**.

15. Install the chrome starter motor cover and secure the cover with the 2 screws.

16. Install the clutch and external gearshift mechanism as outlined in Chapter Six.

17. Install the washer and retaining clip securing the gearshift shaft (**Figure 164**).

18. Install the pistons, cylinder block,

cylinder head and camshafts as outlined in this chapter.

19. Make sure that the spacer is installed on the engine drive shaft. On "L" models, install the large washer next to the spacer. Install the sprocket on the drive shaft. On all except "L" models, the recess is positioned in toward the engine and the countersunk screw heads face out (**Figure 165**). On "L" models, the countersunk screw heads on the sprocket face in toward the engine.

20. Install the drive chain on the sprocket. Install the locking washer (if so equipped) and the sprocket nut. On "L" models, apply blue Loctite (Lock N' Seal No. 2114) to the drive shaft threads before installing the sprocket nut.

21. Connect the return spring to the brake pedal and install the pedal so the punch mark on the shaft is aligned with the split (**Figure 166**). Secure the pedal with the pinch bolt. Torque the bolt to 1.0-1.5 mkg (7.0-11.0 ft.-lb.).

22. Temporarily install the shift lever and shift the transmission into gear. Hold on the rear brake and torque the sprocket nut to 9.0-10.0 mkg (65-73 ft.-lb.). On "L" models, apply blue Loctite (Lock N' Seal No. 2114) to the sprocket retaining bolt and install the bolt and lockwasher. Torque the retaining bolt to 0.6-0.9 mkg (4.5-6.5 ft.-lb.). On all except "L"

models, fold over the locking washer to secure the sprocket nut (**Figure 167**).

23. Install the sprocket cover (**Figure 168**) and tighten the screws evenly and securely.

24. Install the gearshift lever and secure with the pinch bolt.

25. Install the right and left footrests. Torque the bolts to 2.7-4.3 mkg (20-31 ft.-lb.).

26. Connect the throttle cable to the throttle shaft on the carburetors and install the carburetors into the engine flanges. Carefully install the air box flanges over the carburetor throats. Secure the air box to the frame with the 2 bolts (**Figure 169**).

27. Slide the throttle cable into the cable bracket (**Figure 170**). Rotate the cable

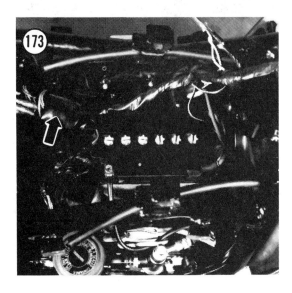

adjuster for 0.5-1.0 mm (1/32-1/16 in.) of cable free play and secure the adjuster with the locknuts.

28. Connect the choke cable to the carburetors and secure the cable to the bracket as shown in **Figure 171**.

29. Connect the battery leads (**Figure 172**).

30. Connect the following wires and cover the connections with the rubber boots (**Figure 173**):

    a. White/green, white blue and yellow alternator wires

    b. Yellow/green starter motor wire

31. Connect the following wires behind the rear master cylinder (**Figure 174**):

    a. Signal generator wire connector (green and blue wires)

    b. Green/yellow oil pressure sensor wire

32. Connect the following connectors near the upper frame tube (**Figure 175**):

a. Blue neutral indicator wire

b. Gear position indicator connector

33. Connect the main starter lead to the starter relay (**Figure 176**).

34. Install the air filter chamber and secure the chamber with the forward clamp (**Figure 177**) and the rear bolt (**Figure 178**). Tighten the bolt securing the rear brake master cylinder reservoir.

35. Make sure the large carburetor vent tubes are routed through the seat brackets as shown in **Figure 179**. Ensure that the tubes are not pinched shut where they fit between the air box and the frame.

36. Slide the exhaust pipes into the cylinder ports and install the rear footrest/muffler mounting bolts to secure the rear of the exhaust system. Leave the bolts loose at this time so the exhaust system can be shifted around as it is secured. Install the 2-piece rings around each inboard exhaust pipe. Hold the exhaust pipes into the cylinder ports and secure the pipes with the flanges. Tighten the bolts finger-tight at this time.

37. Tighten the bolts securing the rear footrests and mufflers to the frame. Torque the bolts to 2.7-4.3 mkg (20-31 ft.-lb.).

38. Make sure all the exhaust pipe flanges are correctly positioned and the exhaust pipes are correctly aligned. Torque the flange nuts to 1.5-2.0 mkg (11-15 ft.-lb.). Torque the clamp bolts securing the inboard pipes to the mufflers to 0.9-1.4 mkg (7-10 ft.-lb.).

39. Connect the tachometer cable to the tachometer drive unit (**Figure 180**).

40. Make sure breather cover gasket is installed with the opening facing forward. Install the breather cover and secure with the 4 bolts (**Figure 181**). Connect the breather hose to the breather cover and air box.

41. Install the horn and bracket to the frame. Connect the horn wires.

42. Screw the clutch cable adjuster into the crankcase fitting finger-tight. Install the clutch release arm on the clutch pinon shaft and

secure with the pinch bolt (**Figure 182**). Leave the adjuster locknuts loose at this time.

43. Lightly lubricate the fuel tank mounting pads with rubber lubricant or WD-40 and install the fuel tank. Connect the fuel line and engine vacuum line to the fuel valve before

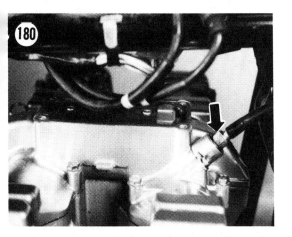

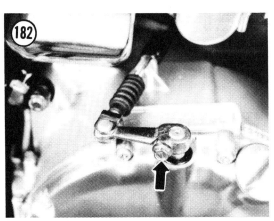

securing the rear of the fuel tank to the frame. Connect the black/white and yellow/black fuel gauge wires near the left rear corner of the air filter chamber (**Figure 183**).

44. Refer to Chapter Three and perform the following procedures:

   a. Install the oil filter and add engine oil.

   b. Perform *Clutch Adjustment.*

   c. Perform *Drive Chain Adjustment and Lubrication.*

ENGINE LOWER END

It is necessary to split the crankcase to gain access to the crankshaft, connecting rods, transmission and inner gearshift components.

The following procedures represent a complete step-by-step process that should be followed if an engine is to be completely reconditioned. However, if you are replacing a known failed part, the disassembly need only be carried out until the failed part is accessible. Further disassembly is unnecessary as long as you know that the remaining components are in good condition and that they were not affected by the failed part.

Disassembly

1. Perform the complete engine removal procedure as outlined in this chapter. Several preliminary disassembly steps are performed during engine removal.

2. Remove the cylinder head, cylinder block and pistons as described in this chapter, if not previously removed.

5

3. Bend back the tabs securing the seal retainer bolts (**Figure 184**). Remove the bolts and the seal retainer.

4. Refer to Chapter Six and remove the clutch and external gearshift mechanism, if not previously removed.

5. Remove the screws securing the ignition cover and remove the cover.

6. Remove the 3 screws securing the signal generator unit to the crankcase and remove the unit. Disengage the ignition wires from under the retaining clips secured to the oil sump.

> *NOTE*
> *Do not mix the bearing and seal retainer screws with the screws removed from the gearshift cam guide and gearshift pawl retainer. The 7 bearing and seal retainer screws are 16 mm long, while the 4 gearshift component screws are 12 mm long.*

7. Remove the screws securing the bearing and seal retainers as indicated in **Figure 185**. Take care that the gasket behind the large retainer is not damaged.

8. If oil passage cleaning is desired, remove the oil control jets from the upper crankcase (**Figure 186**). Use needlenose pliers and pull the jet straight out; do not attempt to turn the jet out. Note that each jet is fitted with an O-ring (**Figure 187**).

9. Refer to **Figure 188** and remove thirteen 6 mm bolts and one 8 mm bolt securing the upper crankcase.

> *NOTE*
> *Before removing the crankcase bolts, cut a cardboard template the approximate size and shape of the engine. Punch holes in the template for each bolt location. Place the bolts in the template holes as they are removed. This will greatly speed up the assembly time by eliminating the search for the correct length bolt.*

10. Turn the engine over to gain access to the bottom crankcase bolts.

> *NOTE*
> *Have plenty of rags handy. Approximately*

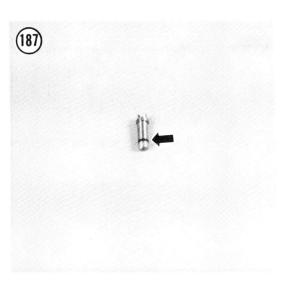

1/2 pint of oil is trapped in the engine and will run out when the engine is turned over.

11. Gradually and evenly loosen the bolts securing the oil sump (**Figure 189**). Remove the bolts and remove the oil sump. It may be necessary to tap around the edge of the sealing surface with a plastic or rubber mallet to help break the sump loose from the crankcase.

12. Remove the screws securing the oil pickup screen (**Figure 190**) and remove the screen.

13. If desired, remove the oil pressure relief valve (**Figure 191**).

14. Remove the seven 6 mm bolts and the twelve 8 mm bolts securing the lower crankcase. Refer to **Figure 192** and remove the bolts in descending order. The numbers are also cast in the crankcase. The two center 8 mm Allen bolts are accessible through the oil filter sump (**Figure 193**). Use a cardboard template as previously described to keep all the bolts in order as they are removed.

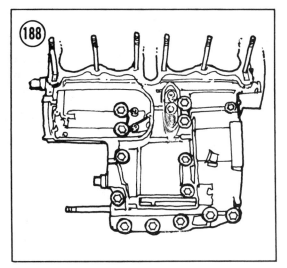

NOTE
If using an Allen wrench fitted to a socket, it is usually necessary to fit the Allen wrench into the bolt through the filter opening and then install a socket extension down through the crankcase opening. Most sockets are too large to pass through the crankcase bolt holes.

15. Remove the nut located by the drive shaft (**Figure 194**). This nut is often covered with dirt and grease.

16. Gently tap around the bottom crankcase half with a rubber or plastic mallet to break it loose, then lift off the crankcase half.

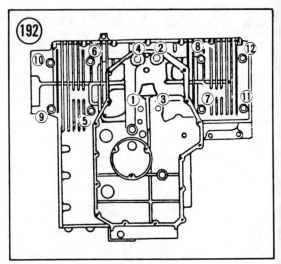

CAUTION
Never attempt to pry the crankcase halves apart with a screwdriver or similar tool. Serious damage will result to the crankcase sealing surfaces. The crankcase halves are a matched set and are very expensive. Damage to one crankcase half necessitates replacing the entire set.

17. At this point of disassembly, major service can be performed on the crankshaft, connecting rods, transmission and gearshift components. All crankshaft and connecting rod insert bearings can be removed and replaced and all major inspections can be performed. If transmission and/or gearshift repairs are desired, refer to Chapter Six.

18. Remove and discard the oil passage O-ring (**Figure 195**). If cleaning is desired, unscrew the oil control jet from the oil passage (**Figure 196**).

19. If connecting rod removal is desired, remove the nuts securing each connecting rod to the crankshaft (**Figure 197**). Carefully lift off each bearing cap and remove each rod assembly.

CAUTION
Use a felt tip pen or scribe and carefully mark the location of each connecting rod and rod cap as well as the position of the bearing inserts if they are to be reused. Do not mark on the bearing surface, mark on the exterior of the connecting rod and bearing cap. All parts must be installed in the exact position and location from which they were removed as wear patterns have

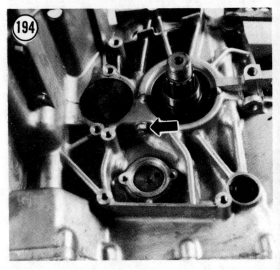

developed on all parts. If the parts are intermixed with other like connecting rod components, rapid and excessive wear may result.

CAUTION
Do not attempt to remove the bolts from the connecting rods. The bolts are factory fit and aligned with each bearing cap. If the bolts are disturbed, the bearing cap alignment will be disturbed.

20. If crankshaft removal is desired, carefully lift out the crankshaft assembly.

21. To determine the condition of the connecting rods and the crankshaft, refer to the following inspection procedures. If new bearing inserts are to be installed on the connecting rods and crankshaft main bearings, refer to the appropriate bearing selection procedures following.

Crankshaft and Connecting Rod Inspection

NOTE
Some steps in the following procedure require the use of highly specialized and expensive measuring equipment. If such equipment is not available, have a dealer or machine shop perform the measurements.

NOTE
If new engine crankcases are to be installed on 1981 and earlier models, refer to the Chapter Five section of the Supplement at the end of this book.

1. Carefully examine the main bearing inserts (**Figure 198**) and connecting rod bearing inserts (**Figure 199**). The bearings should be

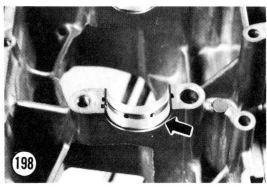

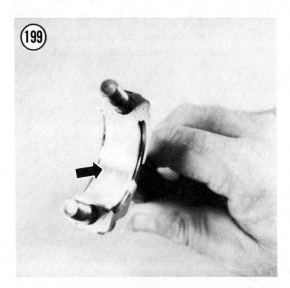

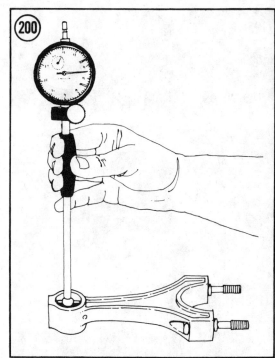

replaced if there are any signs of bluish tint (burned), flaking, abrasion or scoring. If the bearing inserts are good they may be reused, provided the bearing clearance is within tolerance. Refer to the appropriate bearing clearance inspection procedure following. If any insert is questionable, replace the entire set.

2. Use a bore gauge or inside micrometer and measure the piston pin bore in each connecting rod (**Figure 200**). Use a micrometer and measure the diameter of each piston pin (**Figure 201**). If the clearance exceeds 0.080 mm (0.0031 in.) replace the out-of-tolerance connecting rods and piston pins as a set.

3. Use a feeler gauge and measure the side clearance between each connecting rod and the crankshaft (**Figure 202**). If the clearance exceeds 0.3 mm (0.012 in.), the connecting rod or crankshaft must be replaced. Perform the following to determine which component is worn excessively:

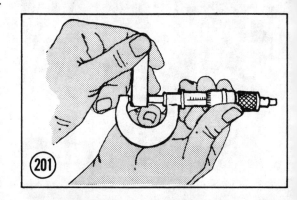

   a. Use a micrometer and measure the width of the big end of the connecting rod (**Figure 203**). If the big end width is not as specified in **Table 7**, replace the connecting rod.
   b. Use an inside micrometer and measure the inside width of the crank pin journal (**Figure 204**). If the journal width is not as specified in **Table 8**, replace the crankshaft.

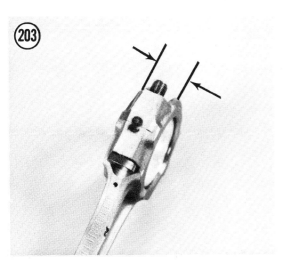

5

4. Place the crankshaft on 2 V-blocks, one on each end, and position a dial indicator against one of the center main bearing journals. Rotate the crankshaft to determine the amount of runout or deflection. If the runout exceeds 0.05 mm (0.002 in.), the crankshaft must be replaced.

5. Temporarily install the crankshaft in the crankcase. Use a feeler gauge and measure the side thrust (end play) clearance between crankshaft and the No. 2 main bearing (**Figure 205**) on the magneto side of the engine. If the clearance exceeds 0.5 mm (0.02 in.) the crankshaft or the crankcases must be replaced. If the clearance is excessive, perform the following to determine which component must be replaced:

    a. Use an inside micrometer and measure the width of the No. 2 crankshaft main bearing journal (**Figure 206**). If the width exceeds the specifications in **Table 8**, replace the crankshaft.

    b. Use a caliper or micrometer and measure the width of No. 2 main bearing journal in the crankcase (**Figure 207**). If the width of the journal is not within the specified tolerance (**Table 8**), the crankcase must be replaced. The crankcase consists of 2 matched halves. Both halves must be replaced as a set.

6. Use a micrometer and *accurately* measure the diameter of each main bearing journal (**Figure 208**) and crank pin journal (**Figure 209**). All main and crank pin journals must be within the specifications in **Table 8** or the crankshaft must be replaced. Write

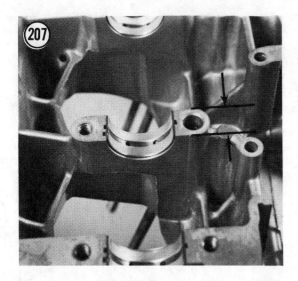

down all measurements. The measurements can be used to determine the required bearing inserts, if new inserts are to be installed.

Connecting Rod Bearing Clearance Inspection

1. To accurately measure the bearing clearance it is necessary to use Plastigage. A strip of Plastigage is installed between the bearing surface and the crankshaft and is compressed when the bearing cap is tightened to the proper torque. The thickness of the compressed Plastigage is then measured with the Plastigage wrapper. This method, when properly performed, results in an accurate measurement of the bearing clearance.

2. Remove the nuts securing the connecting rod bearing cap and carefully remove the bearing cap and connecting rod (**Figure 210**).

CAUTION
Use a felt tip pen or scribe and carefully mark the location of each connecting rod and rod cap as well as the position of the bearing inserts if they are to be reused. Do not mark on the bearing surface; mark on the exterior of the connecting rod and bearing cap. All parts must be installed in the exact position and location from which they were removed as wear patterns have developed on all parts. If the parts are intermixed with other like connecting rod components, rapid and excessive wear may result.

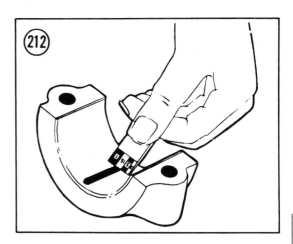

5

CAUTION
Do not attempt to remove the bolts from the connecting rods. The bolts are factory-fit and aligned with each bearing cap. If the bolts are disturbed, the bearing cap alignment will be disturbed.

3. Clean the connecting rod bearing surface as well as the crank pin journal with solvent or contact cleaner.

4. Place a strip of green Plastigage on the top or bottom (TDC or BDC) of the crank pin journal. Make sure the strip does not cover the oil hole in the journal. Use a strip as long as the journal so the clearance can be checked at both ends of the bearing.

NOTE
Plastigage is available in different colors, corresponding to the range of measurement possible. Green Plastigage provides the proper range of measurement necessary to determine the connecting rod bearing clearance.

5. Carefully install the connecting rod and bearing cap on the crank pin journal. Make sure the connecting rod is installed with the oil hole (**Figure 211**) toward the *rear* of the engine.

NOTE
Do not allow the crankshaft to turn or the Plastigage strip will be ruined. The connecting rod must then be removed and a new strip of Plastigage installed.

6. Tighten the bearing cap nuts in 2 steps to make sure they are properly torqued. Tighten

each bearing cap nut a little at a time to 1.2-1.8 mkg (8.5-13.0 ft.-lb.) then torque each nut to the final value of 3.0-3.4 mkg (21.5-25.0 ft.-lb.).

7. Carefully remove the nuts securing the bearing cap and remove the cap and connecting rod.

8. Use the Plastigage wrapper and read the clearance at both ends of the Plastigage strip as shown in **Figure 212**. If the clearance indicated by the Plastigage exceeds the service limit of 0.080 mm (0.0031 in.), the bearing inserts must be replaced. If the indicated clearance varies more than 0.025 mm (0.001 in.) on each end of the Plastigage strip, the crank pin journal is tapered excessively. The crankshaft must be reground or replaced.

NOTE
The Plastigage may adhere to the bearing cap, connecting rod or crank pin journal. Any of these positions will provide an accurate indication of bearing clearance.

9. If the bearing inserts must be replaced, proceed to *Connecting Rod Bearing Insert Selection and Installation.* If the bearing clearance is within tolerance and the bearing inserts appear serviceable, install the connecting rods and bearing caps as outlined in *Assembly.*

Crankshaft Main Bearing Clearance Inspection

1. To accurately measure the bearing clearance it is necessary to use Plastigage. A

strip of Plastigage is installed between the bearing insert and the crankshaft and is compressed when both crankcase halves are bolted together and the bolts are tightened to the proper torque. The thickness of the compressed Plastigage is then measured with the Plastigage wrapper. This method, when properly performed, results in an accurate measurement of the bearing clearance.

2. Remove the crankshaft as described under *Disassembly*. Do not remove the bearing inserts at this time.

3. Use solvent or contact cleaner and clean the main bearing journals on the crankshaft as well as the main bearing inserts in both crankcase halves.

4. Clean all the sealant residue from the sealing surfaces of both crankcase halves.

CAUTION
Make sure all sealant residue is removed from the crankcase sealing surfaces. Left-over sealant residue may "bunch up" in places and not allow the crankcase halves to be bolted together completely. The Plastigage may then not be completely compressed between the bearing surfaces, resulting in an incorrect bearing clearance indication.

5. Place the upper crankcase half on a workbench and carefully install the crankshaft in the upper crankcase half.

CAUTION
Make sure the crankshaft is installed correctly or inaccurate bearing clearance indications will result. When the engine is viewed from the inside with the crankshaft at the top, the alternator end of the crankshaft must be on the right end (Figure 213).

6. Place a strip of green Plastigage on each crankshaft main bearing journal. Make sure the strip does not cover the oil hole in the journal. Use a strip as long as the journal so the clearance can be checked at both ends of the bearing.

NOTE
Plastigage is available in different colors, corresponding to the range of measurement possible. Green Plastigage provides the proper range of measurement necessary to determine the connecting rod bearing clearance.

7. Carefully install the lower crankcase half over the upper half. Install all the crankcase bolts finger-tight.

NOTE
Do not allow the crankshaft to turn or the Plastigauge strips will be ruined. The lower crankcase must then be removed and new strips of Plastigauge installed on all the main bearing journals.

8. Tighten the crankcase bolts in 2 steps to make sure they are properly torqued. Tighten all the 8 mm bolts in the order designated in **Figure 192**. Tighten each 6 mm bolt a little at a time to 0.6 mkg (4.5 ft.-lb.) then the 8 mm bolts (in designated order) to 1.3 mkg (9.5 ft.-lb.). Torque each 6 mm bolt to the final value of 0.9-1.1 mkg (6.5-8.0 ft.-lb.) and each 8 mm bolt to 2.0-2.4 mkg (14.5-17.5 ft.-lb.).

9. Remove the bolts securing the crankcase halves and carefully lift off the lower crankcase half.

10. Use the Plastigage wrapper and read the clearance at both ends of the Plastigage strip as shown in **Figure 214**. If the clearance indicated by the Plastigage exceeds the service limit of 0.080 mm (0.0031 in.), the bearing

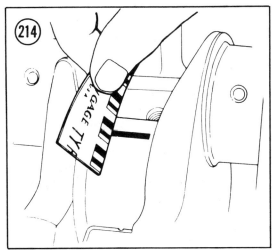

5

**Connecting Rod Bearing Insert
Selection and Installation**

Refer to **Table 9** for this procedure.

NOTE
Before purchasing new connecting rod bearing inserts, refer to the Chapter Five section of the Supplement at the end of this book.

1. Perform *Crankshaft and Connecting Rod Inspection* to determine if crank pin journals and connecting rods are serviceable.
2. Perform *Connecting Rod Bearing Clearance Inspection* to determine if the bearing clearance is within tolerances specified in **Table 7**. If bearing clearance is not as specified, the bearing inserts must be replaced as a set.
3. Each connecting rod is etched with a code number "1" or "2" as shown in **Figure 215**.
4. Each crank pin journal on the crankshaft is stamped with a code number "1", "2" or "3" as shown in **Figure 216**.

NOTE
Do not confuse the crank pin code numbers "1", "2" and "3" with the letters "A", "B" or "C" on the crankshaft. The letter codes are used to select crankshaft main bearing inserts.

inserts must be replaced. If the indicated clearance varies more than 0.025 mm (0.001 in.) on each end of the Plastigage strip, the main bearing journal is tapered excessively. The crankshaft must be reground or replaced.

NOTE
The Plastigage may adhere to the bearing insert or the crankshaft journal. Either location will provide an accurate indication of bearing clearance.

11. If the bearing inserts must be replaced, proceed to *Crankshaft Main Bearing Insert Selection and Installation*. If the bearing clearance is within tolerance and the bearing inserts appear serviceable, install the crankshaft as outlined in *Assembly*.

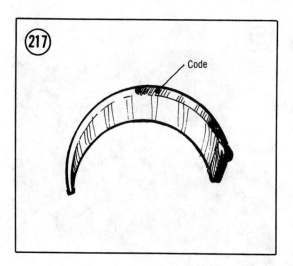

Code

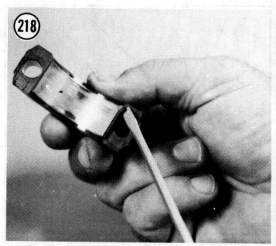

5. Each bearing insert is color-coded on the edge of the bearing (**Figure 217**).

6. Bearing selection is determined by the connecting rod code and crank pin code as shown in **Table 9**. If the crank pin dimensions are within the tolerances stated for each number code, the bearings can be simply selected by color-code. For example: the crank pin shown in **Figure 216** is stamped "1". It was determined with a micrometer, during inspection, that this crank pin measured 35.997 mm (1.4172 in.). This is within the tolerances stated in **Table 9** for a number "1" crank pin. The connecting rod used on this crank pin is etched "2" as shown in **Figure 215**. The required bearing insert for a "2" connecting rod and a "1" crank pin journal is color-coded *black* as specified in **Table 9**.

7. If any crank pin measurements taken during inspection do not fall within the tolerance range for the stamped numbered code, the serviceability of the crankshaft must be carefully examined. If the crank pin journal in question is not tapered, out-of-round or scored the crankshaft may still be used, however, the bearing selection will have to be made based on the measured diameter of the crank pin and not by the stamped number code. Suzuki recommends the crankshaft be replaced whenever a crank pin journal dimension is beyond the specified range of the stamped code number.

CAUTION
*The oil hole in the bearing insert (**Figure 220**) must be aligned with the oil hole in the connecting rod (**Figure 221**).*

8. To install new connecting rod bearing inserts, perform the following:
  a. Use a small screwdriver or awl and carefully pry out each old insert by the "tab" as shown in **Figure 218**.

CAUTION
Do not touch the bearing surface of new inserts. The bearing surfaces are easily contaminated and damaged by dirt, grit and skin acids.

  b. Make sure the inner surfaces of each connecting rod and bearing cap are perfectly clean. Engage the "tab" on the insert with the notch in the connecting rod or bearing cap and carefully press the other end of the insert into place. Make sure the "tabs" are correctly positioned in the notches as shown in **Figure 219**.

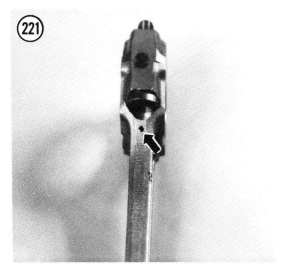

NOTE
Both connecting rod bearing inserts are equipped with oil holes, therefore, the inserts are interchangeable; they can be installed in either the connecting rod or the bearing cap. The bearing cap is not fitted with an oil hole.

c. Make sure each insert is flush with the edge of the connecting rod or bearing cap.

9. Install the connecting rods as outlined in *Assembly*.

Crankshaft Main Bearing Insert Selection and Installation

Refer to **Table 10** for this procedure.

NOTE
Before purchasing new crankshaft main bearing inserts, refer to the Chapter Five section of the Supplement at the end of this book.

1. Perform *Crankshaft and Connecting Rod Inspection* to determine if the crankshaft main bearing journals are serviceable.

2. Perform *Crankshaft Main Bearing Clearance Inspection* to determine if the bearing clearances are within tolerances specified in **Table 8**. If bearing clearances are not as specified, the bearing inserts must be replaced as a set.

3. Each crankcase main bearing is identified by a letter code "A" or "B" stamped on panels at the rear of the upper crankcase half as shown in **Figure 222**. These stamped letter codes correspond to each crankcase bearing in the order shown in **Figure 223**.

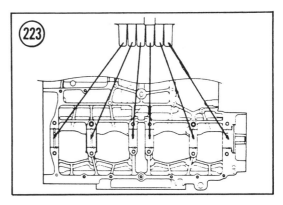

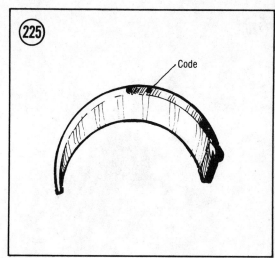

Code

4. Each main bearing journal on the crankshaft is identified by a code letter "A", "B" or "C" stamped on the crankshaft counterweight as shown in **Figure 224**. The letter code for each journal is always stamped on the counterweight closest to the journal.

> *NOTE*
> *Do not confuse the main bearing code letters "A", "B" and "C" with the numbers "1", "2" or "3" on the crankshaft counterweights. The number codes are only used to select connecting rod bearing inserts.*

5. Each bearing insert is color-coded on the edge of the bearing (**Figure 225**).

6. Bearing selection is determined by the crankcase code and the crankshaft counterweight code as shown in **Table 10**. If the crankshaft main bearing dimensions are within the tolerances stated for each letter code, the bearings can be simply selected by color-code. For example: the main bearing journal as shown in **Figure 224** is stamped "B". It was determined with a micrometer, during inspection, that this journal measured 35.989 mm (1.4168 in.). This is within the tolerances stated in **Table 10** for a letter "B" main bearing journal. The crankcase code for this main bearing is stamped "B" as shown in **Figure 222**. The required bearing insert for a "B" crankcase bearing and a "B" crankshaft main bearing journal is color-coded *brown* as specified in **Table 10**.

7. If any main bearing journal measurements taken during inspection do not fall within the tolerance range for the stamped letter codes, the serviceability of the crankshaft must be carefully examined. If the main bearing journal in question is not tapered, out-of-round or scored the crankshaft may still be used, however, the bearing selection will have to be made based on the measured diameter of the bearing journal and not by the stamped letter code. Suzuki recommends the crankshaft be replaced whenever a main bearing journal dimension is beyond the specified range of the stamped code letter.

8. To install new main bearing inserts, perform the following:

  a. Use a small screwdriver or awl and carefully remove each old insert by prying up on the locating "tab" (**Figure 226**).

> *CAUTION*
> *Do not touch the bearing surface of new inserts. The bearing surfaces are easily contaminated and damaged by dirt, grit and skin acids.*

  b. Make sure the inner bearing surfaces of both crankcase halves are perfectly clean. Engage the "tab" on the insert with the notch in the crankcase and carefully press the other end of the insert into place.

NOTE
Both main bearing inserts are equipped with oil holes, therefore, the inserts are interchangeable; they can be installed in either crankcase half.

c. Make sure each insert is flush with the edge of the crankcase.

9. Install the crankshaft as outlined in *Assembly.*

Assembly

CAUTION
Never use STP or similar friction reducing products as assembly lubricant. Even a small amount will combine with the engine oil and destroy the friction properties of the clutch. If this should occur, the engine's lubrication system must be completely flushed and new clutch plates installed.

CAUTION
During all phases of engine assemby, frequently rotate the crankshaft and other moving parts. If any binding or stiffness is present, find out why and correct the problem before continuing the assembly. An engine that feels rough or tight when rotated by hand will not "wear in." Such an engine will likely cause expensive damage to itself if run.

CAUTION
Use a thread locking compound such as blue Loctite (Lock N' Seal No. 2114) on all internal fasteners during engine

assembly. A small bolt or screw working loose inside the engine could have disastrous and expensive consequences.

1. Make sure all engine parts are clean and all fasteners are in good condition. Replace all bolts, nuts and screws that have damaged heads or threads.

2. Carefully remove all traces of old sealant residue from the sealing surfaces on both crankcase halves. Use a wooden scraper or similar device to clean off the old sealant. Never use a metal scraper or the sealing surfaces can be damaged. Wipe the surfaces clean with solvent or lacquer thinner.

3. If the crankshaft was removed, perform the following:

    a. Apply a thin film of molybdenum disulfide lubricant (such as Bel-Ray Moly Lube) on the bearing inserts in both crankcase halves as well as on the main bearing journals on the crankshaft.

    b. Install the cam chain over the crankshaft.

NOTE
On engines undergoing a complete rebuild, it is recommended that a new cam chain be installed.

    c. Route the cam chain into the chain tunnel and carefully place the crankshaft into the upper crankcase half (**Figure 227**).

4. If the connecting rods were removed from the crankshaft, perform the following:

    a. Apply engine assembly oil or Bel-Ray Moly Lube to both halves of each

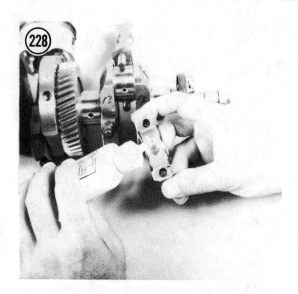

connecting rod bearing insert (**Figure 228**).

b. Carefully install each connecting rod over the correct crank pin journal with the oil hole (**Figure 229**) toward the *rear* of the engine. Install the bearing cap over the connecting rod bolts with the etched numbers on the connecting rods together as shown in **Figure 230**.

> *CAUTION*
> *Make sure all connecting rod components are installed exactly as removed. Intermixing connecting rod components may cause serious and excessive engine wear.*
> *If the connecting rods are not installed with the oil holes (Figure 229) toward the rear of the engine, expensive engine damage will result.*

c. Install all connecting rod nuts finger-tight. Tighten each nut a little at a time to a torque value of 1.2-1.8 mkg (8.5-13.0 ft.-lb.). Gradually and evenly torque the nuts to a final torque value of 3.0-4.0 mkg (21.5-25.0 ft.-lb.) as shown in **Figure 231**.

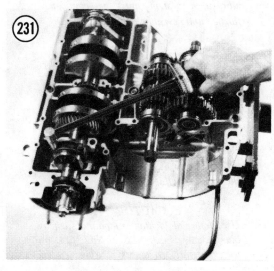

5. If transmission or internal gearshift components were removed for repair, install the C-rings and seal retainers (**Figure 232**) at this time. Install the transmission and gearshift components. Refer to Chapter Six

for applicable installation procedures. Make sure the locating pins on the transmission bearings are properly fitted into the crankcase notches (**Figure 233**).

6. Slide the rear cam chain tensioner into place (**Figure 234**). Make sure the ends of the tensioner completely engage the notches in the crankcase.

7. Install the 2 rubber cushions over the ends of the chain tensioner (**Figure 235**). The small tips of the cushions must point toward the inside of the engine.

8. Install a new O-ring in the crankcase oil passage (**Figure 236**). Install the oil control jet, if removed.

9. Carefully apply a thin layer of Suzuki Bond No. 4 (or equivalent) to the sealing surfaces on the lower crankcase half.

> *CAUTION*
> *Apply crankcase sealant with care. All surfaces must be covered or oil leaks may occur. **Do not** allow any sealant to contact any of the bearing surfaces. Use only a thin layer of sealant or the excess may squeeze into the crankshaft or transmission bearing areas.*

10. Make sure that all transmission and gear shift parts are correctly installed as outlined in Chapter Six. Ensure that the bearing locating pins are properly engaged in the crankcase notches. Make sure that the sealing surface of the upper crankcase half is clean and all the old sealant has been removed.

> *CAUTION*
> *Hold the slack out of the cam chain and rotate the crankshaft several times. The crankshaft and transmission shafts should rotate freely and easily with no binding or stiff spots. If something does not feel right, **stop** and correct the problem now. Do not attempt to run an engine that does not feel right when rotated by hand or serious and expensive damage may result.*

11. Carefully install the lower crankcase half over the upper half. Gently tap the crankcase halves together with a rubber mallet or block of wood. The dowel pins should align and both sealing surfaces should fit together. If the lower crankcase half does not fit down fully, stop and investigate the interference.

> *CAUTION*
> *The crankcase halves should fit together without force. If they do not fit together fully, do not attempt to pull them together with the crankcase bolts or the crankcases will be damaged. Remove the bottom half and investigate the cause of the interference. The upper and lower crankcases are a matched set and are very expensive. Do not risk damage by trying to force the cases together.*

12. Install all the crankcase bolts finger-tight. Tighten the crankcase bolts in 2 steps to make sure they are properly torqued. Tighten all the 8 mm bolts in the order designated in **Figure 237**. Tighten each 6 mm bolt a little at a time to 0.6 mkg (4.5 ft.-lb.) then the 8 mm bolts (in designated order) to 1.3 mkg (9.5 ft.-lb.). Torque each 6 mm bolt to the final value of 0.9-1.1 mkg (6.5-8.0 ft.-lb.) and each 8 mm bolt to 2.0-2.4 mkg (14.5-17.5 ft.-lb.).

13. Turn the engine over. Refer to **Figure 238** and install the thirteen 6 mm bolts and one 8 mm bolt securing the upper crankcase. Tighten the upper crankcase bolts in the same manner and to the same torque values as the lower crankcase bolts.

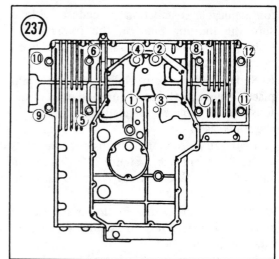

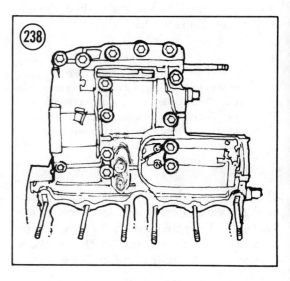

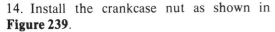

14. Install the crankcase nut as shown in **Figure 239**.

15. Install the external seal retainer (**Figure 240**). Fold over the tabs to secure the retainer bolts.

16. Install both bearing and seal retainers as shown in **Figure 241**. Apply a small amount of blue Loctite (Lock N' Seal No. 2114) to the seven 16 mm retainer screws before installing them. Make sure the gasket behind the large retainer is correctly installed.

NOTE
Do not mix the bearing and seal retainer screws with the screws removed from the gearshift cam guide and gearshift pawl retainer. The 7 bearing and seal retainer screws are 16 mm long, while the 4 gearshift component screws are 12 mm long. long.

17. Install the oil pressure release valve, if removed (**Figure 242**).

18. Install the oil pump pick-up screen (**Figure 243**). Use a small amount of blue Loctite on the screws securing the screen.

19. Make sure the sealing surfaces on the oil sump and crankcase are clean and free of old gasket residue. Use a new gasket and install the oil sump (**Figure 244**). Gradually and evenly tighten all the oil sump bolts in a crisscross pattern. Torque the bolts to 1.0 mkg (7.0 ft.-lb.).

20. Install the signal generator unit and secure with the 3 screws. Route the wires along the edge of the oil sump. Secure the wires to the sump with the retainer clips.

21. Install the oil control jets in the crankcase, if removed (**Figure 245**). Lightly oil the O-ring on the jet and push the jet into position.

22. Refer to *Engine Installation and External Assembly* and complete the engine assembly after the engine is installed in the frame.

OIL PUMP

The GS750 TSCC engine is fitted with a high pressure oil pump. The pump is not repairable and should be carefully cleaned, inspected and/or replaced if the engine is undergoing a complete rebuild.

If abnormal oil pressure is suspected, have the pressure checked by a dealer. Normal oil pressure is 3.0-5.5 kg/cm^2 (43-78 psi) at 3,000 rpm and 60° C (140° F).

Removal/Installation

1. To gain access to the oil pump, refer to Chapter Six and perform *Clutch Removal.*

2. Remove the snap ring securing the pump drive gear (**Figure 246**) and remove the gear.

3. Remove the gear drive pin and thrust washer (**Figure 247**) from the pump shaft.

4. Remove the 3 screws securing the oil pump (**Figure 248**) and remove the pump.

5. Installation is the reverse of these steps. Keep the following points in mind:

    a. Use grease to hold the special O-ring seal in the pump body (**Figure 249**).

    b. Apply a small amount of blue Loctite (Lock N' Seal No. 2114) to the 3 screws securing the pump.

5

c. Make sure the thrust washer is installed between the pump body and the drive gear (**Figure 250**).

Disassembly/Inspection/Assembly

The following procedure is provided to determine the overall wear of the oil pump. The pump is not repairable and must be replaced if any tolerance is greater than specified.

1. Remove the 3 screws securing the pump body together.

2. Gently tap on the pump shaft to separate the pump components.

3. Push the shaft back through the pump body. Disassemble the pump inner and outer rotors from the pump body. See **Figure 251**.

4. Clean the pump components in solvent. Carefully examine the pump body for wear or signs of damage (**Figure 252**).

5. Assemble the 2 pump rotors as shown in **Figure 253** and carefully examine the rotors for signs of excessive wear or damage.

6. Install the pump rotors into the pump body. The chamfered edge of the rotor is positioned toward the inside of the pump.

7. Use a feeler gauge and measure the clearance between the inner and outer rotors (**Figure 254**). The clearance limit is 0.2 mm (0.008 in.).

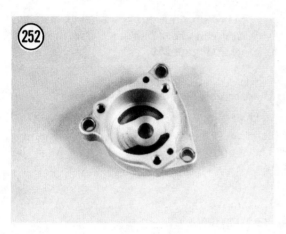

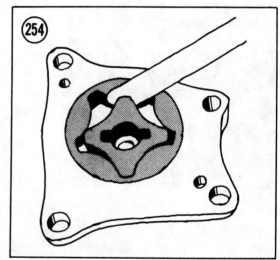

8. Measure the outer rotor clearance as shown in **Figure 255**. The clearance limit is 0.25 mm (0.0098 in.).

9. Use a straightedge with a feeler gauge and measure the pump side clearance (**Figure 256**). The clearance must not exceed 0.15 mm (0.0059 in.).

10. When reassembling the pump, use blue Loctite (Lock N' Seal No. 2114) on the 3 screws securing the pump assemby.

CAM CHAIN TENSIONER

Removal/Installation

> *NOTE*
> *If the engine is still installed in the motorcycle, it is necessary to remove the carburetors to gain access to the tensioner assembly. Refer to Chapter Seven and perform **Carburetor Removal.***

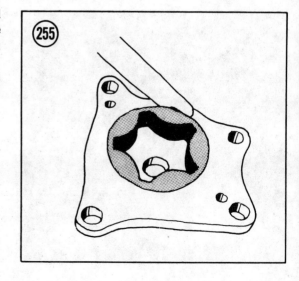

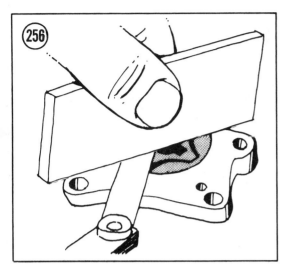

1. Loosen the locknut securing the lockscrew and tighten the lockscrew to hold the tensioner plunger (**Figure 257**).
2. Remove the 2 bolts securing the tensioner to the cylinder and remove the tensioner assembly (**Figure 258**).
3. Before installing the tensioner, completely compress the spring-loaded plunger and secure it with the lockscrew (**Figure 259**).
4. Make sure the gasket is installed on the tensioner assembly and secure the assembly to the cylinder with the 2 bolts.
5. Loosen the locknut securing the lockscrew and back off the lockscrew 1/4 turn to allow the spring-loaded plunger to move in against the internal chain tensioner. Tighten the locknut to secure the lockscrew.

NOTE
Do not back out the lockscrew more than 1/2 turn or the spring-loaded plunger may become disengaged from the tensioner body. If this should occur, it will be necessary to remove the tensioner assembly and reinstall the plunger into the tensioner body.

Disassembly/Inspection/Assembly

Refer to **Figure 260** for this procedure.
1. Loosen the locknut securing the lockscrew and remove the lockscrew from the tensioner body.
2. Remove the plunger, spring and O-ring.

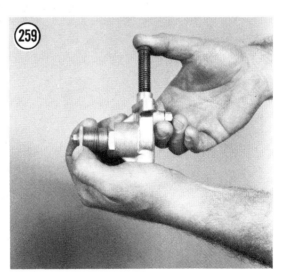

3. Clean the parts in solvent and inspect the plunger and tensioner body for damage or excessive wear. Replace the worn parts as necessary.

4. Install a new O-ring on the lockscrew. Oil the O-ring and lockscrew and install the lockscrew a few turns into the tensioner body.

5. Lightly grease the plunger and tensioner body. Install the spring and plunger and secure the plunger in the compressed position with the lockscrew.

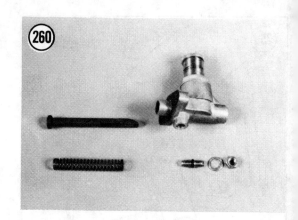

Table 1　ENGINE TORQUE SPECIFICATIONS

Item	mkg	ft.-lb.
Camshaft cover bolt	0.9-1.0	6.5-7.0
Ignition advance governor	1.3-2.3	9.5-16.5
Cylinder head nut	3.5-4.0	25.5-29.0
Cylinder head bolt (10 mm)	0.7-1.1	5.0-8.0
Valve adjuster locknut	0.9-1.1	6.5-8.0
Camshaft bearing cap bolts	0.8-1.2	6.0-8.5
Camshaft sprocket bolt	0.9-1.2	6.5-8.5
Rocker arm shaft stopper bolt	0.8-1.0	6.0-7.0
Cam chain tensioner bolts	0.6-0.8	4.5-6.0
Cam chain adjuster locknut	0.9-1.4	6.5-10.0
Alternator rotor bolt	6.0-7.0	43.5-50.5
Starter clutch Allen bolts	1.5-2.0	11.0-14.5
Connecting rod nuts	3.0-4.0	21.5-25.0
Crank web No. 4 nut	2.6-3.0	19.0-21.5
Crankcase bolts		
(6 mm)	0.9-1.3	6.5-9.5
(8 mm)	2.0-2.4	14.5-17.5
Starter motor bolts	0.4-0.7	3.0-5.0
Oil sump bolts	1.0	7.0
Oil pressure sensor	1.3-1.7	9.5-12.5
Clutch sleeve hub nut	5.0-7.0	36.0-50.5
Clutch spring bolt	1.1-1.3	8.0-9.5
Drive sprocket nut	9.0-10.0	65.0-72.5
Neutral cam stopper bolt	1.8-2.8	13.5-20.0
Oil filter cover nut	0.6-0.8	4.5-6.0
Muffler bracket nut	1.5-2.0	11.0-14.5
Muffler clamp bolts	0.9-1.4	6.5-10.0
Engine mount bolts		
Main front bolt	4.5-5.5	32.5-40.0
8 mm	2.0-3.0	14.5-21.5
10 mm	3.0-3.7	21.5-27.0
Spark plugs	1.5-2.0	11.0-14.0
Gearshift lever bolt	1.3-2.3	9.5-16.5
Clutch release arm bolt	0.6-1.0	4.5-7.0

Table 2　CAMSHAFT SPECIFICATIONS

Item	Standard	Service limit
Cam lobe height		
Intake	34.360-34.400 mm (1.3528-1.3543 in.)	34.060 mm (1.3409 in.)
Exhaust	34.360-34.400 mm (1.3528-1.3543 in.)	34.060 mm (1.3409 in.)
Camshaft deflection	—	0.10 mm (0.004 in.)
Camshaft journal clearance	0.020-0.054 mm (0.0008-0.0021 in.)	0.150 mm (0.0059 in.)
Camshaft journal diameter	21.959-21.980 mm (0.8645-0.8654 in.)	—
Camshaft bearing cap inside diameter	22.000-22.013 mm	—

5

Table 3　ROCKER ARM AND ROCKER SHAFT SPECIFICATIONS

Item	Standard	Service limit
Rocker arm inside diameter	12.000-12.018 mm (0.4724-0.4731 in.)	—
Rocker shaft diameter	11.973-11.984 mm (0.4714-0.4718 in.)	—

Table 4　VALVE SPECIFICATIONS

Item	Standard	Service limit
Valve face (margin)	—	0.5 mm (0.02 in.)
Valve stem deflection	—	0.05 mm (0.02 in.)
Valve head deflection	—	0.03 mm (0.001 in.)
Valve-to-guide clearance		
Intake	0.025-0.052 mm (0.0010-0.0020 in.)	0.090 mm (0.0035 in.)
Exhaust	0.040-0.067 mm (0.0016-0.0026 in.)	0.100 mm (0.0039 in.)
Valve stem diameter		
Intake	5.460-5.475 mm (0.2150-0.2156 in.)	—
Exhaust	5.445-5.460 mm (0.2144-0.2150 in.)	—
Valve seat width	0.9-1.1 mm (0.035-0.043 in.)	—
Valve spring free length		
Inner	—	31.9 mm (1.26 in.)
Outer	—	35.6 mm (1.40 in.)

Table 5 PISTON AND CYLINDER SPECIFICATIONS

Item	Standard	Limit
Piston pin bore	18.002-18.008 mm (0.7087-0.7090 in.)	18.030 mm (18.030 in.)
Piston pin diameter	17.995-18.000 mm (0.7085-0.7087 in.)	17.980 mm (0.7079 in.)
Piston diameter	66.945-66.960 mm (2.6356-2.6362 in.)	66.880 mm (2.6331 in.)
Piston measuring point	15 mm (0.6 in.) from piston skirt end	
Cylinder inner diameter	67.000-67.015 mm (2.6378-2.6384 in.)	67.080 mm (2.6410 in.)
Piston-to-cylinder clearance	0.050-0.060 mm (0.0020-0.0024 in.)	0.120 mm (0.0047 in.)
Cylinder distortion		0.2 mm (0.008 in.)
Piston pin/Pin bore clearance		0.12 mm (0.0047 in.)

Table 6 PISTON RING SPECIFICATIONS

Item	Standard	Limit
Ring-to-groove clearance		
Top ring	—	0.180 mm (0.0071 in.)
Middle ring	—	0.150 mm (0.0059 in.)
Ring thickness		
Top ring	1.175-1.190 mm (0.0463-0.0469 in.)	—
Middle ring	1.170-1.190 mm (0.0461-0.0469 in.)	—
Ring groove width		
Top ring	1.21-1.23 mm (0.047-0.048 in.)	—
Middle ring	1.21-1.23 mm (0.047-0.048 in.)	—
Oil ring	2.51-2.53 mm (0.099-0.100 in.)	—
Ring end gap		
Top and middle rings	0.10-0.30 mm (0.004-0.012 in.)	0.7 mm (0.03 in.)
Ring free end gap		
Top ring	Approx. 9.5 mm (0.37 in.)	7.6 mm (0.30 in.)
Middle ring	Approx. 10.0 mm (0.39 in.)	8.0 mm (0.31 in.)

Table 7 CONNECTING ROD SPECIFICATIONS

Item	Standard	Service limit
Small end inside diameter	18.006-18.014 mm (0.7089-0.7092 in.)	18.040 mm (0.7102 in.)
Piston pin outside diameter	17.995-18.000 mm (0.7085-07087 in.)	17.980 mm (0.7079 in.)
Connecting rod small end/piston pin clearance	—	0.080 mm (0.0031 in.)
Big end width	20.95-21.00 mm (0.825-0.827 in.)	—
Big end side clearance	0.10-0.20 mm (0.004-0.008 in.)	0.30 mm (0.012 in.)
Big end bearing clearance	0.024-0.048 mm (0.0009-0.0019 in.)	0.080 mm (0.0031 in.)
Crankshaft crank pin (rod journal) width	21.10-21.15 mm (0.831-0.833 in.)	—
Crankshaft crank pin (rod journal) outside diameter	35.976-36.000 mm (1.4164-1.4173 in.)	—

Table 8 CRANKSHAFT SPECIFICATIONS

Item	Standard	Service limit
Crankshaft runout	—	0.05 mm (0.0020 in.)
Crankshaft main bearing journal width	24.00-24.10 mm (0.945-0.949 in.)	—
Crankcase main bearing journal width	23.70-23.90 mm (0.933-0.941 in.)	—
Crankshaft thrust clearance	0.10-0.40 mm (0.004-0.016 in.)	0.5 mm (0.02 in.)
Crankshaft main bearing clearance	0.020-0.044 mm (0.0008-0.0017 in.)	0.080 mm (0.0031 in.)
Crank pin (rod journal) outside diameter	35.976-36.000 mm (1.4164-1.4173 in.)	—
Crankshaft main bearing journal outside diameter	35.976-36.000 mm (1.4164-1.4173 in.)	—

Table 9 CONNECTING ROD BEARING SELECTION

Bearing Color Code Determination			
Connecting rod code	Crank pin code		
	1	2	3
1	Green	Black	Brown
2	Black	Brown	Yellow
Connecting rod inside diameter			
	Code 1	39.000-39.008 mm (1.5354-1.5357 in.)	
	Code 2	39.008-39.016 mm (1.5357-1.5361 in.)	
Crankshaft crank pin diameter			
	Code 1	35.992-36.000 mm (1.4170-1.4173 in.)	
	Code 2	35.984-35.992 mm (1.4167-1.4170 in.)	
	Code 3	35.976-35.984 mm (1.4164-1.4167 in.)	
Bearing color code/thickness			
Color	Suzuki part Number	Bearing thickness	
Green	12164-45400-010	1.484-1.488 mm (0.0584-0.0586 in.)	
Black	12164-45400-020	1.488-1.492 mm (0.0586-0.0587 in.)	
Brown	12164-45400-030	1.492-1.496 mm (0.0587-0.0589 in.)	
Yellow	12164-45400-040	1.496-1.500 mm (0.0589-0.0591 in.)	

Table 10   CRANKSHAFT MAIN BEARING SELECTION

Bearing Color Code Determination

Crankcase journal code	Crankshaft main bearing journal code		
	A	B	C
A	Green	Black	Brown
B	Black	Brown	Yellow

Crankcase main bearing inside diameter		
	Code A	39.000-39.008 mm (1.5354-1.5357 in.)
	Code B	39.008-39.016 mm (1.5357-1.5361 in.)

Crankshaft main bearing diameter		
	Code A	35.992-36.000 mm (1.4170-1.4173 in.)
	Code B	35.984-35.992 mm (1.4167-1.4170 in.)
	Code C	35.976-35.984 mm (1.4164-1.4167 in.)

Bearing color code/thickness		
Color	Suzuki Part Number	Bearing thickness
Green	12229-45400-010	1.486-1.490 mm (0.0585-0.0587 in.)
Black	12229-45400-020	1.490-1.494 mm (0.0587-0.0588 in.)
Brown	12229-45400-030	1.494-1.498 mm (0.0588-0.0590 in.)
Yellow	12229-45400-040	1.498-1.502 mm (0.0590-0.0591 in.)

CLUTCH, TRANSMISSION AND KICKSTARTER

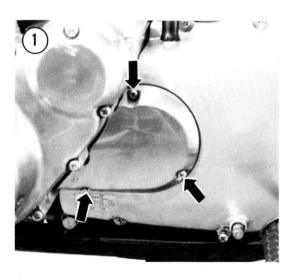

This chapter provides maintenance procedures for the clutch, transmission, gearshift mechanism and the kickstarter. **Tables 1-3** are at the end of the chapter.

All clutch components and some gearshift and kickstarter components can be removed with the engine installed in the motorcycle. To remove the transmission and insternal components of the kickstarter and gearshift mechanism it is necessary to remove and disassemble the engine. Refer to Chapters Four or Five for engine removal and disassembly procedures.

NOTE
The following procedures provide coverage for the 2 types of GS750 engines. All 1979 and earlier models share one style engine. Starting with 1980 models ("T" models), all machines are fitted with a TSCC (Twin Swirl Combustion Chamber) engine. Throughout this chapter these machines are identified as "TSCC" models.

Most maintenance and repair procedures are very similar for both engine types. All minor differences, where applicable, are specified within the procedures. Where significant differences exist, a separate procedure is provided for each type of engine. Before starting any repair or maintenance work, read completely all applicable procedures and note the differences between the models.

CLUTCH

Cable Replacement

1. Remove the fuel tank as outlined in Chapter Seven.
2. On all 1977-1979 models, perform the following:
   a. Remove the screws securing the clutch adjuster cover (**Figure 1**) and remove the cover.

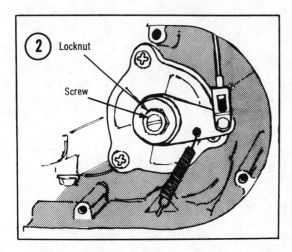

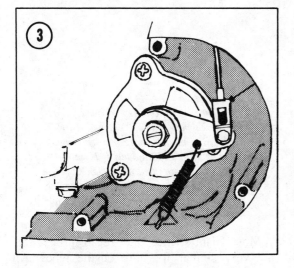

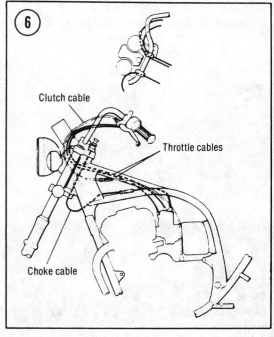

b. Refer to **Figure 2** and loosen the locknut on the adjuster screw. Turn in on the adjuster screw to provide some slack in the clutch cable.

c. Straighten the tab inside the clevis that secures the cable and disconnect the cable (**Figure 3**).

3. On all models with an external cable adjuster, remove the cotter pin, washer and clevis pin securing the cable end to the clutch release arm (**Figure 4**).

4. Unscrew the cable adjuster until the cable can be removed completely from the engine.

5. Loosen the large knurled locknut and screw in the cable adjuster on the clutch lever (**Figure 5**). Disengage the cable end from the lever.

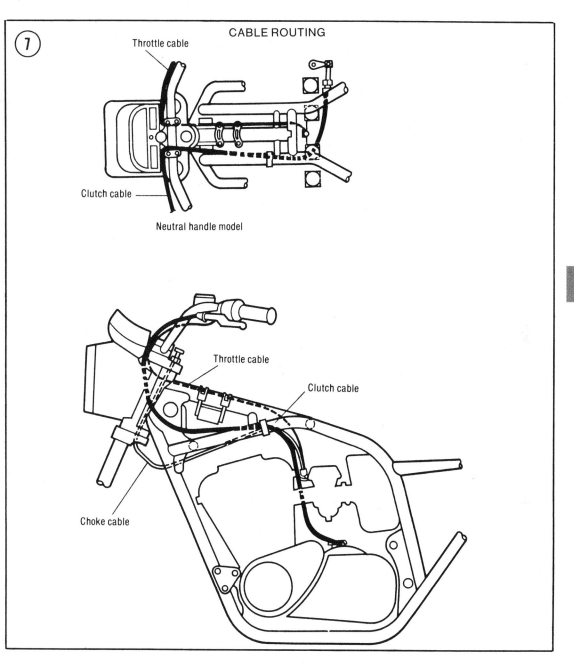

⑦ CABLE ROUTING

Throttle cable

Clutch cable

Neutral handle model

Throttle cable

Clutch cable

Choke cable

6. Route the new cable alongside the old cable. Loosen or remove all the straps securing the cable to the motorcycle frame.

7. Cable installation is the reverse of these steps. Keep the following points in mind:

a. Ensure that the new cable is routed exactly like the old cable and is properly secured with cable straps. Refer to **Figure 6** for 1979 and earlier models and **Figure 7** for all TSCC engines.

b. Screw in handlebar cable adjuster completely and secure the adjuster with the knurled locknut.

c. Refer to Chapter Three and perform the applicable clutch adjustment procedure.

Clutch Removal/Installation

Special preparation should be made before performing a complete clutch removal. A

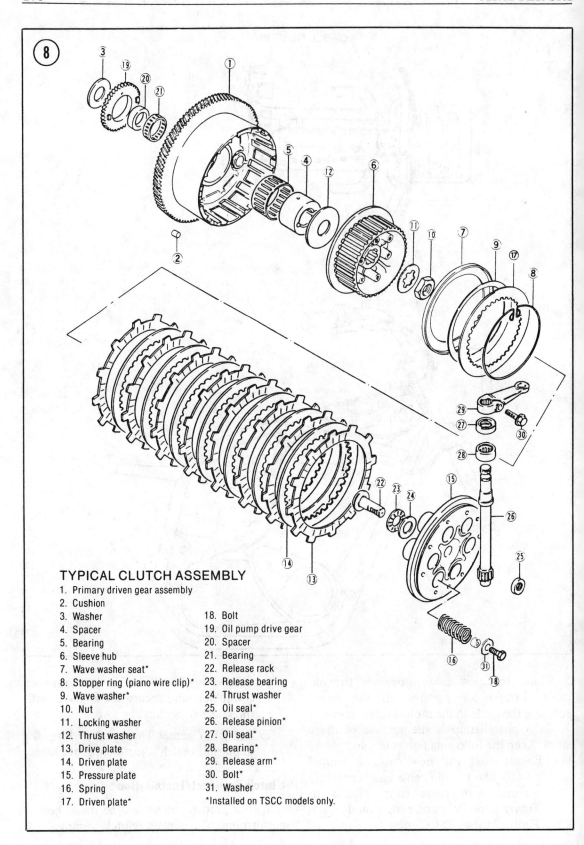

TYPICAL CLUTCH ASSEMBLY
1. Primary driven gear assembly
2. Cushion
3. Washer
4. Spacer
5. Bearing
6. Sleeve hub
7. Wave washer seat*
8. Stopper ring (piano wire clip)*
9. Wave washer*
10. Nut
11. Locking washer
12. Thrust washer
13. Drive plate
14. Driven plate
15. Pressure plate
16. Spring
17. Driven plate*
18. Bolt
19. Oil pump drive gear
20. Spacer
21. Bearing
22. Release rack
23. Release bearing
24. Thrust washer
25. Oil seal*
26. Release pinion*
27. Oil seal*
28. Bearing*
29. Release arm*
30. Bolt*
31. Washer
*Installed on TSCC models only.

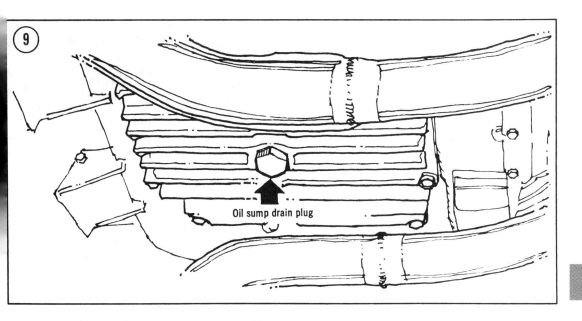

Oil sump drain plug

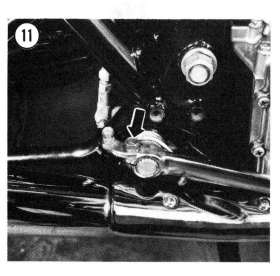

6

special holding tool or access to an impact wrench (air or electric) is necessary to remove the nut securing the clutch sleeve hub. Read the following procedure first to determine what option is best suited for your situation.

Refer to **Figure 8** for this procedure.

1. If the engine has not been removed from the motorcycle, perform the following:

   a. Use a 13/16 in. spark plug socket and remove the oil drain plug from the engine (**Figure 9**). Allow several minutes for the oil to drain completely.

   b. Remove the bolts securing the right footrest and remove the footrest (**Figure 10**).

   c. Remove the pinch bolt securing the brake pedal (**Figure 11**).

   d. Disengage the pedal return spring and slide the pedal off the shaft. Note that the punch mark on the shaft is aligned with the split opening on the brake pedal (**Figure 12**).

   NOTE
   On some earlier models, the punch mark on the pedal shaft is aligned with a punch mark on the pedal.

   e. On all models with external clutch adjusters, pull back the rubber boot and loosen the locknut securing the clutch cable adjuster (**Figure 13**). Turn in on the cable adjuster to provide maximum cable slack. Remove the cotter pin, washer and clevis pin securing the cable end to the clutch release arm (**Figure 14**).

> *NOTE*
> *As an alternate method, the clutch release arm may be removed from the pinion shaft. To remove the clutch release arm, completely remove the pinch bolt securing the arm to the shaft (**Figure 14**).*

2. On models equipped with a kickstarter, remove the pinch bolt (**Figure 15**) and remove the kickstarter lever.

3. Use a hammer-driven impact tool to loosen all the screws securing the right engine cover (clutch cover) as shown in **Figure 16**. Identify the location of the different length screws as the screws are removed. Gently tap around the edge of the cover with a soft-faced mallet to help break the cover loose from the engine and remove the cover. Have a few rags ready as some oil is bound to run out.

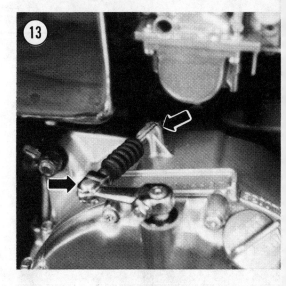

> *NOTE*
> *On all models with a clutch release arm, rotate the arm in the direction of the clutch cable pull to help break the cover loose from the engine.*

> *CAUTION*
> *Do not attempt to pry the cover loose with a screwdriver or similar object as the sealing surface on the cover and/or the engine will be damaged.*

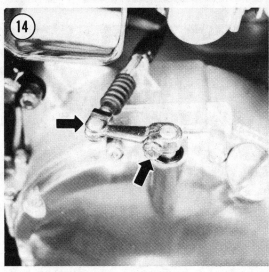

4. Work in a crisscross pattern and gradually and evenly loosen the 6 bolts securing the pressure disc (**Figure 17**). Remove the bolts, washers and springs (**Figure 18**).

5. Lift out the pressure disc and remove the release bearing assembly as shown in **Figure 19**.

6. Remove the clutch drive and driven plates (**Figure 20**). If only plate replacement or inspection is desired, further disassembly is unnecessary.

7. Use a chisel or screwdriver and fold back the tab on the locking washer (**Figure 21**).

> *NOTE*
> *To remove the nut securing the sleeve hub, it is necessary to use a special holding tool or an impact wrench (air or electric). A simple tool can be fabricated locally by welding a rod to a steel driven plate as shown in **Figure 22**. A universal holding tool (part No. 09920-53710) is available from Suzuki; however, the tool is expensive.*

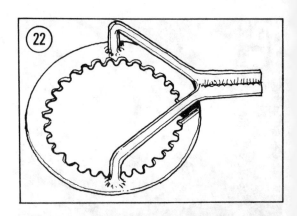

8. Slide the holding tool over the sleeve hub. Hold the sleeve hub securely with the tool and loosen the hub nut. The hub nut requires a 32 mm socket.

> *CAUTION*
> *While holding the sleeve hub nut with the holding tool, make sure that no part of the tool bears against the clutch housing/ primary driven gear assembly or the clutch housing may be damaged.*

9. Remove the sleeve hub nut and folding lockwasher (**Figure 23**).

10. Lift out the sleeve hub (**Figure 24**) and the large washer behind the hub (**Figure 25**). Note that the 2 large machined grooves in the washer face in toward the engine.

NOTE
On all TSCC engines, the innermost driven plate is secured to the sleeve hub with a stopper ring (piano wire clip). Do not remove the stopper ring unless the plate must be replaced. Removal of the stopper ring is described under **Inspection**.

11. Install a 6 mm bolt or screw into the large clutch spacer as shown in **Figure 26**. Engine cover screws work well for this task. Pull out on the screw and remove the large spacer (**Figure 27**).

12. Hold the clutch housing in place and carefully remove the large bearing (**Figure 28**).

13. Slide the clutch housing/primary driven gear assembly off center and disengage the driven gear assembly from the crankshaft drive gear. Lift out and remove the clutch housing assembly.

14. Remove the oil pump drive gear (**Figure 29**).

15. Remove the oil pump gear bearing (**Figure 30**).

16. Remove the spacer and large washer next to the transmission bearing (**Figure 31**).

17. Perform *Inspection*.
18. Installation is the reverse of these steps.
Keep the following points in mind:

  a. Make sure the notches in the clutch housing (**Figure 32**) engage the drive dogs on the oil pump drive gear (**Figure 33**).

  b. Install the large washer between the clutch housing and sleeve hub. Make sure the grooves on the washer (**Figure 34**) face in toward the engine.

  c. Hold the sleeve hub with the holding tool and torque the sleeve hub nut as specified in **Table 1**.

  d. Fold over the locking tab to secure the hub nut as shown in **Figure 21**.

  e. Install a clutch drive plate first then install the remaining plates alternately.

6

f. Install the bolts securing the pressure disc. Torque the bolts evenly in a crisscross pattern as specified in **Table 1**.

CAUTION
If it is necessary to replace a clutch retaining bolt, always use the exact Suzuki replacement bolt. They are specially hardened for that application. Using an incorrect bolt may cause clutch failure and subsequent expensive engine damage.

g. Make sure the release bearing assembly is installed as shown in **Figure 35** for all TSCC engines and **Figure 36** for all other models.

h. On all TSCC engines, position the release rack as shown in **Figure 37** to enable proper alignment with the clutch release pinion shaft inside the clutch cover.

i. Before installing the right engine cover gasket, apply a 2 in. wide film of Bond No. 4 sealant or equivalent over the crankcase seam as shown in **Figure 38**.

19. Use a new gasket and install the right engine cover.

20. Refer to Chapter Three and add engine oil and perform *Clutch Adjustment*.

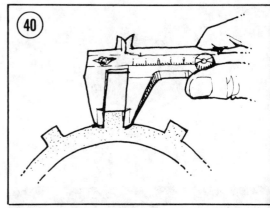

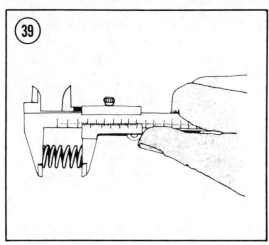

Inspection

Refer to **Table 2** for clutch component specifications.

1. Measure the free length of the clutch springs as shown in **Figure 39**. Replace any springs that are not within the limits specified in **Table 2**. It is recommended that all springs be replaced as a set if any one is not within the specified tolerance.

2. Measure the drive plate claw width as shown in **Figure 40**. Replace any drive plates worn beyond the service limits specified in **Table 2**.

3. Measure the thickness of the clutch drive plates as shown in **Figure 41**. Replace any plates worn beyond the specified service limits.

4. Measure each driven plate for distortion with a feeler gauge on a piece of plate glass as shown in **Figure 42**. Replace any plate that is warped beyond the limits specified in **Table 2**.

5. Carefully examine the large and small bearings (**Figure 43** and **Figure 44**). Replace the bearings if worn or damaged.

6. Check the condition of the clutch housing (**Figure 45**). Deep grooves on the housing edges caused by the drive plates will prevent proper clutch operation. Replace the clutch housing if deep grooves are present.

7. Examine the rubber dampers (**Figure 46**) and springs (**Figure 47**) in the clutch housing. Replace the housing if these springs and rubber dampers appear damaged or defective.

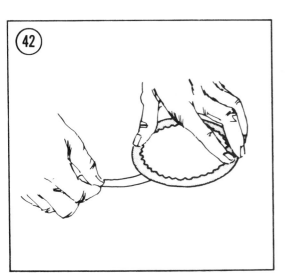

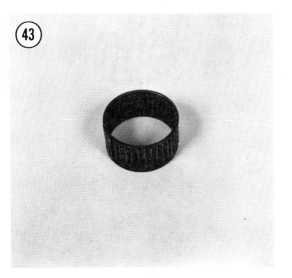

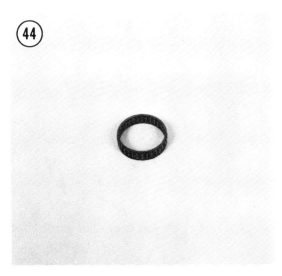

6

8. Examine the clutch release bearing assembly. See **Figure 48** for all TSCC engines and **Figure 49** for all 1979 and earlier models. Replace all worn or damaged components.

9. Check the pressure disc (**Figure 50**) for signs of excessive wear or damage. Replace if defective.

10. Inspect the sleeve hub (**Figure 51**) for damage or abnormal wear. On all TSCC engines, it is not necessary to routinely remove the driven plate, wave washer and washer seat from the sleeve hub. These items should only be removed if component replacement is required. If removal is desired, perform the following:

   a. Pry out the stopper ring (piano wire clip) from the sleeve hub (**Figure 52**).

   b. Remove the driven plate, wave washer and washer seat.

   c. When installing the components always use a new piano wire clip. Ensure the clip ends are properly secured in the sleeve hub (**Figure 53**). Make sure the clip is completely installed in the sleeve hub groove (**Figure 54**).

11. On all 1979 and earlier models, roll the clutch pushrod (**Figure 55**) on a smooth surface to check for bends or other damage. Replace the pushrod if necessary.

12. Examine the teeth and drive dogs on the oil pump drive gear (**Figure 56**). Replace the gear if worn or damaged.

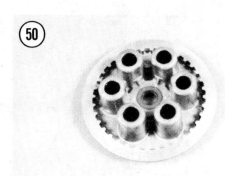

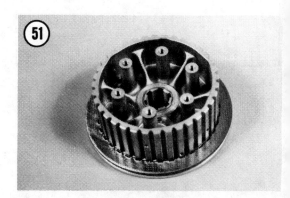

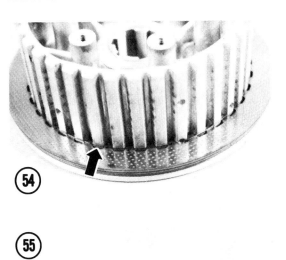

(54)

(55)

(58)

(56)

(57)

6

TRANSMISSION

The countershaft (also known as the input shaft) is connected to the clutch. All the gears on the countershaft are identified as "drive" gears. The drive shaft (also known as the output shaft) is connected to the drive chain. All the gears on the drive shaft are identified as "driven" gears.

CAUTION
Minor differences exist between models concerning the number and location of bushings and spacers. Pay particular attention to how the transmission is disassembled to avoid any problems during assembly.

Removal/Installation

1. Remove the engine and separate the crankcase halves as outlined in Chapters Four and Five.
2. If a dial indicator is available, measure the backlash of each of the gears as shown in **Figure 57**. Record the actual lash and refer to **Table 3** for standard and service limit specifications. Replace any gear combinations with excessive backlash.
3. Before removing gear sets carefully note the position of the bearing locating pins, oil seals, seal retainers and shift forks. Carefully lift out the countershaft gear set (next to the crankshaft) and the drive shaft gear set (**Figure 58**). Place each gear set on a clean rag.

4. Perform *Inspection*. If any gears or bearings must be replaced, refer to the applicable gear set disassembly procedure following. Certain gears and bearings are a press fit and require special tools and expertise for removal and installation.

> NOTE
> *If gear replacement is required due to damage, excessive wear or worn engagement dogs, it is recommended that the mating gears and the corresponding gearshift forks also be replaced.*

5. Installation is the reverse of these steps. Keep the following points in mind:

   a. Make sure the drive shaft bearing is installed with the sealed side facing out as shown in **Figure 59**.

   b. Ensure that the bearing retainer C-rings are properly positioned in the crankcase (**Figure 60**).

   c. Position the locating pins on the countershaft and drive shaft bearings in the notches in the crankcase as shown in **Figure 61**.

   d. Make sure the gear set seals are correctly positioned as shown in **Figure 62**. The large drive shaft seal must be secured by the outer retainer C-ring.

   e. Assemble the engine as outlined in Chapters Four and Five.

Inspection

1. Clean and carefully inspect all gears for burrs, chips or roughness on the teeth.
2. Closely examine all bearings for wear or cracks in the races.
3. Carefully check all the gear engagement dogs. See **Figure 63** for outside dogs and **Figure 64** for inside dogs. Both gears in a "dog set" must be replaced if the engagement dogs are damaged or rounded on the corners. Worn or rounded engagement dogs will cause the transmission to fail to shift or to jump out of gear.

> CAUTION
> *If both gears in a "dog set" are not replaced at the same time, the newly replaced gear will be damaged.*

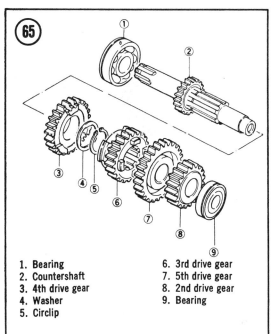

1. Bearing
2. Countershaft
3. 4th drive gear
4. Washer
5. Circlip
6. 3rd drive gear
7. 5th drive gear
8. 2nd drive gear
9. Bearing

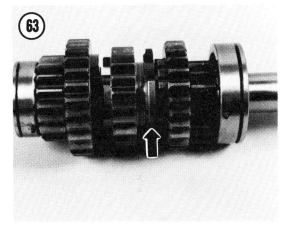

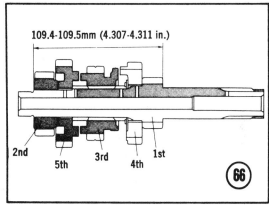

109.4-109.5mm (4.307-4.311 in.)

2nd 5th 3rd 4th 1st

Countershaft Gear Set
Disassembly/Assembly

Refer to **Figure 65** for this procedure.

The 2nd drive gear is pressed on the countershaft. A hydraulic press is required to remove the 2nd gear so that the countershaft can be disassembled. The task of removing and installing the gear should be referred to a dealer or competent machine shop. If gear replacement is performed, ensure that the distance between 1st and 2nd drive gear is 109.4-109.5 mm (4.307-4.311 in.) as shown in **Figure 66**. The 2nd gear can be pressed on and

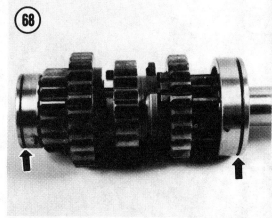

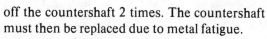

off the countershaft 2 times. The countershaft must then be replaced due to metal fatigue.

If countershaft bearing replacement is desired, carefully pry the bearings from the shaft (**Figure 67**). Gently tap the new bearings in place with the grooves for the C-rings on the outside as shown in **Figure 68**.

Drive Shaft Gear Set Disassembly/Assembly

Refer to **Figure 69** for this procedure.

1. Remove the bearing from the shaft and slide off the 1st driven gear (**Figure 70**).
2. Remove the 4th driven gear (**Figure 71**).
3. Remove the circlip and washer securing the 3rd driven gear (**Figure 72**) and remove the gear.
4. Remove the bushing (on TSCC engines only) and No. 1 and No. 2 lockwashers (**Figure 73**). Slide off the 5th driven gear.
5. Remove the circlip and washer securing the 2nd driven gear. Remove the gear (**Figure 74**). On TSCC engines, remove the shouldered bushing.
6. Assembly is the reverse of these steps. Keep the following points in mind:
   a. If possible, use new circlips to secure the gears. Apply a light film of molybdenum disulfide lubricant (such as Bel-Ray Moly Lube) to the shaft before installing the gears.
   b. On all TSCC engines, install the shouldered bushing into the 2nd drive gear and install the gear on the shaft.

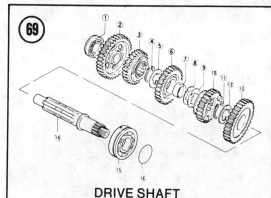

DRIVE SHAFT

1. Bearing	9. Lockwasher No. 2
2. 1st driven gear	10. 5th driven gear
3. 4th driven gear	11. Circlip
4. Circlip	12. Washer
5. Washer	13. 2nd driven gear
6. 3rd driven gear	14. Drive shaft
7. Spacer	15. Bearing
8. Lockwasher No. 1	16. O-ring

The shoulder on the bushing must be **opposite** the threaded end of the shaft. Secure the gear and bushing with the washer and circlip as shown in **Figure 74**.

c. Install the 5th driven gear and the No. 1 and No. 2 lockwashers as shown in **Figure 75**. Turn the No. 2 lockwasher to fit into the shaft groove.

d. Install the No. 1 lockwasher so the ears on the washer engage the notches in the No. 2 lockwasher as shown in **Figure 76**.

e. Slide the bushing on the shaft so the oil hole is aligned with the shaft oil hole as shown in **Figure 73**.

CAUTION
*Failure to correctly align the oil holes as shown in **Figure 73** will result in expensive transmission damage.*

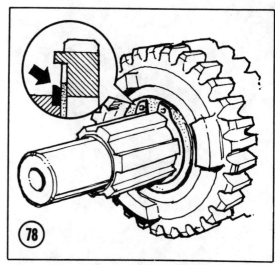

f. Install the 3rd driven gear and the thrust washer (**Figure 77**). Secure the gear and washer with the circlip (**Figure 72**). Make sure the rounded edge of the circlip butts against the thrust washer as shown in **Figure 78**.

g. Refer to **Figure 70** and **Figure 71** and complete the shaft assembly.

h. Install a new O-ring on the sprocket end of the drive shaft (**Figure 79**).

GEARSHIFT MECHANISM

Gearshift repair work, except for the shifting cam and shift forks, can be carried out with the engine in the motorcycle. To remove the shifting cam and shift forks, it is necessary to remove the engine and separate the crankcase halves.

Removal/Installation

1. Perform *Clutch Removal.*

2. If the engine has not been removed from the frame, perform the following:

    a. Remove the bolts securing the left footrest (**Figure 80**) and remove the footrest.

    b. Remove the pinch bolt securing the gearshift lever (**Figure 81**). The bolt

must be removed completely, not just loosened. Remove the gearshift lever.

c. Use a hammer-driven impact tool and loosen the screws securing the sprocket cover (**Figure 82**). Note the location of the different length screws and remove the sprocket cover.

3. On all TSCC engines, remove the retaining clip and washer securing the gearshift shaft (**Figure 83**).

4. Slide the gearshift shaft out of the crankcase (**Figure 84**).

5. Use a hammer-driven impact tool and remove the screws securing the gear shifting pawl lifter (**Figure 85**) and remove the pawl lifter.

6. Use the impact tool and remove the screws securing the gearshifting cam guide (**Figure 86**) and remove the cam guide.

7. Carefully grasp and compress the spring-loaded pawl holder (**Figure 87**) and remove the assembly from the engine. Store the pawl holder assembly in a spray paint can top to keep all the components together as shown in **Figure 88**.

> *NOTE*
> *Further disassembly is not required unless it is necessary to remove the gearshifting cam and shift forks. If shifting cam and shift fork removal is desired it is necessary to remove the engine and separate the crankcase halves. Refer to Chapters Four and Five for engine removal and disassembly procedures. If further disassembly is not required, proceed to Step 13.*

8. Perform *Transmission Removal* as outlined in this chapter.

9. Disengage the spring securing the cam stopper. See **Figure 89** for TSCC engines and **Figure 90** for all 1979 and earlier models.

10. Slide out the shift fork shafts (**Figure 91**) and remove the shift forks. Note the position and location of each fork during removal. The shift forks are not interchangeable and must be installed exactly as removed.

11. Remove the spring-loaded cam stopper holder and the cam stopper (**Figure 92**).

12. Carefully slide out the shifting cam (**Figure 93**). Do not loose the thin thrust washer from the end of the shifting cam (**Figure 94**).

13. Perform *Inspection*.

14. Installation is the reverse of these steps. Keep the following points in mind:

   a. Make sure the thrust washer (**Figure 94**) is on the shifting cam and install the cam so the neutral detent (**Figure 95**) is just below the spring-loaded cam stopper. Install the cam stopper (**Figure 96**) and secure with the spring and stopper housing (**Figure 92**).

   b. Ensure that the shift forks are installed in the exact order and position as when being removed. Position the forks so that the pins will engage the slots in the shifting cam as shown in **Figure 97**.

   c. When installing the 3rd gear shift fork, position the cam stopper on the fork shaft as shown in **Figure 98**. On all TSCC engines, make sure the shoulder on the cam stopper faces **out** toward the crankcase as shown in **Figure 99**. On all 1979 and earlier models, the shoulder on the cam stopper faces IN toward the transmission as shown in **Figure 100**.

   d. Secure the spring end as shown in **Figure 101** for all TSCC engines and **Figure 102** for all 1979 and earlier models.

   e. Ensure that the "wheel" of the cam stopper is positioned in the groove in the shifting cam (**Figure 103**).

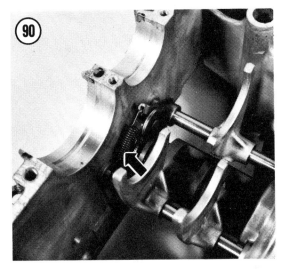

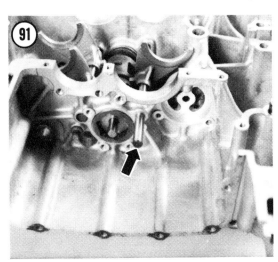

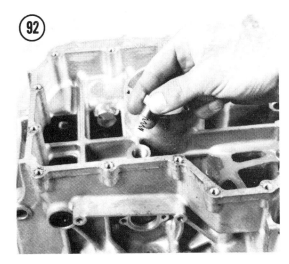

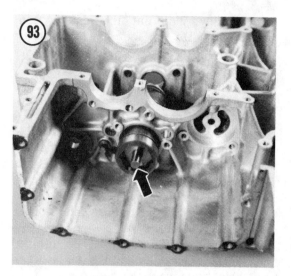

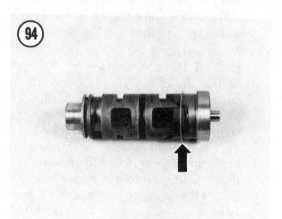

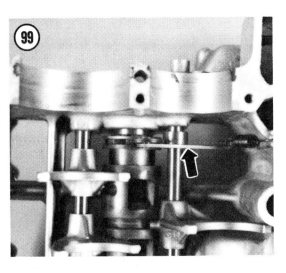

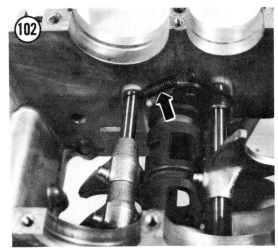

6

f. Make sure all 3 shift forks correctly engage the shifting cam as shown in **Figure 104**. Perform *Transmission Installation* as outlined in this chapter, then refer to Chapters Four and Five and assemble the crankcase halves.

> *CAUTION*
> *Use blue Loctite (Lock N' Seal No. 2114) or equivalent on all the fasteners securing the gearshift components. A loose fastener adrift in the engine could cause serious and expensive damage.*

g. Install the pawl holder (**Figure 105**) with the 5 teeth pointing toward the rear of the engine. Apply blue Loctite to the cam guide and pawl lifter screws and install the cam guide and pawl lifter (**Figure 106**).

h. Install the gearshift shaft so the teeth are centered with the teeth on the pawl holder as shown in **Figure 107**. Make sure the shaft spring is centered over the pin in the crankcase as shown in **Figure 108**. On all TSCC engines, secure the shift shaft with the washer and retaining clip (**Figure 109**).

> *CAUTION*
> *Temporarily install the gearshift lever on the shift shaft. Rotate the transmission counter shaft by hand and upshift and*

downshift the transmission through each gear. Make sure that each gear engages and the shift mechanism works freely without binding or sticking. Stop and correct any shifting malfunctions before continuing engine assembly.

i. Install the engine as outlined in Chapters Four and Five. Install the clutch as outlined in this chapter.

j. Install the sprocket cover and left footrest.

Inspection

1. Clean all gearshift components thoroughly in clean solvent.

2. Examine the gearshift shaft for signs of damage or excessive wear. Roll the shaft on a smooth flat surface and check for bends or distortion. Ensure that the shaft spring is centered on the shaft as shown in **Figure 110**.

3. Carefully inspect the pawl lifter (**Figure 111**) and cam guide (**Figure 112**) for signs of wear and replace them if necessary.

4. Disassemble the pawl holder and inspect the rollers, springs and pawls for wear or damage (**Figure 113**). When reassembling the pawl holder assembly, make sure the rounded ends of the pawl rollers fit in the grooves as

shown in **Figure 114**. The grooves in the pawls are offset. When the pawls are installed, the rear edge of the pawls must be flush with the rear edge of the pawl holder as shown in **Figure 115**.

NOTE
When reassembling pawl holder components, use a piece of tape to hold one of the spring-loaded pawls in position while installing the second pawl.

5. Refer to **Figure 116** and examine the spring-loaded cam stopper components for wear or damage.

6. Carefully examine the grooves in the shifting cam for wear or roughness (**Figure 117**). Replace the shifting cam if the grooves are less than perfect. A defective shifting cam can cause the transmission to shift hard and/or jump out of gear.

7. Check the condition of the cam stopper and replace it if signs of wear are evident. See **Figure 118** for 1979 and earlier models or

Figure 119 for all TSCC engines.

8. Inspect all 3 shift forks for damage or excessive wear. Measure the thickness of the shift forks with a micrometer or calipers as shown in **Figure 120**. The standard dimension for the forks is 4.95-5.05 mm (0.195-0.199 in.). The service limit for all shift forks is 4.85 mm (0.191 in.).

> *CAUTION*
> *It is recommended that marginal shift forks be replaced. Worn forks can cause missed shifts and slipping out of gear which can lead to more serious and expensive damage.*

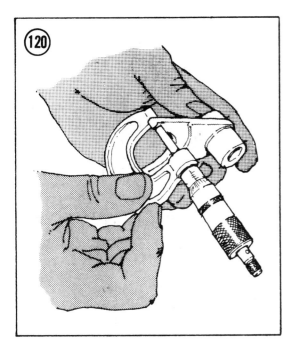

9. Slide the shift forks on the fork shafts and make sure the forks slide freely, but without excessive play (**Figure 121**).

10. Inspect the shifting cam bearing in the crankcase for damaged or worn rollers (**Figure 122**).

> *CAUTION*
> *The shifting cam bearing is a press fit in the crankcase. Do not attempt to remove the bearing for inspection or the bearing will be damaged. If bearing replacement is necessary, refer the task to an dealer or qualified specialist.*

KICKSTARTER

All 1979 and earlier GS750 models are equipped with a kickstarter assembly. The

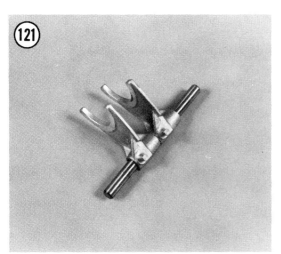

kickstarter was deleted on all 1980 and later models.

To remove the entire kickstarter assembly, it is necessary to remove and disassemble the engine. The kickstarter return spring can be replaced with the engine installed in the frame.

Removal/Installation

Refer to **Figure 123** for this procedure.

1. If is only necessary to replace the kickstarter return spring, perform Steps 1 through 3 of *Clutch Removal* as outlined in this chapter to gain access to the spring. To gain access to other kickstarter components, refer to Chapter Four to remove and disassemble the engine.

2. Pull out and remove the spring guide.

NOTE
On 1977 models, engine numbers 30728 to 38952, a 1.5 mm flat washer is installed between the clutch cover and the spring guide. On later models, engine number 38953 and subsequent, the flat washer was deleted and the spring guide length increased 1.5 mm.

3. Use pliers and disengage the end of the return spring from the kickstarter shaft. Unhook the other spring end from the crankcase and remove the spring.

4. After the engine is disassembled, lift out the kickstarter assembly (**Figure 124**). Note how the starter guide locates the position of the kickstarter.

(123) **KICKSTARTER**

1. Kickstarter lever
2. Pinch bolt
3. Dowel pin
4. Bushing
5. Oil seal
6. Spring guide
7. Spring
8. Starter guide
9. Screw
10. Plate
11. Spring
12. Kickstarter
13. Circlip
14. Kickstarter drive gear
15. Kickstarter shaft
16. Washer

5. Installation is the reverse of these steps. Keep the following points in mind:

    a. If the kickstarter shaft was disassembled, ensure that the punch marks on the shaft and kickstarter unit are aligned as shown in **Figure 125**.

    b. Before assembling the engine, make sure that the kickstarter is located properly by the starter guide as shown in **Figure 124**.

    c. Hook the end of the return spring in the crankcase and rotate the spring until the free end can be installed in the kickstarter shaft hole.

    d. Install the spring guide.

Inspection

1. Carefully examine the starter drive gear for damaged teeth and excessive wear.

2. Check the return spring for signs of cracking or metal fatigue and replace if necessary.

3. Examine the starter shaft for twisted splines or other signs of damage.

4. Inspect the starter guide in the crankcase for excessive wear and replace if necessary.

Tables are on the following page.

Table 1   TORQUE SPECIFICATIONS

Item	mkg	ft.-lb.
Clutch sleeve hub nut		
All TSCC engines	5.0-7.0	36-51
All 1979 and earlier	4.0-6.0	29-43
Clutch spring bolt		
All TSCC engines	1.1-1.3	8-10
All 1979 and earlier	0.4-0.6	3-5
Neutral cam stopper bolt	1.8-2.8	13-20
Gearshift lever bolt	1.3-2.3	10-17
Clutch release arm bolt	0.6-1.0	5-7

Table 2   CLUTCH SPECIFICATIONS

Item	Standard	Limit
Clutch spring free length		
All models	40.4 mm (1.59 in.)	38.8 mm (1.52 in.)
Drive plate thickness		
All TSCC engines	2.7-2.9 mm (0.106-0.114 in.)	2.4 mm (0.094 in.)
All 1979 and earlier	2.9-3.1 mm (0.114-0.122 in.)	2.6 mm (0.102 in.)
Drive plate claw width		
All models	11.8-12.0 mm (0.46-0.47 in.)	11.0 mm (0.43 in.)
Driven plate thickness		
All TSCC engines	1.94-2.06 mm (0.076-0.081 in.)	—
All 1979 and earlier	1.6 mm (0.062 in.)	—
Driven plate distortion (all models)	—	0.10 mm (0.004 in.)

Table 3   GEAR BACKLASH SPECIFICATIONS

Gear	Standard	Limit
1st, 2nd, and 3rd	0-0.05 mm (0-0.002 in.)	0.1 mm (0.004 in.)
4th and 5th	0.05-0.1 mm (0.002-0.004 in.)	0.15 mm (0.006 in.)

FUEL AND EXHAUST SYSTEMS

For correct operation, a gasoline engine must be supplied with fuel and air mixed in proper proportions by weight. A rich mixture is one in which there is an excess of fuel. A lean mixture is one which contains an insufficient amount of fuel. It is the function of the carburetors to supply the correct fuel/air mixture to the engine under all operating conditions.

This chapter includes removal and maintenance of the fuel tank, carburetors and exhaust system. All carburetor adjustments and air cleaner service are outlined in Chapter Three. **Table 1** is at the end of the chapter.

NOTE
The following procedures provide coverage for the 2 types of GS750 machines. All 1979 and earlier models share one style engine as well as most carburetor and exhaust system components.

Starting with 1980 models ("T" models), all GS750 machines are fitted with TSCC (Twin Swirl Combustion Chamber) engines. Throughout this chapter these machines are identified as "TSCC" models.

Except for carburetors, most maintenance and repair procedures are similar for motorcycles with both engine types. All minor differences, where applicable, are specified within the procedures. Where significant differences exist, a separate procedure is provided for each type of motorcycle. Before starting any repair or maintenance work, read completely all applicable procedures and note the differences between the models.

FUEL TANK

Removal/Installation

1. Disconnect the fuel line and vacuum line from the fuel valve.
2. On models equipped with a fuel gauge, disconnect the black/white and yellow/black fuel gauge wires near the left rear corner of the air box (**Figure 1**).
3. Lift up on the rear of the tank and slide the tank back enough to disengage the front rubber mounting pads (**Figure 2**). Make sure the rubber washers on the mounting bolt are not lost.
4. Installation is the reverse of these steps. Lightly lubricate the tank mounting pads with rubber lubricant or WD-40 to aid tank installation.

CARBURETORS

All 1979 and earlier GS750 models are equipped with 4 Mikuni VM26SS carburetors. All TSCC models are equipped with 4 BS32SS

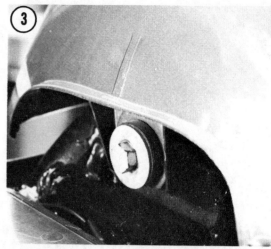

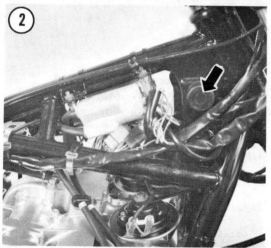

Mikuni carburetors. The VM carburetors use mechanically actuated throttle slide valves directly linked to the throttle cables. The BS carburetors are a constant velocity (CV) type with throttle slide valves controlled by engine vacuum.

> *NOTE*
> *All models **manufactured** after January 1, 1978 are engineered to meet stringent E.P.A. (Environmental Protecting Agency) regulations. The carburetors are flow-tested and preset at the factory for maximum performance and efficiency within E.P.A. regulations. Altering carburetor jet needle and air screw preset adjustments is forbidden by law.. Failure to comply with E.P.A. regulations may result in heavy fines.*

Removal/Installation (1979 and Earlier Models)

1. Raise the seat and unscrew the rear fuel tank mounting bolt (**Figure 3**).
2. Turn the fuel tap to ON or RESERVE and disconnect the fuel line from the carburetor.
3. Slide the tank back and off from the rubber mounts.
4. Unscrew the bolt that attaches the air cleaner box to the frame (**Figure 4**).
5. Loosen the clamping bands between the carburetors and the air cleaner box (**Figure 5**). Disconnect the hoses from the carburetors and remove the air cleaner.
6. Loosen the locknuts on the throttle cable adjusters (**Figure 6**), screw in the adjusters to release tension from the cables and disconnect

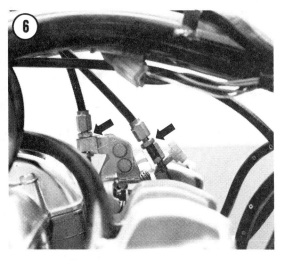

the cables from the quadrant. On models equipped with a choke cable, disconnect the cable from the carburetors.

7. Loosen the clamping bands between the carburetors and the engine (**Figure 7**). Pull rearward to disconnect the carburetors from the engine and remove them from the motorcycle as an assembly. Pull them out carefully so the vent hoses will not be disconnected.

8. Installation is the reverse of the procedures above. Route the vent hoses down between the rear of the engine and the swinging arm pivot. When the installation is complete, refer to Chapter Three and adjust the throttle cables and carburetors.

Removal (TSCC Models)

1. Remove the fuel tank as previously outlined.

2. Loosen the clamp securing the front of the air filter chamber (**Figure 8**). Remove the bolt securing the rear of the air filter chamber (**Figure 9**).

3. Remove the right side cover and loosen the clamp bolt securing the rear master cylinder reservoir enough to allow the reservoir to be moved slightly. Lift out and remove the air filter chamber.

4. Remove the bolt securing the choke cable to the carburetor bracket (**Figure 10**).

5. Refer to **Figure 11** and loosen the locknuts securing the throttle cable. Slide the outer cable end out of the carburetor bracket and disconnect the inner cable end from the throttle shaft.

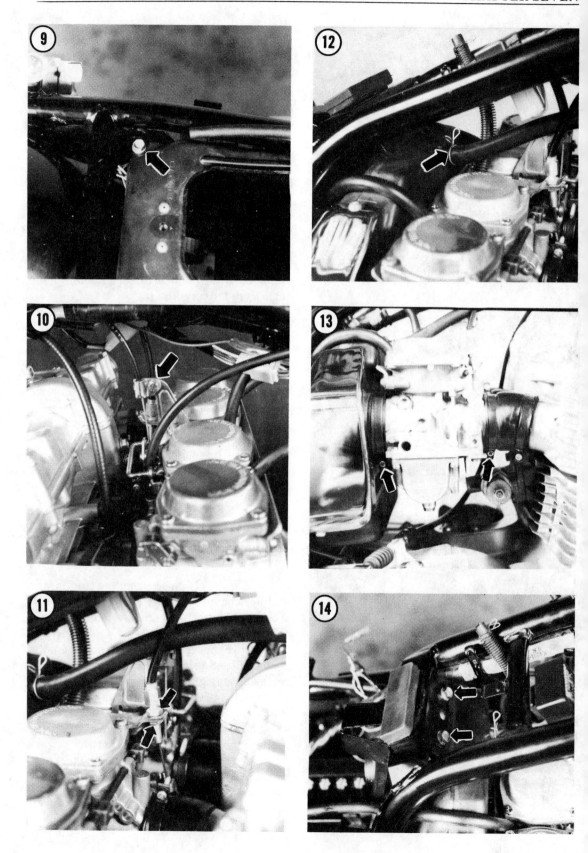

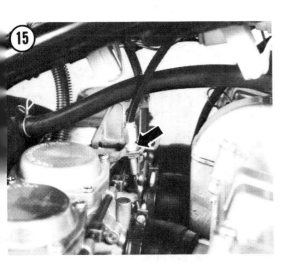

6. Spring open the clamps securing the breather hose to the engine and air box (**Figure 12**) and remove the breather hose.

7. Loosen the clamp screws securing the carburetors to the engine flanges and the air box (**Figure 13**).

8. Remove the 2 bolts (**Figure 14**) securing the air box to the frame. Pull the air box back as far as possible and remove the air box flanges from the carburetor throats.

9. Pull the carburetors back out of the engine flanges. Lower the carburetors enough so that the choke cable bracket clears the wires and the upper frame tube and remove the carburetors. Note that the 2 large carburetor vent tubes are routed back through the seat mounting bracket.

Installation (TSCC Models)

1. Connect the throttle cable to the throttle shaft on the carburetors and install the carburetors into the engine flanges. Carefully install the air box flanges over the carburetor throats.

2. Secure the air box to the frame with the 2 bolts (**Figure 14**).

3. Slide the throttle cable into the cable bracket (**Figure 15**). Rotate the cable adjuster for 0.5-1.0 mm (1/32-1/16 in.) of cable free play and secure the adjuster with the locknuts.

4. Connect the choke cable to the carburetors and secure the cable to the bracket as shown in **Figure 16**.

5. Install the air filter chamber and secure the chamber with the forward clamp (**Figure 17**) and the rear bolt (**Figure 18**). Tighten the bolt

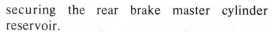

securing the rear brake master cylinder reservoir.

6. Route the large carburetor vent tubes through the seat brackets as shown in **Figure 19**. Ensure that the tubes are not pinched shut where they fit between the air box and the frame.

7. Install the fuel tank.

Disassembly/Assembly (VM Carburetors)

1. Remove the caps from the carburetors (**Figure 20**).

2. Unscrew the lifter lockbolt from each carburetor (**Figure 21**). Unscrew the lifter quadrant bolt.

3. Remove the rubber plugs from the outer carburetors (**Figure 22**).

4. Remove the screw from the throttle lock (**Figure 23**). This lock prevents the rod from

moving side to side. Remove the throttle shaft.

5. Unscrew the flush screws that attach the carburetors to the manifold plate (**Figure 24**). Remove the carburetors from the plate. The throttle quadrant and choke lifter mechanism can be left in place on the plate.

6. Unscrew the screws from the float chamber and remove it (**Figure 25**). Note the sediment trap in the bottom of the float chamber (**Figure 26**). These traps can be cleaned with the carburetors installed on the engine.

7. Remove the throttle shaft bushings from the carburetors (**Figure 27**).

8. Remove the float pin (**Figure 28**).

9. Unscrew the float needle valve (**Figure 29**) and remove the needle valve.

10. Unscrew and remove the main jet (**Figure 30**).

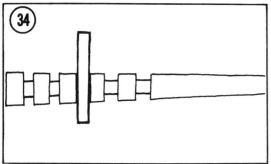

11. Unscrew the pilot jet (**Figure 31**).

> *CAUTION*
> *Do not unscrew or even turn the small jet that is marked with colored paint. This jet is preset at the factory. The position of this jet is calibrated for each individual carburetor, and if disturbed, carburetor adjustment can be severely affected. (See* **Figure 32**.*)*

12. Remove the slide and slide lifter from the carburetor (**Figure 33**) and unscrew the 2 screws that attach the lifter to the slide.

13. Remove the needle from the slide and note the position of the E-clip on the needle (**Figure 34**). Most likely, the E-clip will be in the center groove, but no matter which position it is in, it should be reassembled in the same position from which it was removed if the carburetor adjustment is correct at the time they are disassembled.

14. On models *manufactured* before January 1, 1978, unscrew the idle air screw (**Figure 35**).

15. Unscrew the choke mechanism (**Figure 36**).

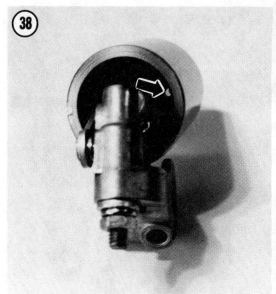

16. Remove the fuel manifold pipe that connects the carburetor float chamber to the chamber of the adjacent carburetor. Carefully remove the O-rings (**Figure 37**).

17. Assembly is the reverse of these steps. Keep the following points in mind:

 a. After installing the needle in the slide, position the slide lifter so that the third hole in the lifter is aligned with the third hole in the slide (**Figure 38**).

 b. When installing the slide lifter assembly, carefully install the needle in the needle jet. Make sure the groove in the carburetor slide engages the pin in the carburetor body (**Figure 39**).

 c. Perform *Float Level Adjustment*.

Disassembly/Assembly (BS Type Carburetors)

1. If it is necessary to separate all 4 carburetors for cleaning and/or repair, perform the following:

 a. Loosen the set screws securing the choke links to the choke shaft (**Figure 40**). Ensure that the set screws are loosened enough for the screw points to clear the indentations in the choke shaft.

 b. Pull out the choke shaft and remove the choke links from each carburetor.

c. Remove the screws securing the upper and lower brackets (**Figure 41** and **Figure 42**).

d. Carefully separate the carburetors. Note how the throttle linkage is fitted. Ensure that the fuel hoses connecting each carburetor are not damaged.

2. Remove the 4 screws securing the diaphragm cover and remove the cover (**Figure 43**). Lift out the diaphragm spring (**Figure 44**).

3. Carefully lift out the diaphragm assembly (**Figure 45**).

4. Remove the 4 screws securing the float chamber and remove the chamber (**Figure 46**).

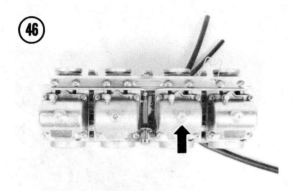

5. Carefully remove the main jet and washer (**Figure 47**).

6. Slide the needle jet out of the carburetor body. Note the O-ring on the needle jet.

7. Push out the hinge pin securing the float assembly and lift out the float (**Figure 48**).

8. Use a socket and remove the needle valve assembly.

9. Perform Cleaning and Inspection.

10. Assembly is the reverse of these steps. Keep the following points in mind:

   a. Install the needle jet so that the groove engages the locating pin as shown in **Figure 49**.

   b. When installing the diaphragm assembly, ensure that the locating tab on the diaphragm is positioned in the locating notch (**Figure 50**).

c. Apply a small amount of blue Loctite (Lock N' Seal No. 2114) to the set screws securing the choke links.

d. Use a caliper and set the float level to 21.4-23.4 mm (0.84-0.92 in.) as shown in **Figure 51** without the float chamber gasket. Reduce the measurement approximately 1 mm if the gasket is still installed. If the float level is not as specified, carefully bend the tang on the float arm until the correct level is achieved.

Cleaning and Inspection

1. Soak all the metal components in carburetor cleaning solution. This solution is available through automotive parts and supply stores in a small resealable tank with a dip basket for just a few dollars. If it is tightly sealed when not in use it will last for several carburetor rebuilds.

> *CAUTION*
> *Do not put non-metallic parts such as floats, gaskets and O-rings in the solution. It may attack them and render them useless.*

2. Check the slides and slide bores for wear. Generally, many thousands of miles of use are necessary before this sort of wear is apparent.

3. Blow out the jets with compressed air. *Do not use wire or sharp instruments to clean them.* They can be easily burred and very likely their sizes will be altered.

4. Inspect all of the O-rings for damage or deterioration and replace any that are less than perfect.

5. Examine the cone on the needle valve and replace the valve and seat if scored or pitted.

6. Inspect the rubber seating surface on the choke plunger. Replace the plunger if the seat is deeply grooved or damaged.

7. On CV carburetors, carefully examine the diaphragm assembly for holes or tears. If the diaphragm is damaged in any way the entire assembly must be replaced.

FLOAT LEVEL ADJUSTMENT

Carburetor floats can be checked with the carburetors installed or removed.

Adjustment (Carburetors Removed)

1. Remove carburetors as outlined in this chapter.

2. Invert carburetors and remove 4 screws securing each float chamber (**Figure 25**). Remove float chamber gaskets.

3. Using vernier calipers, measure float level between float chamber surface and top of float (**Figure 52**). Float level should be as specified in **Table 1**. Carefully bend float tang, if necessary, to achieve specified float level.

Adjustment (Carburetors Installed)

This procedure requires the use of Suzuki special tool, part No. 09913-14511 (fuel level gauge). This inexpensive tool can be ordered

7

from your local Suzuki dealer.

1. Remove drain screw from a carburetor and install fuel level gauge. Place fuel valve in PRIME to fill float chamber, then turn valve back to ON.

2. Start engine and idle at 1,000-1,200 rpm.

3. Hold float level gauge next to the carburetor so that the middle line of the gauge is aligned with the float chamber mating surface as shown in **Figure 53**.

4. With the gauge held in perfect alignment, the fuel level should be below the float chamber mating surface as specified in **Table 1**. Repeat for the other 3 carburetors.

5. If fuel level is not as specified, it is necessary to remove the float chambers and carefully bend float tang until specified level is achieved. Float chambers on the 2 outside carburetors can be removed with the carburetors installed. If a float adjustment is necessary on either inboard carburetor, the carburetors must be removed to gain access to the floats.

FUEL PETCOCK

Replacement

1. Drain the fuel tank into a safe, sealable container.

2. Disconnect the lines from the petcock (**Figure 54**). Remove the petcock.

3. Before installing the petcock, clean the screen thoroughly.

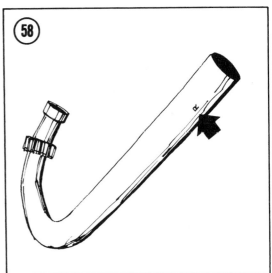

EXHAUST SYSTEM

The exhaust system consists of four exhaust pipes (head pipes) and 2 mufflers. The center exhaust pipes on all TSCC models are connected by a crossover chamber.

Removal

1. Loosen the clamp bolts securing the inner exhaust pipes to the mufflers (**Figure 55**).
2. Loosen the bolts on each side that secure the mufflers to the frame (**Figure 56**). On all TSCC models, these bolts also secure the rear footrests. Do not remove the bolts at this time.
3. Remove the bolts securing each exhaust pipe flange to the engine (**Figure 57**).
4. Support the weight of the exhaust system and remove the rear mounting bolts completely. Spread the mufflers apart slightly while pulling the whole exhaust system forward enough to disengage the exhaust pipes from the engine. On all TSCC models, collect the 2-piece rings installed around each inboard exhaust pipe.
5. Remove the bolts securing the mufflers and remove the entire exhaust system. If desired, the mufflers can be removed from

the exhaust pipes at this time. Note that on 1979 and earlier models, location letters are stamped on the pipes as shown in **Figure 58**.

Installation

1. Slide the exhaust pipes into the cylinder ports and install the rear muffler mounting bolts to secure the rear of the exhaust system. Leave the bolts loose at this time so the exhaust system can be shifted around as it is secured.
2. On all TSCC models, install the 2-piece rings around each inboard exhaust pipe.
3. Hold the exhaust pipes into the cylinder ports and secure the pipes with the flanges. Tighten the nuts finger tight at this time.
4. Tighten the bolts securing the mufflers (and rear footrests on all TSCC models) to the frame. Torque the bolts to 2.7-4.3 mkg (20-31 ft.-lb.).
5. Make sure all the exhaust pipe flanges are correctly positioned and the exhaust pipes are correctly aligned. Torque the flange nuts to 1.5-2.0 mkg (11-15 ft.-lb.). Torque the clamp bolts securing the inboard pipes to the mufflers to 0.9-1.4 mkg (7-10 ft.-lb.).

7

Table 1   CARBURETOR FLOAT LEVEL SPECIFICATIONS

Model	mm	inches
GS750B		
Measured with caliper	26	1.02
Measured with fuel		
level gauge	3	0.12
1978-1979 models		
Measured with caliper	23-25	0.90-0.98
Measured with fuel		
level gauge	3-5	0.12-0.20
CV carburetors		
Measured with caliper	21.4-23.4	0.84-0.92
Measured with fuel		
level gauge	4.5-5.5	0.18-0.22

NOTE: If you own a 1981 and later model, first check the Supplement at the back of the book for any new service information.

CHAPTER EIGHT

ELECTRICAL SYSTEM

The electrical system consists of the following subsystems:

a. Charging system
b. Starting system
c. Ignition system
d. Lighting system
e. Instruments

Complete wiring diagrams are included at the end of the book. **Table 1** and **Table 2** are found at the end of the chapter.

CHARGING SYSTEM

The charging system consists of the battery, alternator, rectifier and regulator. See **Figure 1** for all 1979 and earlier models, except for 1979 "L" models. See **Figure 2** for 1979 "L" models and all TSCC models.

The alternator generates an alternating current (AC) which the rectifier converts to direct current (DC). The regulator controls the voltage going to the battery and the load (lights, ignition, etc.) at a constant voltage regardless of the variations in engine speed and load.

On 1979 "L" models and all TSCC models, the rectifier and regulator are combined in one unit. If either function of the unit fails, the entire unit must be replaced. On all 1979 and earlier models, except 1979 "L" models, the rectifier and regulator are separate units.

Whenever a charging system trouble is suspected, make sure the battery is fully charged and in good condition before beginning any tests. Make sure all connections are clean and tight.

Charging System Output Test
(1979 and Earlier Models,
Except "L" Models)

1. Raise the seat and remove the left side cover. Refer to **Figure 3** and disconnect the yellow wire from the regulator to isolate it from the circuit.
2. Connect the white/green wire from the alternator to the white/red wire from the rectifier.

NOTE
*For U.S. and Canadian models, remove the screw securing the headlamp switch lock cap (**Figure 4**) and turn off the headlamp for this test.*

3. Make sure all lights are switched OFF (this is a no-load test). Start and run the engine at 5,000 rpm. With a voltmeter, check the voltage between the red rectifier wire and ground. If the voltmeter indicates 16.5 volts DC or more, the alternator and the rectifier are good; proceed to the next step to check the

8

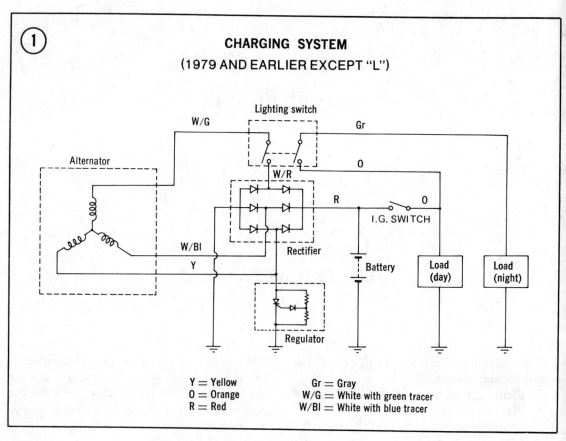

① **CHARGING SYSTEM**
(1979 AND EARLIER EXCEPT "L")

Y = Yellow
O = Orange
R = Red

Gr = Gray
W/G = White with green tracer
W/Bl = White with blue tracer

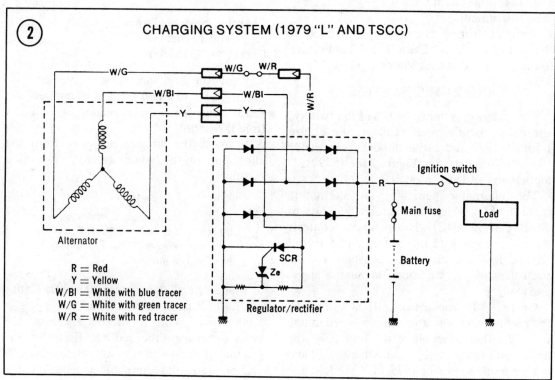

② **CHARGING SYSTEM (1979 "L" AND TSCC)**

R = Red
Y = Yellow
W/Bl = White with blue tracer
W/G = White with green tracer
W/R = White with red tracer

8

regulator. If the voltmeter indication is less than 16.5 volts DC, the alternator or rectifier is defective. Refer to *Rectifier Test.* If the rectifier tests good, the alternator is defective.

4. Shut off the engine and reconnect the wiring in the normal manner. Make sure the light switch is still OFF. Start the engine and run it at 5,000 rpm. With a voltmeter, check the voltage between the positive (+) lead of the battery and a good ground on the frame. If the voltmeter indication is 14-15.5 volts DC, the regulator is good. If the voltage is less than 14 or more than 15.5, the regulator is defective.

5. Before replacing any defective components, recheck all voltages as described to make sure all connections were correct.

6. Install the headlamp switch lock cap and install the left side cover.

Charging System Output Test (1979 "L" Models and All TSCC Models)

1. Remove the left side cover. On 1979 "L" models only, remove the fuse box cover and remove both center fuses (**Figure 5**).

2. Pull back the rubber boot on the main battery lead connected to the starter relay. Connect the positive (+) lead of a voltmeter to the red (+) lead on the starter relay (**Figure 6**). Connect the negative (-) voltmeter lead to a good ground on the frame.

3. Start and run the engine at 5,000 rpm. The voltmeter should indicate 14-15.5 volts DC. An indication of 14-15.5 volts DC signifies that all charging system components are operating correctly.

4. If the voltmeter indicates more than 15.5 volts DC, replace the regulator/rectifier.

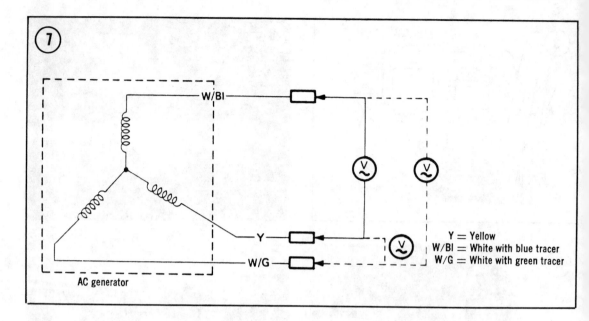

(7)

W/Bl

Y

W/G

AC generator

Y = Yellow
W/Bl = White with blue tracer
W/G = White with green tracer

5. If the voltmeter indicates less than 14 volts DC, the regulator/rectifier or the alternator may be defective. Perform the *No-Load Alternator Test* to determine if the alternator is operating correctly. If the *No-Load Test* is satisfactory, replace the regulator/rectifier to correct the low voltage condition.

6. On 1979 "L" models, replace the fuses in the fuse box and install the fuse box cover.

7. Install the left side cover.

No-Load Alternator Test (1979 "L" Models and All TSCC Models)

1. Remove the left side cover.

2. Pull back the large wire boot and disconnect the white/blue, white/green and yellow alternator wires.

3. Refer to **Figure 7** and alternately connect the leads of an AC voltmeter between the white/blue and yellow, the white/blue and white/green, and white/green and yellow alternator leads. With each test connection, start and run the engine at 5,000 rpm. The AC voltmeter should indicate 75 volts AC (80 volts AC for TSCC models) or more for each test connection. Less than 75 volts AC (80 volts AC for TSCC models) on any test connection indicates a faulty alternator.

4. Reconnect the alternator leads and reinstall the left side cover.

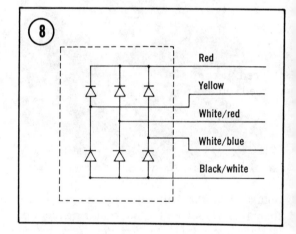

(8)

Red

Yellow

White/red

White/blue

Black/white

Rectifier Test (1979 and Earlier Models Except "L" Model)

The 6 diodes in the rectifier are the electrical equivalent of one-way valves; they permit current to flow in a forward direction and prevent it from flowing in the reverse direction—if they are functioning correctly.

CAUTION
A circuit tester must be used for this test; do not use a megger instrument. Its internal power supply can and most likely will destroy otherwise good diodes.

1. Remove the left side cover and disconnect all of the leads to the rectifier (**Figure 8**).

2. Touch the tester's negative probe to the ground terminal (black/white). Touch the positive probe first to the yellow wire, then the white/red wire, then the white/blue. In each case continuity should be indicated. If not, the rectifier is faulty and must be replaced. If continuity is present in each case, proceed with the next step.

3. Switch the probes—positive probe to the black/white wire and negative probe to the yellow, white/red and white/blue wires in turn. With this hookup, there should be no continuity. If continuity is indicated, the rectifier is faulty and should be replaced. If there is no continuity, check the other 3 diodes, using the red wire as the ground, first with the negative probe on the red and then the positive. If any of the diodes is faulty, the rectifier must be replaced.

CAUTION
Do not run the engine with the rectifier leads disconnected; the alternator is certain to be damaged.

**Alternator Stator
Removal/Installation**

1. Drain the engine oil as outlined in Chapter Three.

2. Use a hammer-driven impact tool and loosen the screws securing the alternator cover (**Figure 9**).

3. Remove the screws, cover and gasket. Note the location of different length screws.

Keep a few rags handy, as some oil is bound to run out when the cover is removed. Note how the alternator wires are routed through the cover and crankcase.

CAUTION
Do not pry the cover loose with a screwdriver or the cover and/or the crankcase sealing surfaces will be damaged. The cover is held tight by the magnetic attraction of the alternator rotor. A strong pull is required to overcome the magnetic field.

4. Remove the screws securing the stator assembly to the alternator case and remove the stator (**Figure 10**). Note how the wiring is routed.

5. Installation is the reverse of these steps. Keep the following points in mind:

   a. Make sure the alternator wires are correctly routed in the alternator cover and the grommet is installed in the notch (**Figure 10**).

   b. Apply a thin layer of Bond No. 4 approximately 1 in. on each side of the crankcase seam behind the alternator cover (**Figure 11**).

   c. Install a new cover gasket and route the alternator wires into the crankcase opening. Hold the gasket in place and install the alternator cover (**Figure 12**).

Alternator Rotor
Removal/Installation

The alternator rotor is a permanent magnet unit. Rotor removal is usually only necessary if the crankshaft must be removed or if the motorcycle has been damaged in an accident. A special puller is required for rotor removal as outlined in Chapters Four and Five.

Regulator/Rectifier
Removal/Installation
(1979 "L" Models
and All TSCC Models)

1. Remove the left side cover.
2. Remove the screws securing the regulator/rectifier unit. See **Figure 13** for 1979 "L" models and **Figure 14** for TSCC models.
3. Disconnect the wires and remove the unit.
4. Installation is the reverse of these steps. Make sure the wires are connected securely.

Regulator Removal/Installation
(1979 and Earlier Models,
Except "L" Models)

1. Remove the left side cover.
2. Disconnect the regulator lead wire.
3. Remove the screws securing the regulator and remove the regulator (**Figure 15**).
4. Installation is the reverse of these steps. Make sure connections are clean and tight.

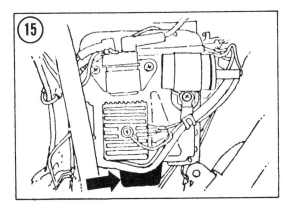

Rectifier Removal/Installation (1979 and Earlier Models, Except "L" Models)

1. Remove the left side cover.

2. Refer to **Figure 16** and disconnect the rectifier leads.

3. Remove the screw securing the rectifier and remove the unit.

4. Installation is the reverse of these steps. Make sure the connections are clean and secure.

STARTING SYSTEM

The starting system consists of the components shown in **Figure 17**. Before checking for suspected trouble in the starting system, make certain all connections are clean and tight. Make certain also that the battery is in good condition, with correct electrolyte level, and fully charged.

If the system is functioning correctly, the relay (**Figure 18**) will make a single audible "clack" when the starter button is pressed and the motor will begin to turn at once.

If the relay makes no sound, and the motor does not turn, and if the battery is fully charged, an open circuit in the relay coil is likely. It must be replaced.

If the relay chatters when the button is pressed, and the motor does not turn, there may be a bad ground connection, the relay contacts may be faulty, or the motor may have an internal open circuit. In such a case, the problem should be referred to a dealer for thorough testing.

Starter Relay Removal/Installation

1. Remove the left side cover.
2. Disconnect the battery and starter motor leads from the relay.
3. Remove the screws securing the relay (**Figure 19**) and remove the relay.
4. Installation is the reverse of these steps. Ensure that the mounting screws and electrical connections are tight.

Starter Motor Removal/Installation

1. Refer to Chapter Seven and perform *Carburetor Removal.*
2. Remove the cam chain tensioner assembly as outlined in Chapters Four and Five.
3. Remove the bolts securing the starter motor cover and remove the cover (**Figure 20**).
4. Disconnect the starter wire from the starter motor.
5. Remove the bolts securing the starter motor and slide out the motor (**Figure 21**).
6. Installation is the reverse of these steps. Before installing the cover, make sure the wires are correctly routed under the cover.

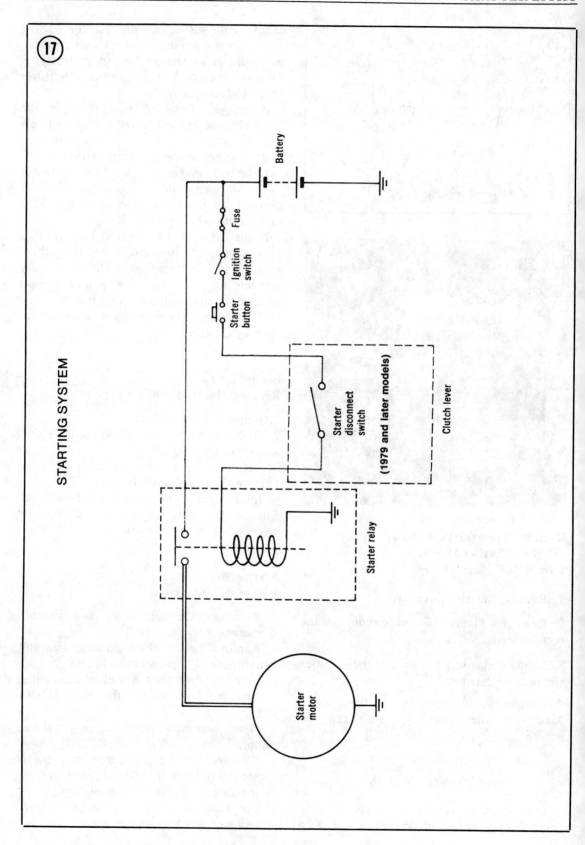

STARTING SYSTEM

(17)

Battery

Fuse

Ignition switch

Starter button

Starter disconnect switch

(1979 and later models)

Clutch lever

Starter relay

Starter motor

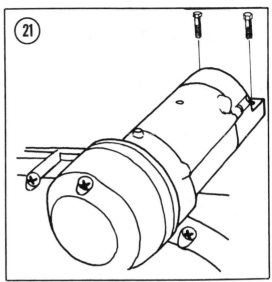

BATTERY SERVICE

Battery Removal
Cleaning/Installation

1. Remove the seat.

2. On all TSCC models, perform the following to gain access to the battery:

   a. Loosen the clamp securing the front of the air filter chamber (**Figure 22**). Remove the bolt securing the rear of the air filter chamber (**Figure 23**).

   b. Remove the right side cover and loosen the clamp bolt securing the rear master cylinder reservoir enough to allow the reservoir to be moved slightly (**Figure 24**).

   c. Lift out and remove the air filter chamber.

3. Remove the battery hold down strap on models so equipped (**Figure 25**).

4. Disconnect the battery terminals—ground first, then the positive. See **Figure 26** for

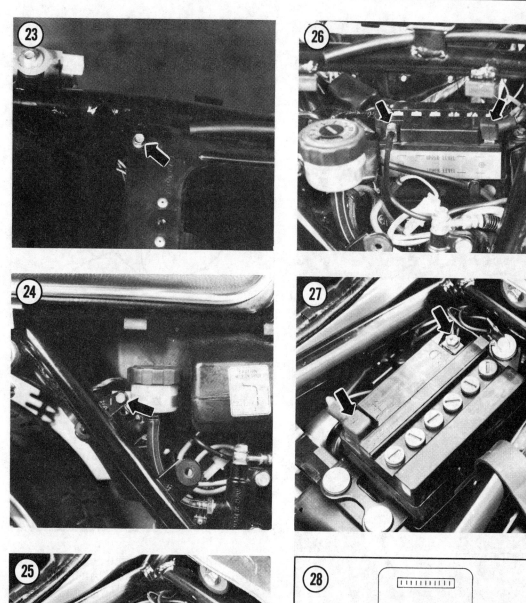

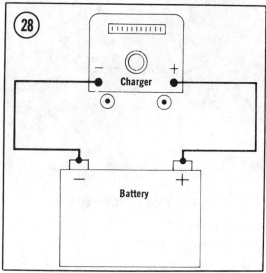

TSCC models and **Figure 27** for all other models. Carefully lift out the battery.

5. Clean the top of the battery with a solution of baking soda and water. Scrub off any stubborn deposits with a wire brush and rinse the battery with clear water. Dry it thoroughly.

> *CAUTION*
> *Keep cleaning solution out of the battery cells or the electrolyte will be severely weakened.*

6. Clean the battery leads with a stiff wire brush.
7. Inspect the battery case for cracks. If any are found, the battery should be replaced. Its condition will deteriorate rapidly and leaking electrolyte could damage painted, plated and polished surfaces as well as electrical insulation.
8. If the battery is in good condition, install it and connect the leads, positive first then ground.
9. Coat the terminals with petroleum jelly, such as Vaseline.
10. Check the electrolyte level and correct it if necessary. Add only distilled water, never electrolyte.

Testing

Hydrometer testing is the best way to check battery condition. Use a hydrometer with numbered graduations from 1.100 to 1.300 rather than one with color-coded bands. To use the hydrometer, squeeze the rubber ball, insert the tip in the cell and release the ball. Draw enough electrolyte to float the weighted float inside the hydrometer. Note the number in line with the surface of the electrolyte; this is the specific gravity for this cell. Return the electrolyte to the cell from which it came. The specific gravity of the electrolyte in each battery cell is an excellent indication of that cell's condition. A fully charged cell will read 1.275-1.280, while a cell in good condition may read from 1.250-1.280. A cell in fair condition reads from 1.225-1.250 and anything below 1.125 is practically dead.

Specific gravity varies with temperature. For each 10° that electrolyte temperature exceeds 80°F, add 0.004 to reading indicated on hydrometer. Subtract 0.004 for each 10° below 80°F.

If the cells test in the poor range, the battery requires recharging. The hydrometer is useful for checking the progress of the charging operation. **Table 1** shows approximate state of charge.

> *CAUTION*
> *Always disconnect both battery connections before connecting charging equipment.*

Charging

The battery can be charged while installed in the motorcycle; however, it is so easily removed after the leads have been disconnected that it is not worth the risk of damaging the motorcycle finish with electrolyte during charging.

> *WARNING*
> *Make certain open flame and cigarettes, etc., are kept away from the battery during charging. Highly explosive hydrogen gas is formed during charging. And never arc the terminals to check the condition of charge; the resulting spark could ignite the gas.*

1. Connect the charger—positive-to-positive and negative-to-negative. See **Figure 28**.
2. Remove the caps from the cells and check the electrolyte level and correct it if necessary by adding only distilled water. Leave the caps off during charging.
3. If the charger output is variable, select a low rate (1.5-3 amps), turn on the charger and allow the battery to charge as long as possible. If it is severely discharged, as long as 8 hours may be required to charge it completely.
4. When charging is complete, test it with a hydrometer as described above. If the specific gravity level is satisfactory, wait an hour and test it again. If the level is still correct, the battery is fully charged and in good condition. If the specific gravity level drops between tests, it is likely that one or more cells are sulfated. In such a case, the battery should be replaced as soon as possible.

IGNITION

Two types of ignition systems are installed on GS750 models. All 1979 and earlier models are fitted with a breaker point system (**Figure 29**). All TSCC models, beginning with 1980 "T" models, are equipped with a Nippon Denso transistorized (breakerless) ignition system (**Figure 30**).

The breaker point system consists of 2 coils with condensers, 2 contact breaker point sets and 4 spark plugs. The transistorized system utilizes ignition coils and spark plugs, however, the breaker points and condensers are replaced with a signal generator and an igniter unit.

The signal generator is driven by the engine and generates pulses which are routed to the igniter unit. The igniter unit amplifies the pulses and triggers the output of the ignition coils.

Ignition timing on the transistorized system is pre-set and non-adjustable; the ignition system requires no periodic maintenance.

Periodic adjustment of breaker points and timing on 1979 and earlier models is outlined under *Engine Tune-up* in Chapter Three.

Ignition Coil Test

The easiest test for a suspected coil is to replace it with a coil that is known to be good. For example, if 2 of the cylinders are operating correctly, exchange the ignition coils and see if the symptoms move to the other 2 cylinders.

Ignition Coil Removal/Installation

1. Remove the fuel tank as outlined in Chapter Seven.
2. Disconnect the primary leads from the coils.
3. Disconnect the high-tension leads (spark plug leads) from the spark plugs. Grasp the spark plug caps, not the wires, to pull them off.
4. Remove the nuts from the coil mounts. Remove the coil mounts and coils with the spark plug leads.

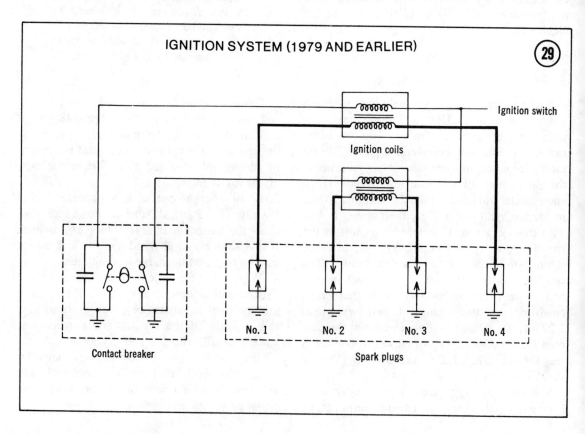

IGNITION SYSTEM (1979 AND EARLIER)

(29)

Ignition switch

Ignition coils

Contact breaker

No. 1   No. 2   No. 3   No. 4

Spark plugs

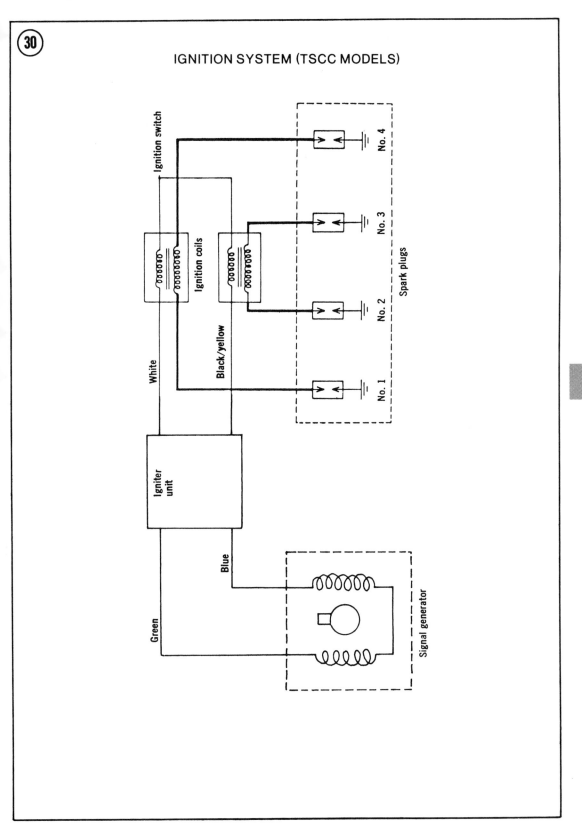

IGNITION SYSTEM (TSCC MODELS)

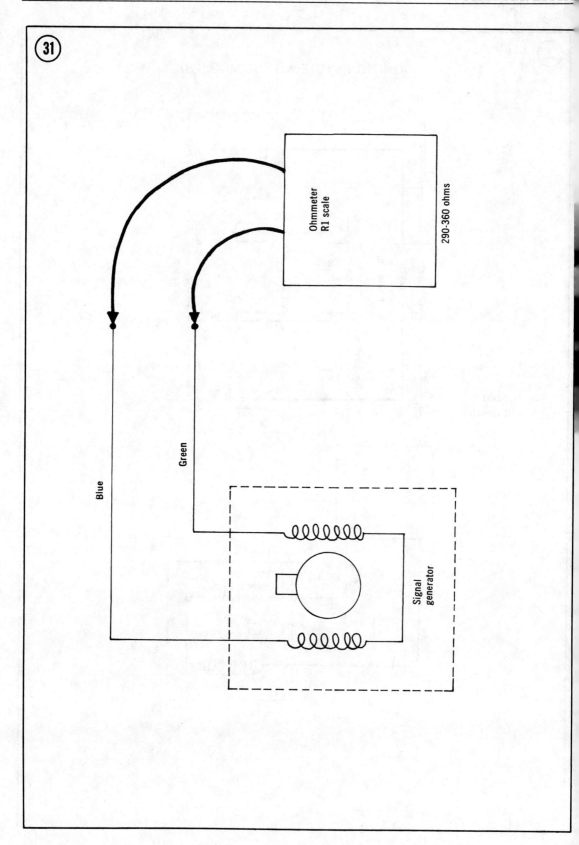

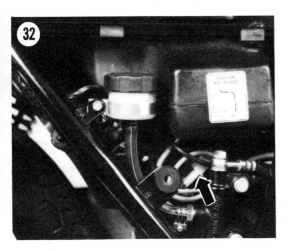

5. Installation is the reverse of these steps. Make sure the spark plug leads are routed to the correct cylinders.

Condenser Test

The condensers can be tested with an ohmmeter equipped with a battery of 12 volts or less. An ohmmeter with a battery of higher output will destroy a good condenser as soon as it is connected.

1. Connect one lead of the ohmmeter to the metal case of the condenser.
2. Touch the other ohmmeter lead to the condenser lead. If the condenser is good, the ohmmeter will first indicate a very low resistance, then start climbing higher and higher. It may reach infinity. Touch the condenser lead to the case to discharge it.
3. If the meter drops to a low value and stays there, or climbs only slightly, the condenser is shorted. If the needle never drops to a low value, but remains high, the condenser is open. In either case, replace the condenser.

Breaker Points and Spark Plugs

Breaker point and spark plug maintenance is outlined in Chapter Three.

Signal Generator Test

Refer to **Figure 31** for this test.
1. Remove the right side cover to gain access to the signal generator wire connectors (**Figure 32**).

2. Disconnect the green and blue signal generator wires.
3. Connect an accurate ohmmeter between the blue and green signal generator wires and switch the ohmmeter to the R1 scale. The ohmmeter should indicate 290-360 ohms.
4. If the ohmmeter indication is not as specified, replace the signal generator. Connect the wire connectors and reinstall the side cover.

Igniter Unit Test

Refer to **Figure 33** for this test.
1. Carefully remove spark plug leads from the spark plugs on No. 3 and No. 4 cylinders (the 2 cylinders on the right-hand side of the motorcycle).
2. Remove No. 3 and No. 4 spark plugs and reconnect the spark plug leads.
3. Lay both spark plugs against the cylinder head so that each plug is grounded on the head.
4. Remove the right side cover and disconnect the blue and green leads from the igniter unit (**Figure 34**).
5. Turn on the motorcycle ignition.

NOTE
This test utilizes the 1-1/2 volt battery in the ohmmeter to simulate the pulse from the signal generator. A 1-1/2 volt power source such as a dry cell battery can also be used for this test.

CAUTION
Ensure that proper polarity is observed for this test or the igniter unit will be destroyed. The positive lead connects to the blue wire and the negative lead connects to the green wire.

6. Set the ohmmeter to the R1 scale and connect the positive (+) lead to the blue igniter unit wire. Connect the negative (-) meter lead to the green igniter unit wire. As the negative lead is connected, the No. 4 spark plug should fire. As the negative lead is disconnected, the No. 3 spark plug should fire. If both spark plugs are properly grounded and one or both fail to fire, replace the igniter unit.

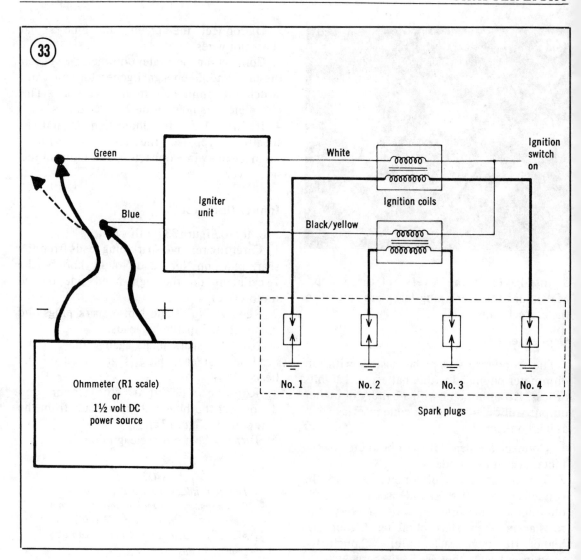

Green

White

Ignition switch on

Blue

Igniter unit

Ignition coils

Black/yellow

Ohmmeter (R1 scale)
or
1½ volt DC
power source

No. 1   No. 2   No. 3   No. 4

Spark plugs

7. Install both spark plugs and connect the spark plug leads. Reconnect the igniter unit wires and install the side cover.

**Signal Generator Unit
Removal/Installation**

1. Remove the 3 screws securing the ignition cover and remove the cover.

2. Remove the right side cover and disconnect the blue and green signal generator wires (**Figure 32**).

3. Remove the screws securing the signal generator unit (**Figure 35**) and remove the unit. Note how the wiring is routed along the engine sump and secured with retaining clips.

4. Installation is the reverse of these steps. Ensure that the signal generator leads are

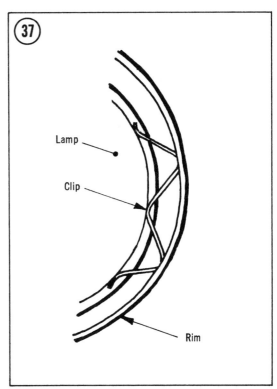

connected properly and the wiring is routed and secured correctly in the retaining clips.

Igniter Unit
Removal/Installation

1. Remove the right side cover and disconnect the leads from the igniter unit (**Figure 34**).
2. Remove the screws securing the unit to the motorcycle frame and remove the unit.
3. Installation is the reverse of these steps. Ensure that the igniter wires are connected securely.

LIGHTING SYSTEM

The lighting system consists of the headlamp (with 2 filaments for high-beam and low-beam operation), the taillamp, stoplamp, directional signals and warning and indicator lamps. **Table 2** lists replacement bulbs for these components.

All 1979 and earlier models, except "L" models are equipped with a sealed beam headlamp. All TSCC models and 1979 "L" models are fitted with a separate halogen headlamp bulb.

Headlamp Replacement
(1979 and Earlier Models,
Except "L" Models)

1. Loosen the lockscrew at the top of the headlamp rim (**Figure 36**) and pull the rim out from the top.
2. Unplug the connector from the rear of the headlamp.
3. Remove the clips that lock the lamp into the rim (**Figure 37**) and remove the lamp.
4. Installation is the reverse of the above. Adjust the headlamp beam as described below.

8

Headlamp Adjustment
(1979 and Earlier Models)

Adjust the headlamp beam horizontally and vertically according to the motor vehicle regulations in your area.

To adjust it horizontally, turn the screw (**Figure 38**). To adjust it vertically, loosen the mounting bolts on either side (**Figure 39**), move the headlight body as required, and tighten the bolts without further moving the headlight body.

Halogen Headlamp
Bulb Replacement

1. On "L" models only, remove the screws securing the headlamp rim and pull the rim out from the top.

2. On all other TSCC models, remove the 3 screws securing the headlamp assembly to the housing (**Figure 40**).

3. Carefully withdraw the headlamp assembly (**Figure 41**).

4. Roll back the rubber boot and disconnect the bulb retaining spring. Carefully pull out the bulb.

CAUTION
Use a clean rag when removing and installing the halogen bulb to avoid getting finger prints on the bulb. Fingerprints will cause hot spots and lead to early bulb failure.

5. Installation is the reverse of these steps. Perform the applicable headlamp adjustment procedure.

Headlamp Adjustment
(TSCC Models, Except "L" Models)

Adjust the headlamp beam horizontally and vertically according to the motor vehicles regulations in your area.

Refer to **Figure 42** and rotate the upper adjusting screw for horizontal movement and the lower screw for vertical movement.

Turn Signal Relay
Removal/Installation
(1979 and Earlier Models)

1. Remove the left side cover.
2. On 1978 and 1979 models, slide the relay out of the frame clip (**Figure 43**).
3. On 1977 models, remove the mounting screw securing the relay (**Figure 44**).
4. Disconnect the wires from the relay and remove the relay.
5. Installation is the reverse of these steps.

Turn Signal Relay
Removal/Installation
(TSCC Models)

1. Refer to Chapter Seven and remove the fuel tank.
2. Slide the relay out of the frame clip (**Figure 45**).
3. Disconnect the wires from the relay and remove the relay.
4. Installation is the reverse of these steps.

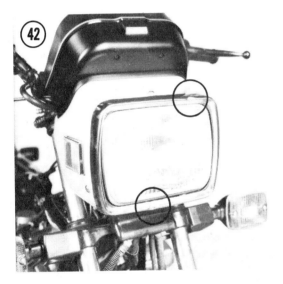

8

Taillamp Replacement

A single bulb functions as a taillamp, stoplamp and license plate illumination lamp. If only one of the 2 filaments fail, the bulb must be replaced. To replace it, remove the lens and turn the bulb counterclockwise to unlock it, clockwise to lock the new bulb into the socket.

Directional Signal Lamp Replacement

To repair any of the 4 directional signal lamps, remove the lens, turn the bulb counterclockwise to unlock it and turn the new bulb clockwise to lock it into the socket. When installing the lens, do not tighten the screws so tightly that the lens cracks.

Front Stoplamp Switch Replacement

The front stoplamp switch is operated by the brake lever when the brake is applied. Refer to **Figure 46** for this procedure.
1. Remove 2 screws securing switch cover to brake lever assembly.
2. Carefully lift off switch housing. Do not lose the spring-loaded switch contact in the switch body. Replace brass switch contact if worn.
3. Installation is the reverse of these steps. Make sure small spring is installed beneath brass contact (**Figure 47**). Switch mounting holes are slightly elongated to allow for switch adjustment.

Rear Stoplamp Switch Replacement

1. Disconnect the wires from the switch (**Figure 48**).
2. Unscrew the locknut from the switch and remove the switch from the bracket. Disconnect it from the return spring.
3. Installation is the reverse of these steps. Adjust the switch locknuts so that the stoplamp comes on when the brake pedal is depressed.

Horn Removal/Installation

1. Disconnect the wires from the horn.

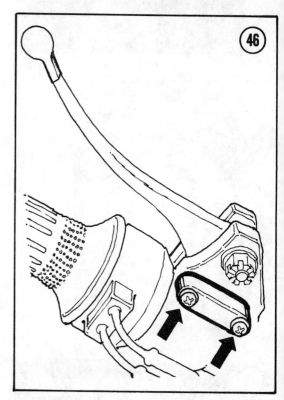

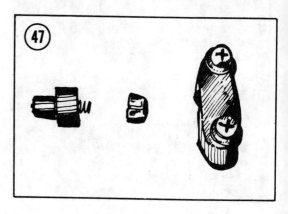

2. Remove the bolts that attach the horn to the frame.

3. Installation is the reverse of these steps.

Horn Testing

1. Disconnect the wires from the horn.

2. Connect jumper wires between a 12-volt battery and the horn terminals. If the horn sounds, it is all right. Check the continuity of the switch.

Horn Switch
Removal/Installation

The horn switch is part of the directional signal control switch assembly. If it is faulty, the entire unit must be replaced.

Directional Switch
Removal/Installation

1. Disconnect the directional signals and horn wires.

2. Remove the mirror from the switch housing.

3. Remove the screws from the switch body (**Figure 49**); separate the halves of the switch.

4. Installation is the reverse of these steps.

FUSE

All 1978 and earlier models are fitted with a single main fuse (**Figure 50**). All 1979 and later models are equipped with a fuse panel as shown in **Figure 51**. To gain access to fuses remove the left side cover. All 1979 models are equipped with a separate accessory fuse terminal.

If a fuse blows, find out why before replacing it. Fuse failure is usually caused by a short circuit in the wiring. Check for worn insulation or a disconnected wire shorting to ground.

> *CAUTION*
> *Never substitute tinfoil or wire for a fuse. Never use a higher amperage fuse than specified. An overload could result in a fire and loss of the motorcycle.*

INSTRUMENTS

Instrument Cluster Removal/Installation (1979 and Earlier and All "L" Models)

1. Refer to Chapter Seven and remove the fuel tank.
2. Remove the headlamp assembly as outlined in this chapter.
3. Disconnect the instrument assembly wiring connectors located below the ignition coils (**Figure 52**). Remove the straps securing the wires to the frame.
4. Disconnect the speedometer and tachometer cables (**Figure 53**).
5. Remove the bolts securing the instrument cluster to the mounting bracket (**Figure 54**) and remove the cluster.

6. Installation is the reverse of these steps. Ensure that all wiring connectors and cables are properly connected.

**Instrument Cluster
Removal/Installation
(TSCC Models,
Except "L" Models)**

1. Remove the headlamp assembly as previously outlined.
2. Refer to Chapter Seven and remove the fuel tank.
3. Disconnect the instrument cluster wiring connectors and remove the straps securing the wires to the frame (**Figure 55**).
4. Disconnect the tachometer and speedometer cables from the instruments (**Figure 56**).
5. Remove the 2 bolts securing the instrument cluster to the upper steering stem head and remove the cluster.
6. Installation is the reverse of these steps.

Fuel Gauge Test

Perform the following test to determine if the fuel tank sending unit or the fuel gauge in the instrument cluster is defective.

> *NOTE*
> *The fuel gauge unit on 1979 "L" models is installed in the tachometer housing. The gauge unit is not available separately, therefore, if the gauge unit is defective, the entire tachometer/fuel gauge assembly must be replaced.*

1. Remove the left side cover.
2. Disconnect the fuel tank sending unit wires near the left edge of the air box (**Figure 57**).
3. Turn on the motorcycle ignition.
4. Use a jumper wire such as a straightened paper clip and short between both the fuel gauge leads (not the tank sending unit leads). If the fuel gauge needle fails to move, the gauge unit or the wiring harness is defective. If the fuel gauge needle does move, the tank sending unit or the wiring harness is defective.
5. To determine if the fuel gauge or the wiring harness is defective, use the jumper wire and ground the yellow/black lead. If the fuel gauge needle does not move, the gauge unit is

8

defective. Extreme needle movement indicates a fault in the wiring or the connectors.

6. To determine if the tank sending unit or the wiring harness is defective, use an accurate ohmmeter and measure the resistance between the tank sending unit leads. A large unstable resistance indication signifies a defective sending unit. A normal resistance of approximately 1-110 ohms (depending on the level of fuel in the tank) signifies the fault lies in the wiring or connectors. An indication of approximately 110 ohms is for an empty tank.

Fuel Gauge Unit
Removal/Installation

The fuel gauge unit is housed in the instrument cluster. To replace the gauge unit, remove the instrument cluster as previously outlined.

Fuel Tank Sending Unit
Removal/Installation

1. Refer to Chapter Seven and remove the fuel tank.
2. Remove the screws securing the sending unit to the fuel tank (**Figure 58**). Carefully remove the sending unit.
3. Installation is the reverse of these steps. Ensure that the sending unit gasket is in good condition and properly positioned before installing the sending unit.

Oil Pressure Sending Unit
Removal/Installation
(1979 and Earlier Models)

1. Disconnect the wire from the sending unit (**Figure 59**).

2. Remove the bolts securing the sending unit and remove the unit.
3. Installation is the reverse of these steps. Make sure the gasket is in good condition and installed properly.

Oil Pressure Sensor
Removal/Installation
(TSCC Models)

1. Remove the nuts securing the oil pressure sensor cover (**Figure 60**) and remove the cover.
2. Remove the screw securing the wire to the sensor and remove the wire (**Figure 61**).
3. Unscrew the oil pressure sensor from the oil filter cover.
4. Installation is the reverse of these steps. Keep the following points in mind:
   a. Apply a small amount of Bond No. 4 or equivalent to the threads on the oil pressure sensor before installing in the filter cover.
   b. Tighten the oil pressure sensor to 1.3-1.7 mkg (9.5-12.5 ft.-lb.).

Table 1   STATE OF CHARGE

Specific Gravity	State of Charge
1.110-1.130	Discharged
1.140-1.160	Almost discharged
1.170-1.190	One-quarter charged
1.200-1.220	One-half charged
1.230-1.250	Three-quarters charged
1.260-1.280	Fully charged

Table 2   LAMP RATINGS

	Watts
Headlamp	
1979 and earlier	**50/40**
TSCC models	**60/55**
Meter lamp	3.4
Turn signal indicator lamp	3.4
High beam indicator lamp	3.4
Oil pressure indicator lamp	3.4
Neutral indicator lamp	3.4
Turn signal lamp	23
Rear combination lamps	
Tail and parking	8 (3 cp)
Stop	23 (32 cp)

8

NOTE: If you own a 1981 and later model, first check the Supplement at the back of the book for any new service information.

CHAPTER NINE

FRONT SUSPENSION AND STEERING

This chapter includes repair, replacement and service procedures for the front wheel, forks and steering components. Work involving the front brake is presented in Chapter Eleven.

Table 1 and **Table 2** are at the end of the chapter.

FRONT WHEEL

Removal/Installation

1. Place the motorcycle on the centerstand and support the engine with a block (**Figure 1**) so the front wheel is clear of the ground.

2. Unscrew the speedometer cable from the wheel (**Figure 2**).

3. Remove cotter key from the axle (**Figure 3**) and discard the key. Loosen the axle nut. On models with leading axle fork legs, remove the axle nut.

4. On models equipped with dual front disc brakes, remove the bolts securing the right or left brake caliper (**Figure 4**). Carefully remove the caliper.

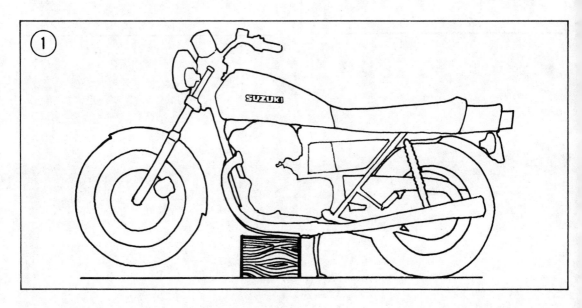

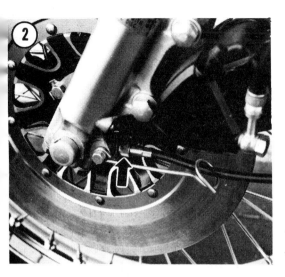

CAUTION
Suspend the brake caliper with a heavy cord or wire. Do not allow the caliper to hang by the brake hose or the hose may be damaged.

NOTE
Do not actuate the front brake with the caliper removed or the brake pads will have to be compressed back into the caliper body.

5. On models with straight fork legs, remove the nuts securing both axle holders and remove the holders from the studs on the fork legs (**Figure 5**). Remove the front wheel.

6. On models with leading axle fork legs, loosen the pinch bolt securing the axle on the right fork leg (**Figure 6**). Slide out the axle and remove the front wheel.

9

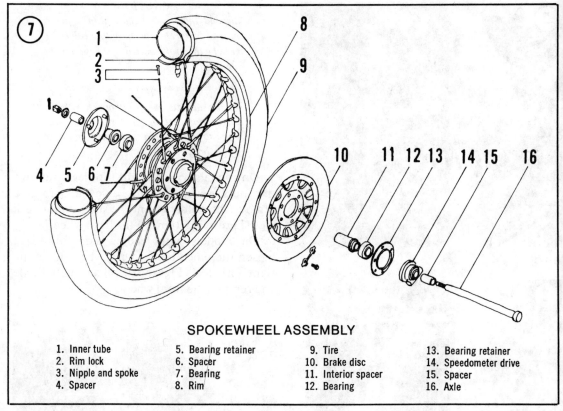

SPOKEWHEEL ASSEMBLY

1. Inner tube
2. Rim lock
3. Nipple and spoke
4. Spacer
5. Bearing retainer
6. Spacer
7. Bearing
8. Rim
9. Tire
10. Brake disc
11. Interior spacer
12. Bearing
13. Bearing retainer
14. Speedometer drive
15. Spacer
16. Axle

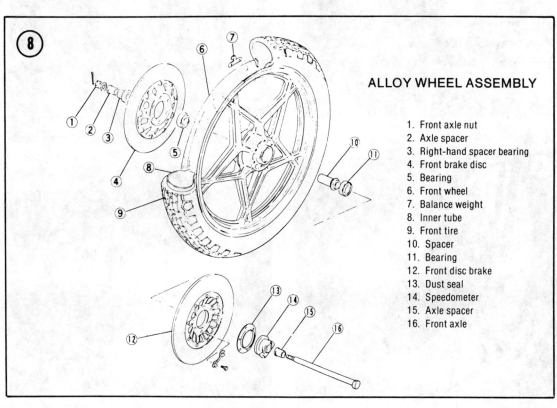

ALLOY WHEEL ASSEMBLY

1. Front axle nut
2. Axle spacer
3. Right-hand spacer bearing
4. Front brake disc
5. Bearing
6. Front wheel
7. Balance weight
8. Inner tube
9. Front tire
10. Spacer
11. Bearing
12. Front disc brake
13. Dust seal
14. Speedometer
15. Axle spacer
16. Front axle

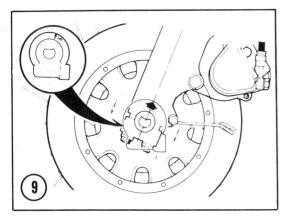

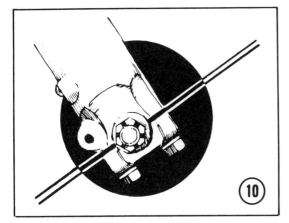

7. Installation is the reverse of these steps. Keep the following points in mind:

a. Assemble the axle and wheel components as shown in **Figure 7** or **Figure 8**.

b. On models with straight fork legs, position the speedometer drive unit as shown in **Figure 9**. Lift the front wheel into place and install the axle holder nuts finger-tight. Make sure that the space between the holder and fork leg is equal on both sides as shown in **Figure 10**.

c. For models with leading axle fork legs, lift the front wheel into place and install the axle from the left side. Make sure the speedometer drive unit is installed with the "ears" aligned with the slots in the hub (**Figure 11**). Position the speedometer drive unit as shown in **Figure 12** and install the axle nut finger-tight.

d. Torque the axle nut, axle pinch bolt, axle holder nuts and brake caliper mounting bolts as specified in Table 1.

CAUTION
Insert a screwdriver shaft or drift through the hole in the axle shaft head to prevent the axle from turning while tightening the axle nut. If the axle turns, the speedometer drive unit may be damaged.

e. When connecting the speedometer cable, make sure the slot in the cable end

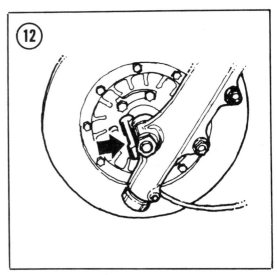

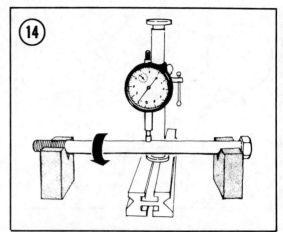

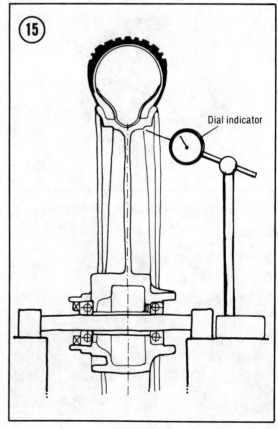

Dial indicator

engages the blade in the speedometer drive unit.

Disassembly

Refer to **Figure 7** or **Figure 8** for this procedure

1. On all models with straight fork legs, remove the axle nut and remove the axle.

2. If brake disc removal is desired, straighten the locking tabs on the disc mounting bolts (**Figure 13**). Unscrew the bolts and remove the brake disc. Remove the right bearing cover.

3. Tap the bearings out of the hub with a long aluminum or brass drift. Collect the spacers.

Inspection

1. Inspect the brake components as described in Chapter Eleven.

2. Clean the hub inside and out with solvent. Clean the bearing covers, the axle and the speedometer drive. Clean the spacers inside and out.

> *CAUTION*
> *Do not clean the bearings in solvent. They are sealed and permanently lubricated.*

3. Turn each bearing by hand and check it for smoothness and play. It should turn smoothly and quietly. Replace the bearings if they are questionable.

4. Inspect the axle for runout (**Figure 14**). If it exceeds 0.25mm (0.010 in.), replace the axle. *Do not attempt to straighten it.*

5. Measure the axial and radial runout of the wheel with a dial indicator as shown in **Figure 15**. Maximum runout in either direction is 2.0 mm (0.08 in.).

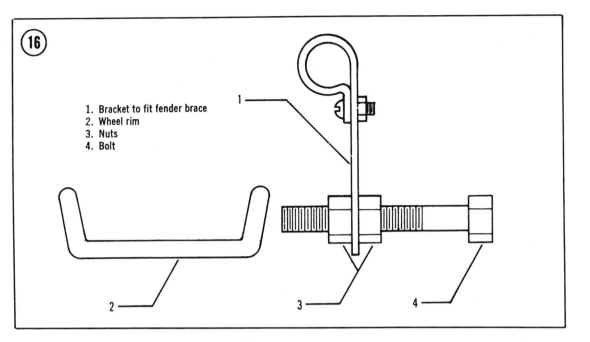

1. Bracket to fit fender brace
2. Wheel rim
3. Nuts
4. Bolt

5g   10g   15g   20g

NOTE
If a dial indicator is not available, a simple gauge can be improvised as shown in **Figure 16**.

6. If the runout on a spoke wheel is excessive, refer to *Spoke Wheels* and attempt to true the wheel.

7. If the runout on an alloy wheel is excessive, check the wheel bearings and/or replace the wheel. The stock Suzuki alloy wheel cannot be serviced; it must be replaced.

Assembly

1. Install the left bearing in the hub using a driver or socket that is only fractionally smaller in diameter than the outer bearing race. This is essential so that the force required to drive the bearing into the hub is applied only to the outer race.

2. Install the interior spacer through the inside of the hub. The shoulder on the spacer rests against the left bearing inner race.

3. Install the right bearing, spacer and bearing retainer.

4. Install the disc. Tighten the bolts to 1.5-2.5 mkg (11-18 ft.-lb.) and bend the lock tabs over against the flats on the bolt heads.

5. Install the speedometer drive so that the tangs on the drive unit line up with the slots in the hub (**Figure 11**). Perform *Front Wheel Installation*.

WHEEL BALANCING

An unbalanced wheel can adversely affect the handling of the motorcycle as well as make the machine very uncomfortable to ride.

Wheels are relatively easy to balance without special equipment. Most dealers or motorcycle accessory shops carry an assortment of balance weights that can be crimped on the spokes as shown in **Figure 17**.

9

Alloy wheels will accept standard automotive type weights or adhesive weights designed for automobile "mag" wheels. Buy a couple of each weight available. If the weights are unused they can usually be returned.

Many dealers now have high-speed spin balancing services available. This type of balancing is very fast and accurate. Have your wheels balanced by the high-speed spin method if such services are available.

Before attempting to balance a wheel, make sure the wheel bearings are in good condition and properly lubricated. If balancing is to be performed with the wheels still installed on the motorcycle, ensure that the brakes do not drag. A brake that drags will prevent the wheel from turning freely, resulting in an inaccurate wheel balance. Before the rear wheel can be balanced, the drive chain must be removed.

1. Rotate the wheel slowly and allow it to come to rest by itself. Make a chalk mark on the tire at the 6 o'clock position and rotate the wheel as before, several times, noting the position of the chalk mark each time the wheel comes to rest. If the wheel stops at different positions each time, the wheel is balanced.

NOTE
*If desired, the wheel may be removed from the motorcycle and supported on a stand as shown in **Figure 18**.*

2. If the chalk mark stops at the same position—6 o'clock—each time, add weight to the 12 o'clock position until the chalk mark stops at a different position each time.
3. Install the wheel, if removed, and road test the motorcycle on a smooth, straight road. Repeat the balance procedure if necessary.

SPOKE WHEELS

Spokes should be routinely checked for tightness. The "tuning fork" method for checking spoke tightness is simple and works well. Tap each spoke with a spoke wrench or the shank of a screwdriver and listen to the tone. A correctly tightened spoke will emit a clear, ringing tone, while a loose spoke will sound flat. All of the spokes in a correctly tightened wheel will emit tones of similar

pitch but not necessarily the same precise tone.

Bent, broken or stripped spokes should be replaced as soon as they are detected, as they can cause the destruction of an expensive hub.

NOTE
Most professional motorcycle mechanics use and recommend the Rowe Products spoke wrench. It will not round off the square edges of the spoke nipples and fits virtually all sizes of spokes.

Runout Adjustment (Truing)

1. To measure the runout of the rim, support the wheel in a stand as shown in **Figure 18** or support the motorcycle so that the wheel being checked is free of the ground.
2. Install a dial indicator (**Figure 15**) or locally fabricated runout indicator (**Figure 16**). Adjust the position of the bolt until it just clears the rim.
3. Rotate the rim and note whether the clearance between the rim and the indicator increases or decreases. Mark the tire with chalk or crayon at areas where the clearance is large or small. Maximum runout on the edge and/or the face of the rim is 2.0 mm (0.08 in.).
4. To pull or "true" the rim, tighten spokes which terminate on the same side of the hub and loosen the spokes which terminate on the

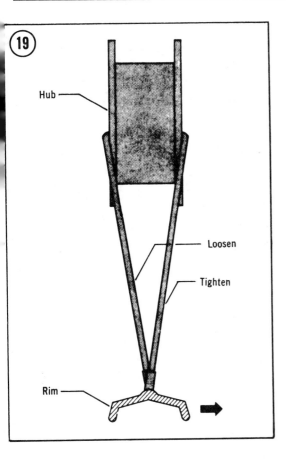

6. After tightening spokes, always check the runout to make sure that the rim has not been pulled out of true.

Spoke Replacement

A stripped or broken spoke can usually be replaced with the tire still installed on the wheel, providing the spoke nipple is in good condition. If the nipple is damaged or more than 2 or 3 spokes need replacing, the tire must first be removed from the wheel. If several spokes need replacing, the rim is also probably damaged. Unless you are skilled in wheel lacing and rim replacement, this task is best left to a dealer or motorcycle shop skilled in wheel repair.

To replace one or 2 damaged spokes with the tire still mounted, perform the following procedure.
1. Inflate the tire to at least 30 psi to help hold the spoke nipple in the rim.
2. Unscrew the nipple from the damaged or broken spoke. If the old spoke is not broken, press the nipple into the rim far enough to free the end of the damaged spoke. Take care not to push the nipple back into the rim. Remove the old spoke.
3. Trim the threaded end of the new spoke so that it is about 2 or 3 turns shorter than the old spoke. This permits the new spoke to stretch without the risk of puncturing the inner tube.
4. Install the new spoke into the hub and gently bow it so it can be inserted into the nipple.
5. Tighten the spoke nipple until the tone of the new spoke is similar to the other spokes in the wheel.
6. The tightness of the new spoke must be checked frequently. The spoke will stretch and must be retightened several times before it takes a final "set." Make the first check after 30 minutes to one hour of riding.

opposite side of the hub as shown in **Figure 19**. In most cases, only a slight amount of adjustment is necessary. After adjustment, rotate the rim and make sure that another area of the rim has not been pulled out of true. Continue adjusting and checking until runout does not exceed 2.0 mm (0.08 in.). Be patient and thorough, adjusting the position of the rim a little at a time.

NOTE
If rims cannot be trued within 2.0 mm (0.08 in.) of edge or face runout, the rim is damaged and must be replaced. Unless you are experienced in wheel lacing, this task is best left to a dealer or motorcycle shop experienced in wheel repair.

5. Always tighten spokes gradually and evenly in a crisscross pattern on one side of the hub then the other. One-half to one turn should be sufficient; do not overtighten.

FRONT FORK

Removal/Installation

1. Remove the front wheel as outlined under *Front Wheel Removal*.

2. Remove the bolts securing the brake caliper (**Figure 20**) and remove the caliper. Support the caliper from the handlebars with a piece of wire or Bungee cord. Do not allow the caliper to hang by the hose.

NOTE
On models with dual front disc brakes, remove both calipers if both fork legs are to be removed.

3. Remove the fender bolts and remove the fender.

4. If the forks are being removed for disassembly, perform the following:

   a. On models equipped with air valves, remove the protective cap from the valves (**Figure 21**) and gently bleed off the fork air pressure.

NOTE
*Failure to bleed off the fork air pressure **gently** usually results in a "quick squirt" of fork oil.*

   b. Loosen the fork cap bolts (**Figure 22**).

   c. Remove the drain screw (**Figure 23**) and drain the oil from each fork leg. Allow several minutes for the forks to drain completely.

5. Loosen the upper and lower pinch bolts securing each fork leg (**Figure 24** and **Figure 25**). Pull down and remove each fork leg.

6. Installation is the reverse of these steps. Torque the fork pinch bolts and fork cap bolts as specified in **Table 1**.

Disassembly/Assembly

Refer to **Figure 26** for this procedure.

NOTE
Preparation should be made prior to starting the disassembly as an impact tool (air or electric) or a special holding tool is necessary to remove the Allen retaining bolt in the bottom of each fork leg. The Allen bolt is secured with a thread locking compound (such as Loctite) and is often difficult to remove because the damper rod will turn inside the fork tube. Have a local dealer remove the Allen bolts with an impact tool or with an Allen wrench and the special holding tool. Use Suzuki part No. 09940-34561 (Attachment "D") inside the fork tube to hold the damper rod. Attachment "D" can be used with the Suzuki handle (Suzuki part No. 09940-34520) or with one or two long 3/8 inch drive socket extensions.

Each fork leg assembly on all TSCC models contains 2 "DU" Teflon-coated metal rings. These "DU" rings are used to decrease the internal friction between the inner fork tube and the outer slider unit. These "DU" rings are generally damaged when the fork tubes are removed, therefore Suzuki recommends the rings be replaced each time the forks are disassembled.

1. Remove the front forks as outlined in this chapter.

2. Remove the fork cap bolt (**Figure 27**) from the inner tube.
3. Remove the upper and lower fork springs (**Figure 28**) complete with the spring seat (**Figure 29**).
4. Tip up the fork tube and drain the fork oil. Stroke the fork several times over a drain pan to pump out all the remaining oil. Let the fork tube drain for several minutes.
5. On all TSCC models, perform the following:
   a. Remove the outer dust cover to gain access to the seal retaining snap ring.
   b. Use snap ring pliers and remove the snap ring securing the fork seal.
6. Use the special tools or an impact tool and remove the Allen bolt from the bottom of the fork outer tube (**Figure 30**).
7A. On all 1979 and earlier models, perform the following:
   a. Slide out and remove the inner tube from the outer tube (**Figure 31**).
   b. Remove the oil lock piece from the end of the damper rod (**Figure 32**).

NOTE
The oil lock piece is often stuck to the bottom of the outer tube. Make sure the piece is not lost.

   c. Tip up the inner tube and slide out the damper rod assembly complete with the rebound spring (**Figure 33**).

9

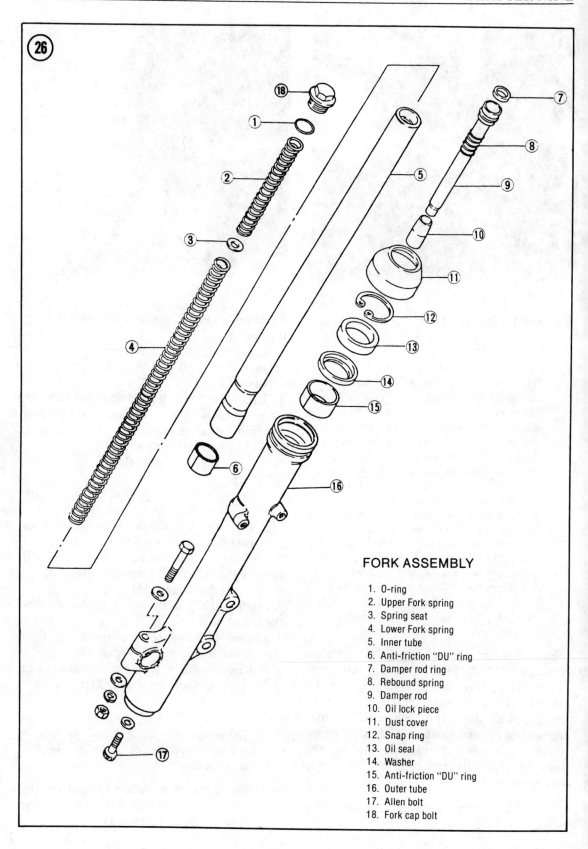

FORK ASSEMBLY

1. O-ring
2. Upper Fork spring
3. Spring seat
4. Lower Fork spring
5. Inner tube
6. Anti-friction "DU" ring
7. Damper rod ring
8. Rebound spring
9. Damper rod
10. Oil lock piece
11. Dust cover
12. Snap ring
13. Oil seal
14. Washer
15. Anti-friction "DU" ring
16. Outer tube
17. Allen bolt
18. Fork cap bolt

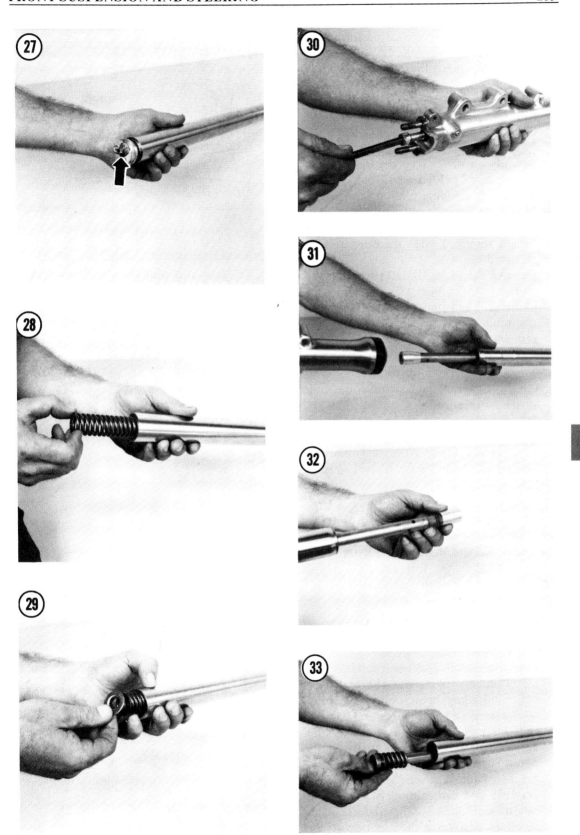

7B. On all TSCC models, perform the following:

   a. Tip up the inner tube and slide out the damper rod assembly complete with rebound spring and oil lock piece.

   b. Pad the jaws of a vise with wooden blocks or soft aluminum plates. Place the fork leg in the vise and clamp the vise securely on the brake caliper mounting lugs as shown in **Figure 34**.

   c. With a quick sliding motion remove the inner tube from the outer tube. The seal, seal washer and upper "DU" ring are usually removed when the outer tube is removed.

   d. Remove the lower "DU" ring from the end of the inner tube.

   e. If the seal and upper "DU" ring were not removed when the inner tube was removed, proceed to Step 9.

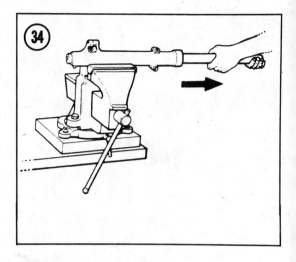

8. On 1979 and earlier models, perform the following to gain access to the fork seals.

   a. Carefully pry off and remove the fork dust boot (**Figure 35**).

   b. Remove the snap ring securing the oil seal (**Figure 36**).

   c. Lift out and remove the seal retaining washer on models so equipped (**Figure 37**).

9. Carefully pry out the old seal with a large blade screwdriver or tire tool as shown in **Figure 38**. Pad the edge of the outer fork tube with a rag or piece of aluminum (**Figure 39**) to prevent damage to the fork tube. On TSCC models, remove the washer and upper "DU" ring.

10. Perform *Inspection*.

11. Assembly is the reverse of these steps. Keep the following points in mind:

   a. Ensure that all fork components are clean and dry. Wipe out the seal bore before installing the new oil seal. Lightly oil the inner and outer tubes and damper rod assembly before assembling the parts. Apply a light film of grease to the outer edge and lips of each fork seal before installing the seals.

   b. On 1979 and earlier models, install the new oil seal (open end down) and tap the seal into position with a seal driver or

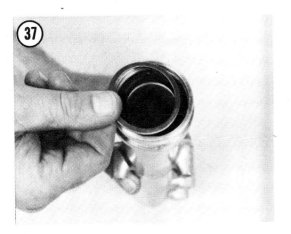

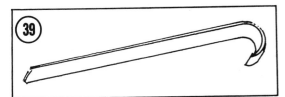

suitably sized socket. Install the seal retaining washer (on models so equipped) and secure the seal with the snap ring.

c. Make sure the rebound (top-out) spring is installed on the damper rod before installing the rod in the inner fork tube.

NOTE
Temporarily install the fork springs and the fork cap bolt. The tension of the fork springs will keep the damper rod extended through the end of the fork tube and ease fork assembly.

d. On TSCC models, carefully install the lower "DU" ring on the *inner* fork tube and slide the inner tube into the outer tube.

e. Apply blue Loctite (Lock N' Seal No. 2114) to the Allen retaining bolt before installing the bolt. Ensure that the washer is fitted to the bolt. Torque the bolt to 1.5-2.5 mkg (11-18 ft.-lb.).

f. On TSCC models, slide the upper "DU" ring, washer and seal over the inner tube and carefully tap the components into place in the outer tube. Make sure the seal is fully seated in the outer tube. Secure the seal with the snap ring.

NOTE
If Suzuki special tools are available, use the oil seal driver (part No. 09940-54910) with attachment (part No. 09940-54920).

g. Install the dust cover over the seal.

13. Remove the fork springs. Refer to **Table 2** and add the specified amount and type of fork oil to each fork tube. Use a graduate or a baby bottle (**Figure 40**) to ensure the oil amount is correct for each fork tube. Oil level can also be measured from the top of the fork tube. Use an accurate ruler or the Suzuki oil level gauge (part No. 09943-74110) to ensure the oil level is as specified in **Table 2**. The oil level must be measured with the forks completely compressed and without springs.

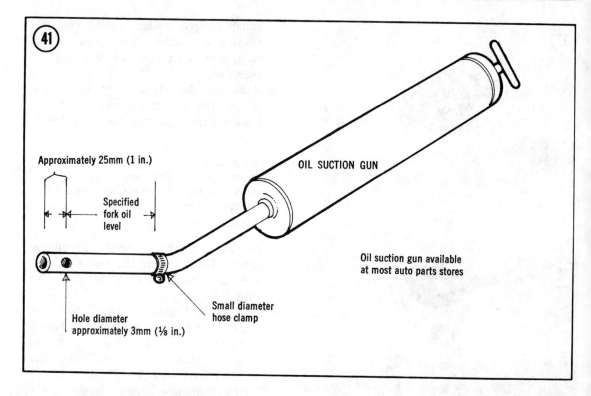

Approximately 25mm (1 in.)

Specified fork oil level

OIL SUCTION GUN

Oil suction gun available at most auto parts stores

Small diameter hose clamp

Hole diameter approximately 3mm (⅛ in.)

NOTE
*An oil level measuring device can be locally fabricated as shown in **Figure 41**. Fill the fork with a few cc's more than the required amount of oil. Position the hose clamp on the top edge of the fork tube and draw out the excess oil. Oil is sucked out until the level reaches the small diameter hole. A precise oil level can be achieved with this simple device.*

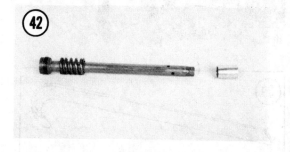

14. Install the long fork spring, the spring seat and the short spring. Make sure the closer coils on the short spring are pointed up.

15. Ensure the O-ring on the fork cap is in good condition. Install the fork cap finger-tight. The cap can be tightened after the forks have been installed on the motorcycle.

Inspection

1. Thoroughly clean all parts in solvent and dry them completely. Lightly oil and assemble the inner and outer fork tubes, then slide the tubes together. Check for looseness, noise or binding. Replace any defective parts.

2. Carefully examine the area of the inner fork tube that passes through the fork seal. Any scratches or roughness on the tube in this area will damage the oil seal. If the inner fork tube is scratched or pitted it should be replaced.

3. Inspect the damper rod assembly for damage or roughness (**Figure 42**). Check for signs of galling, deep scores or excessive wear. Replace the parts as necessary. Make sure all the oil passages are clean and free of any sludge or oil residue.

4. Inspect the dust cover on the fork tube for holes or abrasive damage. A damaged cover may allow dirt and moisture to pack up next to the fork seal. Packed-in dirt can scratch the surface of the fork tubes as well as damage the fork seal. Install new dust covers if any damage exists.

5. Accurately measure the fork springs. If any spring is shorter than the length specified in **Table 2**, replace the springs as a set.

STEERING HEAD

The steering head should be disassembled periodically and the bearings packed with new grease. All 1979 and earlier models use 18 uncaged ball bearings in each of the upper and lower bearing races. All TSCC models are equipped with tapered roller bearings in both upper and lower bearing races.

Use a good heavy grade of grease such as wheel bearing grease when lubricating the bearings; on 1979 and earlier models, the grease is also used to hold the bearing balls in position during installation.

Disassembly/Lubrication/
Assembly

Refer to **Figure 43** or **Figure 44** for this procedure.

1. Remove the front forks.
2. Remove the fuel tank as outlined in Chapter Seven to avoid possible damage to the tank.
3. Remove the instrument cluster and headlamp assembly as outlined in Chapter Eight.
4. Loosen the pinch bolt securing the large steering stem bolt or nut (**Figure 45**).
5. Remove the large steering stem bolt or nut (**Figure 46**).
6. Lift up on the handlebars and lift off the upper steering stem head.
7. Remove the steering stem nut and lift off the dust cover. Use a locally improvised tool similar to **Figure 47** or Suzuki special tool part No. 09940-14910 to remove the stem nut. If care is exercised, a hammer and punch may also be used to tap off the nut.
8. On 1979 and earlier models, remove the upper bearing outer race. On TSCC models, lift out the upper roller bearing.
9. The entire steering stem can now be partially withdrawn from the frame. On 1979 and earlier models, place a container under the steering head to catch any ball bearings that may fall out. To lubricate the bearings, further disassembly is unnecessary.

NOTE
*To completely remove the steering stem it is necessary to remove the brake hose manifold (**Figure 48**) and disconnect cable and wire retainers, directional light wiring and all other components secured to the lower steering stem bracket.*

10. Assembly is the reverse of disassembly. Keep the following points in mind:
  a. Pack the upper and lower roller bearings with heavy duty grease.
  b. On 1979 and earlier models, ensure that 18 bearing balls are installed in each bearing race.
  c. On TSCC models, use the Suzuki special tool (part No. 09940-14940) or equivalent and temporarily torque the steering stem nut to 4.0-5.0 mkg (29-36 ft.-lb.) to seat the roller bearings. Turn the steering lock to lock a few times to ensure that the movement is smooth without excessive play. Back off the steering stem nut approximately 1/4 turn.
  d. On 1979 and earlier models, tighten the steering stem nut fully to seat the bearing balls. Back off the nut just enough for smooth steering movement without any perceptible free play.
  e. Install the large steering stem nut or bolt and torque to 3.6-5.2 mkg (26-38 ft.-lb.). Check that the steering stem moves easily and smoothly from side to side and no vertical play is present. Readjust the steering stem nut if necessary.
  f. Torque the steering stem pinch bolt to 1.5-2.5 mkg (11-18 ft.-lb.).
  g. If the lower steering bracket was removed, install all wire and cable retainers and the brake hose manifold. Bleed the brakes as outlined in Chapter Eleven if any brake hoses were opened.

Inspection

1. Clean the bearing races and bearings with solvent.
2. Check the frame welds around the steering head for cracks and fractures. If any are found, have them repaired by a competent frame shop or welding service.

9

STEERING STEM (1979 AND EARLIER)

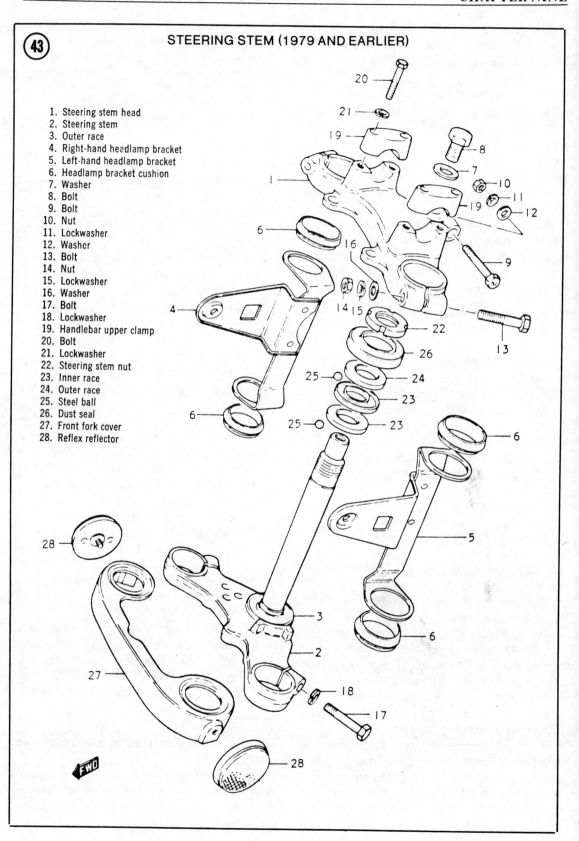

1. Steering stem head
2. Steering stem
3. Outer race
4. Right-hand headlamp bracket
5. Left-hand headlamp bracket
6. Headlamp bracket cushion
7. Washer
8. Bolt
9. Bolt
10. Nut
11. Lockwasher
12. Washer
13. Bolt
14. Nut
15. Lockwasher
16. Washer
17. Bolt
18. Lockwasher
19. Handlebar upper clamp
20. Bolt
21. Lockwasher
22. Steering stem nut
23. Inner race
24. Outer race
25. Steel ball
26. Dust seal
27. Front fork cover
28. Reflex reflector

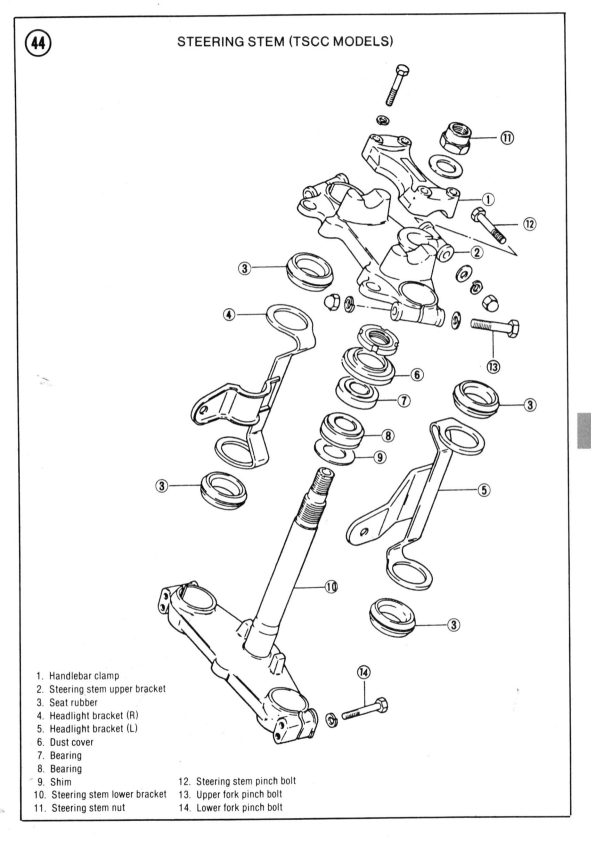

STEERING STEM (TSCC MODELS)

1. Handlebar clamp
2. Steering stem upper bracket
3. Seat rubber
4. Headlight bracket (R)
5. Headlight bracket (L)
6. Dust cover
7. Bearing
8. Bearing
9. Shim
10. Steering stem lower bracket
11. Steering stem nut
12. Steering stem pinch bolt
13. Upper fork pinch bolt
14. Lower fork pinch bolt

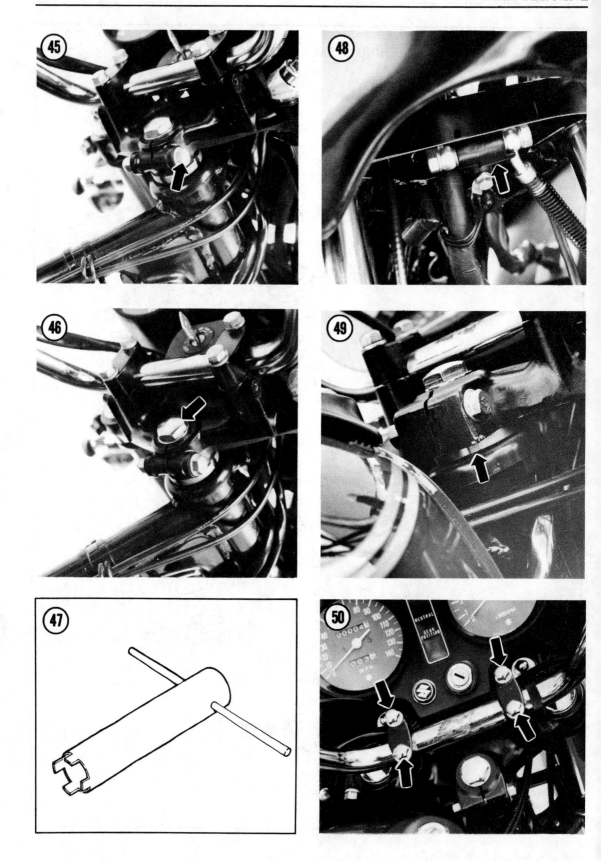

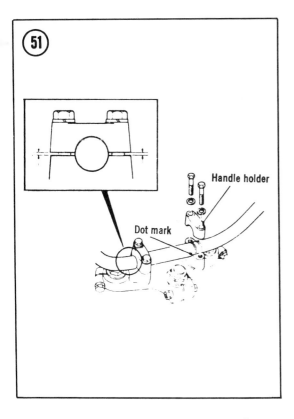

(51)

Handle holder

Dot mark

3. Check the bearings for pitting, scratches or signs of corrosion. If they are less than perfect, replace them as a set.

4. Check the races for pitting, galling and corrosion. If any of these conditions exist, replace the races. See the applicable bearing replacement procedure.

5. Check the steering stem for cracks, damage or wear.

Steering Head Adjustment

1. Place the motorcycle on the centerstand and place a block under the engine until the front wheel is clear of the ground. Grasp each fork leg at the lower end and attempt to move the front end back and forth. If any fore and aft movement of the front end is detected, the steering stem locknut will have to be adjusted.

2. Loosen the pinch bolt securing the steering stem head bolt or nut (**Figure 45**) and loosen the head bolt or nut (**Figure 46**).

3. Use the Suzuki spanner wrench (part No. 09940-10122) and adjust the steering stem locknut (**Figure 49**) until all play is removed

from the steering head, yet the front end turns freely from side to side under its own weight. If the Suzuki spanner is not available the steering locknut can be gently tapped with a hammer and a punch or screwdriver. Take care not to damage the locknut.

4. Torque the steering stem head bolt or nut and the steering stem pinch bolt as specified in **Table 1**.

Handlebar Removal/ Installation

1. If the handlebars are to be replaced, it is necessary to remove the clutch lever, front master cylinder and throttle grip.

2. Remove the bolts securing the handlebar clamps (**Figure 50**) and remove the handlebars.

3. Install the handlebar with the dot and handlebar clamps positioned as shown in **Figure 51**. Torque the clamp bolts to 1.2-2.0 mkg (9-15 ft.-lb.).

4. Install the clutch lever, front master cylinder and throttle grip if removed.

Bearing Race Replacement (1979 and Earlier Models)

1. Insert a hardwood dowel or brass drift into the steering head as shown in **Figure 52** and tap around the race to drive it out. Do the same with the opposite race.

2. Install new races by tapping them into the steering head with a hardwood block (**Figure 53**). Make sure the races are seated squarely before tapping them into place. Tap them in until they are fully seated in the steering head.

3. Use 2 screwdrivers and carefully pry off the lower race from the lower steering stem. Carefully tap a new race into place with a wooden block.

Bearing Replacement (TSCC Models)

Several special tools and considerable expertise are required to replace the steering head bearings and bearing races. It is recommended that this task be referred to an authorized dealer or competent specialist equipped with the necessary tools.

9

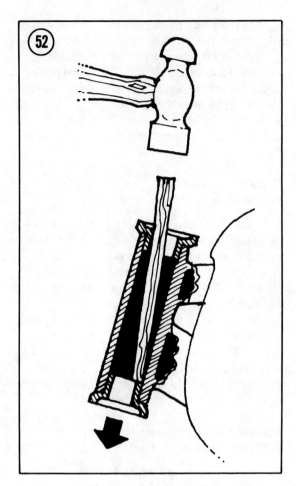

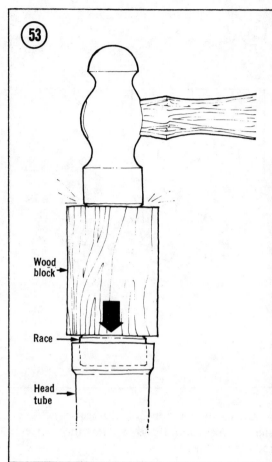

Table 1   FRONT SUSPENSION TORQUE SPECIFICATIONS

Item	mkg	ft.-lb.
Front axle nut	3.6-5.2	26-38
Front axle holder nut	1.5-2.5	11-18
Front caliper mounting bolt	2.5-4.0	18-29
Front caliper axle bolt		
1979 and earlier models	2.5-3.5	18-26
TSCC models	1.5-2.0	11-15
Upper fork pinch bolt	2.0-3.0	15-22
Lower fork pinch bolt		
1979 and earlier models	2.0-3.0	15-22
TSCC models	1.5-2.5	11-18
Steering stem pinch bolt	1.5-2.5	11-18
Steering stem head bolt or nut	3.6-5.2	26-38
Handlebar clamp bolt	1.2-2.0	9-15
Fork cap bolts	1.5-3.0	11-22
Brake disc mounting bolt	1.5-2.5	11-18

Table 2   FRONT FORK SPECIFICATIONS

Recommended Fork Oil			
SAE 10, 20 or 30 weight fork oil or 50:50 mix with A.T.F. (automatic transmission fluid)			
Fork Oil Capacity			
1979 "L" models	280 cc	9.5 U.S. oz.	9.9 Imp. oz.
TSCC models	237 cc	8.0 U.S. oz.	8.3 Imp. oz.
1979 and earlier models	180 cc	6.0 U.S. oz.	6.3 Imp. oz.
Fork oil level (See Notes)			
1979 "L" models	202 mm (8.0 in.)		
TSCC models	229 mm (9.0 in.)		
1979 and earlier models	206 mm (8.1 in.)		
Fork spring length	Standard	Service limit	
All TSCC models			
short spring	153 mm (6.0 in.)	—	
long spring	451 mm (17.8 in.)	—	
1979 "L" models			
short spring	167.0 mm (6.6 in.)	154 mm (6.1 in.)	
long spring	475.8 mm (18.7 in.)	460 mm (18.1 in.)	
1979 and earlier models			
short spring	166 mm (6.5 in.)	—	
long spring	370 mm (14.6 in.)	—	

NOTES:
1. The maximum allowable difference in oil level between the right and left fork tubes is 1 mm (0.04 in.).

2. Measure oil level from the top of the fork leg with the fork leg held vertical, spring removed and fork leg fully compressed.

CHAPTER TEN

REAR SUSPENSION

This chapter includes repair and replacement procedures for the rear wheel and rear suspension components. Refer to Chapter Nine for wheel balancing and spoke adjustment procedures. All rear brake repair is outlined in Chapter Eleven.

REAR WHEEL

Removal/Installation

1. Place the motorcycle on the centerstand. If desired, the exhaust system can be removed as outlined in Chapter Seven to provide better access to the rear wheel components.
2. Remove the bolts securing the chain guard and remove the guard (**Figure 1**).
3. Loosen the locknuts securing the chain adjuster bolts (**Figure 2**) and loosen the adjuster bolts.
4. Remove the cotter pin or lynch pin securing the rear axle nut (**Figure 3**) and loosen the axle nut.
5. Remove the adjuster support bolts from each side (**Figure 4**).
6. Remove the cotter pin securing the torque link bolt (**Figure 5**). Remove the bolt and nut securing the torque link to the brake caliper.
7. Remove the bolts securing the brake caliper (**Figure 6**) and lift the caliper off the mounting bracket.

CAUTION
Support the caliper from the frame with a piece of wire or Bungee cord. Do not allow the caliper to suspend from the brake hose or the hose may be damaged.

8. Swing the chain adjusters down and push the rear wheel as far forward as possible to gain maximum chain slack. Disengage the drive chain from the rear sprocket. Tilt the top of the wheel to the left as shown in **Figure 7** and remove the rear wheel.

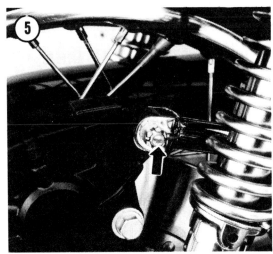

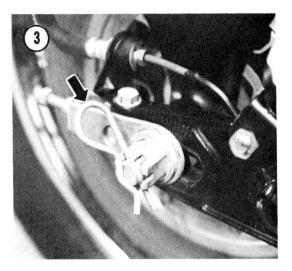

10

9. Installation is the reverse of these steps. Keep the following points in mind:

  a. Turn the chain adjuster bolts equally on both sides until the chain deflection is 20-30 mm (3/4-1 3/16 in.) as shown in **Figure 8**. Make sure the index marks on the adjusters are aligned equally on both sides (**Figure 9**). Tighten the adjuster locknuts.

  b. Torque the axle nut, caliper mounting bolts, torque link nut and adjuster support bolts as specified in **Table 1**.

  c. Secure the rear axle nut with a new cotter pin or lynch pin. Secure the torque link nut with a new cotter pin.

Disassembly/Assembly

  Refer to **Figure 10** or **Figure 11** for this procedure.

1. Remove rear wheel.

2. Lift out sprocket mounting drum and remove bearing holder. Remove cushion plate on models so equipped (**Figure 12**).

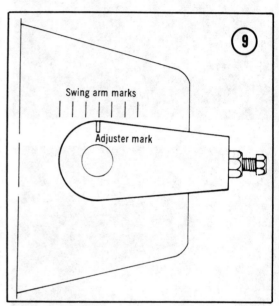

Swing arm marks

Adjuster mark

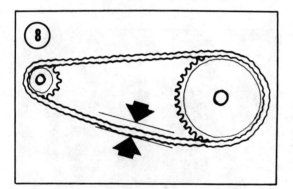

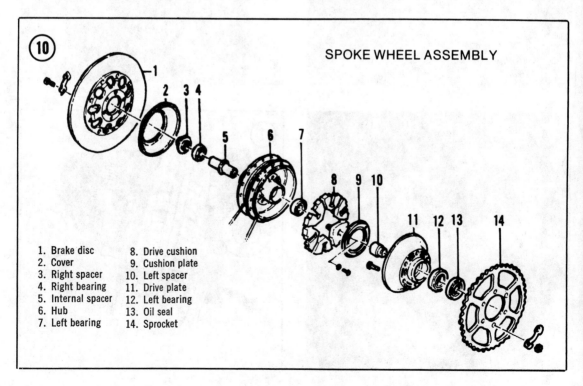

SPOKE WHEEL ASSEMBLY

1. Brake disc
2. Cover
3. Right spacer
4. Right bearing
5. Internal spacer
6. Hub
7. Left bearing
8. Drive cushion
9. Cushion plate
10. Left spacer
11. Drive plate
12. Left bearing
13. Oil seal
14. Sprocket

3. Remove the 6 rubber shock absorbers.

4. Fold back locking tabs securing 6 sprocket nuts (**Figure 13**). Remove nuts and bolts and remove the sprocket.

5. If brake disc removal is desired, perform the following:

    a. Fold back locking tabs on the bolts securing the disc.

    b. Remove bolts and nuts securing disc to hub assembly and lift off disc.

6. Assembly is the reverse of these steps. Secure sprocket bolts with locking tabs. Inspect brake components as outlined in Chapter Eleven. Torque sprocket nuts and nuts securing the brake disc as specified in **Table 1**.

Inspection

1. Rotate bearings by hand and check for roughness. If bearings turn smoothly, they

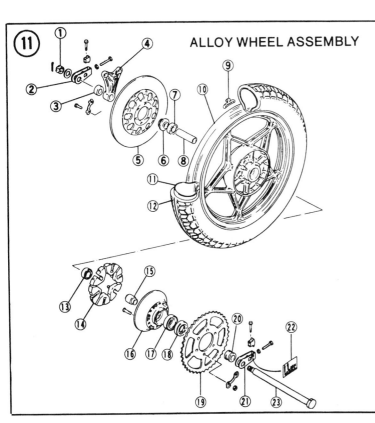

ALLOY WHEEL ASSEMBLY

1. Rear axle nut
2. Right-hand chain adjuster
3. Spacer
4. Rear caliper bracket
5. Rear brake disc
6. Right-hand axle spacer
7. Right-hand bearing
8. Spacer
9. Balance weight
10. Rear wheel
11. Inner tube
12. Rear tire
13. Left-hand bearing
14. Rear hub cushion
15. Bearing holder
16. Sprocket mounting drum
17. Bearing
18. Oil seal
19. Rear sprocket
20. Left-hand axle spacer
21. Left-hand chain adjuster
22. Chain wear indicator label
23. Rear axle

10

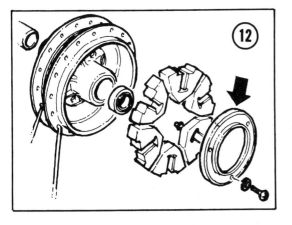

need not be removed. However, if roughness is apparent, drive the sealed bearings out of the hub from the inside using a soft drift or from the outside with a bearing puller.

2. Check sprocket for wear and replace it if teeth show signs of undercutting (**Figure 14**).

3. Check axle for straightness (**Figure 15**). If deflection is greater than 0.25mm (0.010 in.), replace the axle.

4. Check for bent, broken or loose spokes. Replace any that are bent or broken and tighten loose spokes so that all spokes will have an equal "ring" when tapped with a wrench. Refer to *Spoke Wheels* in Chapter Nine.

Wheel Balancing

Refer to *Wheel Balancing* as outlined in Chapter Ten.

SUSPENSION UNITS

The rear suspension units (spring/shock absorber assemblies) are non-repairable items. If units fail to dampen adequately, replace them as a set.

Removal/Installation

1. Place motorcycle on the centerstand and set the spring preload to the softest position.

2. Remove upper and lower mounting fasteners and washers (**Figure 16**) and remove suspension units.

> *NOTE*
> *Remove and install one unit at a time; the unit that remains in place will maintain the correct relationship between the top and bottom mounts and make the job easier.*
>
> *To ease suspension unit removal first slide upper mount off mounting boss then raise rear wheel to allow lower mount to clear muffler.*

3. Installation is the reverse of these steps. Torque upper and lower mounting fasteners to 2.0-3.0 mkg (15-22 ft.-lb.).

SWINGING ARM

The swinging arm pivot is equipped with pressed-in needle bearings. If correctly maintained (periodic cleaning, greasing and

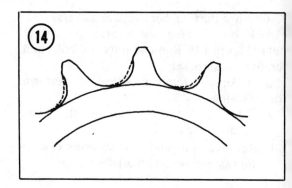

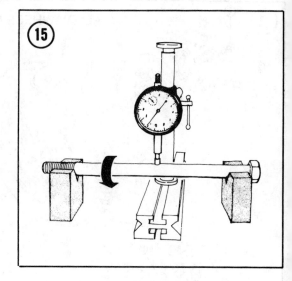

adjustment), these bearings should last the life of the motorcycle. However, if they must be replaced, the swinging arm should be removed and entrusted to a dealer; a special puller is required to remove the bearings and it is unlikely that you would ever use it more than once.

Removal/Installation

Refer to **Figure 17** for this procedure.

1. Perform *Rear Wheel Removal* and *Suspension Unit Removal* as outlined in this chapter.

2. Refer to Chapter Eleven and perform *Rear Master Cylinder Removal.*

> *NOTE*
> *Unless desired, do not remove brake hose from rear master cylinder or it will be necessary to bleed brake system after swinging arm installation.*

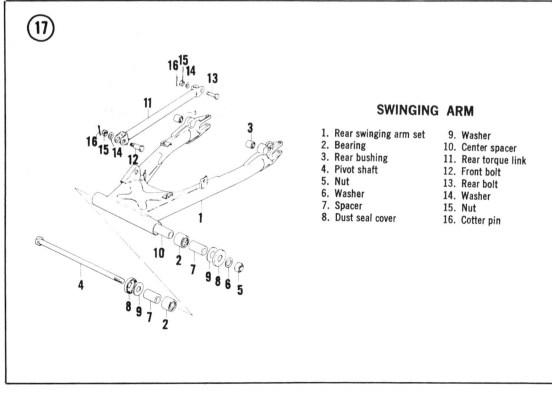

10

SWINGING ARM

1. Rear swinging arm set
2. Bearing
3. Rear bushing
4. Pivot shaft
5. Nut
6. Washer
7. Spacer
8. Dust seal cover
9. Washer
10. Center spacer
11. Rear torque link
12. Front bolt
13. Rear bolt
14. Washer
15. Nut
16. Cotter pin

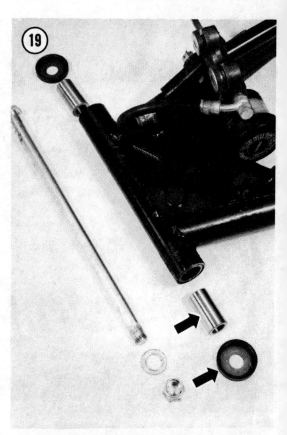

3. Remove nut securing swinging arm pivot bolt (**Figure 18**) and remove bolt. Remove swinging arm assembly from frame.

> *NOTE*
> *If necessary, tap bolt out of frame with a drift. Remove bolt with care to prevent damage to swinging arm bearings and/or pivot bolt.*

4. Remove dust cover, washer, and inner bearing race (spacer) from each side of swinging arm (**Figure 19**).
5. Check condition of needle bearings (**Figure 20**) and replace them if they are worn, galled or feel rough. Refer bearing replacement to a dealer.
6. Disconnect the brake line from the clips at the front and rear of the swinging arm and remove the master cylinder, line, and caliper (**Figure 21**).
7. Installation is the reverse of these steps. Keep the following points in mind:

> *NOTE*
> *Do not forget to install the drive chain before installing the swinging arm in the frame.*

a. Grease pivot bolt and bearings with a good grade of waterproof grease such as marine wheel bearing grease.

b. Install pivot bolt from the left side. Use a screwdriver shaft or drift to help align center and outer spacers as pivot bolt is installed. Torque pivot nut to 5.0-8.0 mkg (36-58 ft.-lb.).

SPROCKET REPLACEMENT

Rear sprocket removal is outlined under *Rear Wheel Disassembly*. Remove engine drive sprocket as described in *Engine Removal*, Chapters Four or Five.

DRIVE CHAIN

Drive chain care is very important. The chain and sprockets should be cleaned, inspected and adjusted at least every 1,000 km (600 miles). If chain or sprocket wear is

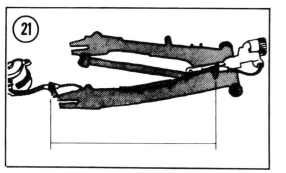

evident they must be replaced as a set. An excessively stretched chain will cause severe vibration and will be difficult if not impossible to adjust properly.

The drive chain is a long-life continuous (no master link) type with internal lubrication, between the rollers and pins, sealed in with O-rings. See **Figure 22** for a cross-section of a typical link.

Cleaning and Lubrication

1. Wash chain with clean kerosene and dry it thoroughly. This can be done with the chain installed.

CAUTION
Use only kerosene to wash the chain. Do not use gasoline, benzine, or non-petroleum solvent; they will attack the O-ring seals and enter the permanently lubricated spaces between the pins and rollers, severely shortening the service life of the chain.

2. Lubricate outside of chain with motor oil. Do not use specially compounded chain lubricants *unless* they are specifically designated for use on O-ring chains. After chain has been throughly oiled, wipe off excess lubricant with a clean rag.

10

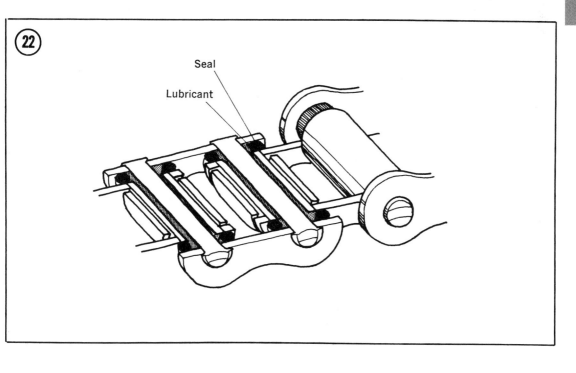

Seal

Lubricant

3. Check sprockets for undercutting of the teeth (**Figure 23**). If wear is evident, replace the sprockets.

Inspection

1. Carefully examine the chain for loose pins, damaged rollers, dry or rusty links, kinked links and missing O-rings. The chain must be replaced if any of these conditions exist.
2. To check the stretch of the chain refer to *Drive Chain Adjustment and Lubrication* in Chapter Three and tighten both chain tensioners until all chain slack is removed.
3. With an accurate ruler or a locally improvised measuring gauge, measure the distance between 21 pins on the chain as shown in **Figure 24**. The service limit for all 1979 and earlier models is 384.8 mm (15.15 in.). The service limit for TSCC models is 383.0 mm (15.08 in.). The chain must be replaced if it is stretched beyond the service limits.

> *WARNING*
> *Do not attempt to shorten the chain by removing links and installing a master link; the chain could easily fail. Such a chain failure could cause the rear wheel to lock up, resulting in a serious accident.*

> *CAUTION*
> *Always replace both sprockets as a set if either is worn excessively or when installing a new drive chain. Never run a new chain on old sprockets or an old chain*

on new sprockets. Rapid and uneven wear will result and seriously damage the new components.

4. Readjust the chain slack as outlined in Chapter Three.

Removal/Installation

To remove chain it is necessary to remove the swinging arm and chain guard. Refer to *Swinging Arm, Removal/Installation.*

Adjustment

Adjust chain as outlined under *Drive Chain Adjustment and Lubrication* in Chapter Three.

> *CAUTION*
> *Always replace both sprockets as a set if either is worn excessively or when installing a new drive chain. Never run a new chain on old sprockets or an old chain on new sprockets. Rapid and uneven wear will result and seriously damage the new components.*

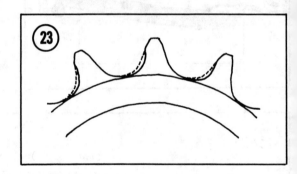

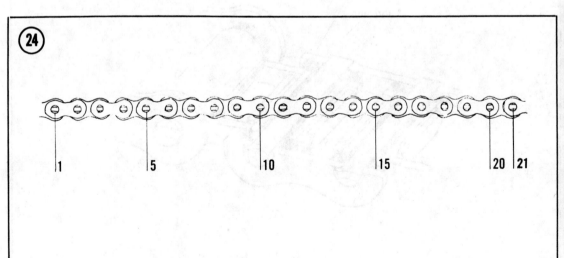

Table 1   REAR SUSPENSION TORQUE SPECIFICATIONS

Item	mkg	ft.-lb.
Rear sprocket nut	2.5-4.0	18-29
Swinging arm pivot nut	5.0-8.0	36-58
Shock absorber nut	2.0-3.0	15-22
Rear axle nut	8.5-11.5	62-83
Torque link nut	2.0-3.0	15-22
Rear brake caliper mounting bolts		
1979 and earlier models	2.0-3.0	15-22
TSCC models	2.5-4.0	18-29
Brake disc bolts	1.5-2.5	11-18
Chain adjuster support bolts	1.5-2.0	11-15

10

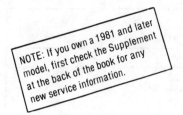
NOTE: If you own a 1981 and later model, first check the Supplement at the back of the book for any new service information.

CHAPTER ELEVEN

BRAKES

All GS750 models are equipped with hydraulic disc brakes front and rear. All 1978 and 1979 "E" and "L" models as well as all TSCC models are fitted with double disc/caliper units on the front wheel. Single disc units are installed on the rear of all models.

Two types of front brake calipers are used on GS750 models. All 1979 and earlier models share one style, while all TSCC models are fitted with a newer "square pad" style caliper. All front calipers are single piston units. All rear brake calipers use 2 pistons.

> ### WARNING
> *If it is necessary to top off either master cylinder reservoir, only use brake fluid marked DOT 3 or DOT 4. All GS750 models use a glycol-based brake fluid. Mixing a glycol-based fluid with a petroleum-based or silicon-based fluid may cause brake component damage leading to brake failure.*

Tables 1-3 are at the end of the chapter.

BRAKE PAD REPLACEMENT

Replace both front pads as a set when they are worn down to the red line as shown in **Figure 1**. The rear pads should be replaced as a set when the shoulder on either pad is worn down (**Figure 2**).

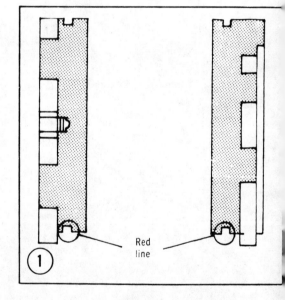

(1) Red line

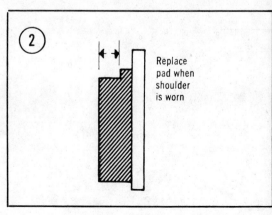

(2) Replace pad when shoulder is worn

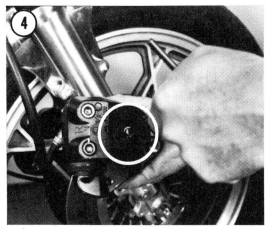

**Front Pad Replacement
(1979 and Earlier Models)**

1. Remove the bolts securing either front caliper to the fork leg (**Figure 3**) and slide the caliper off the disc.

> *NOTE*
> *Do not actuate the front brake lever while a caliper is removed or the caliper piston may be pushed completely out of the caliper body.*

2. Remove the screw securing the pad lock plate (**Figure 4**) and remove the plate.
3. Press out and remove the stationary pad (**Figure 5**).
4. Pry up and remove the sliding pad (**Figure 6**).
5. Remove the cover from the front master cylinder reservoir. Wrap a rag around the reservoir to catch any brake fluid spills.
6. Slowly press the caliper piston back into the caliper as far as it will go.
7. Apply a *light* film of PBC-based brake pad grease (Suzuki part No. 99000-25110) to the back of the sliding pad and to the surface of the caliper piston.

> *NOTE*
> *Suzuki recommends a light film of PBC-based (copper-colored) Brake Pad Grease (part No. 99000-25110) be applied between the pad and piston when*

11

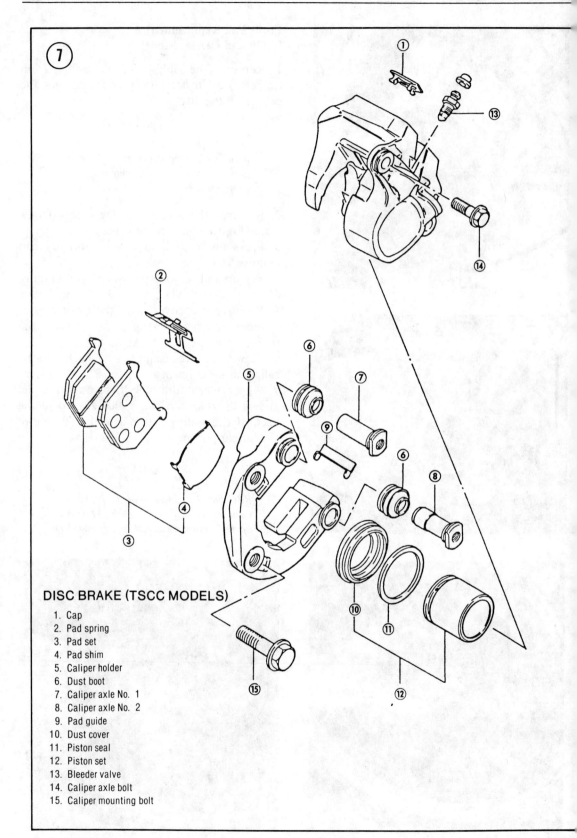

DISC BRAKE (TSCC MODELS)

1. Cap
2. Pad spring
3. Pad set
4. Pad shim
5. Caliper holder
6. Dust boot
7. Caliper axle No. 1
8. Caliper axle No. 2
9. Pad guide
10. Dust cover
11. Piston seal
12. Piston set
13. Bleeder valve
14. Caliper axle bolt
15. Caliper mounting bolt

new pads are installed. The grease acts as
a cushion and helps prevent brake squeal
due to metal-to-metal contact.

CAUTION
*Do not allow any grease to get on the pad
friction material or the pad will be ruined.*

8. Install the sliding pad into the caliper body.
Make sure that the notch in the pad engages
the locating tab in the caliper.
9. Install the stationary pad and secure it with
the pad lock plate.
10. Install the caliper. Torque the caliper
mounting bolts as specified in **Table 1**. Top up
the master cylinder reservoir, if necessary.
11. Spin the front wheel and apply the front
brakes a few times to ensure that the brakes
operate properly and the pads adjust correctly.

**Front Pad Replacement
(TSCC Models)**

Refer to **Figure 7** for this procedure.

NOTE
*Suzuki recommends the use of a small
amount of silicon-base (colorless) Caliper
Axle Grease (part No. 99000-25100) on
the caliper axles when the caliper is
disassembled for pad replacement. Use
the grease sparingly or pad and disc may
become contaminated with grease,
resulting in loss of braking power. The
following procedure describes pad
replacement by removing the entire caliper
unit. The caliper can also be partially
disassembled while on the motorcycle.
Once disassembled, the actual pad
replacement is essentially the same for
either method. To partially disassemble
the caliper on the motorcycle, remove the
bolts securing the caliper axles (A, **Figure
8)** and remove the moveable half of the
caliper.*

1. Remove the bolts securing the front caliper
(B, **Figure 8**) and carefully remove the caliper
from the fork leg.
2. Carefully separate the piston assembly as
shown in **Figure 9**.
3. Disengage the stationary pad from the pad
spring and remove the pad (**Figure 10**). Take
care that the small pad guide springs are not
lost or misaligned.

4. Disengage the sliding pad from the pad spring and remove the pad as shown in **Figure 11**. Note the metal plate attached to the back of the sliding pad.

5. Remove the cover from the front master cylinder reservoir. Wrap a rag around the reservoir to catch any brake fluid spills.

NOTE
If the reservoir is full, brake fluid may overflow slightly when the caliper piston is pushed completely back into the caliper.

6. Apply a *light* film of colorless Caliper Axle Grease (part No. 99000-25100) to the caliper axles. Do not allow any grease to get on the pad friction material or the pad may be ruined.

7. Slowly press the caliper piston back into the caliper as far as it will go.

8. Install the sliding pad into the caliper body.

9. Install the stationary pad against the pad spring in the caliper.

10. Hold both pads in position and carefully slide the piston assembly into the caliper mounting bracket (**Figure 9**).

11. Install the caliper unit or the moveable half of the caliper. Torque the caliper mounting bolts to 2.5-4.0 mkg (18-29 ft.-lb.). Torque the caliper axle bolts, if removed, to 1.5-2.0 mkg (11-15 ft.-lb.).

12. Top up the master cylinder reservoir with approved brake fluid, if necessary, and install the reservoir cap.

13. Spin the front wheel and apply the front brake a few times to ensure that the brakes operate properly and the pads adjust correctly.

Rear Pad Replacement

1. Use a screwdriver and gently pry off the plastic inspection cover on the rear caliper (**Figure 12**).

2. Remove the snap clips securing the pad retainer pins (**Figure 13**).

3. Use a small punch or needlenose pliers and push the retainer pins back out of the caliper (**Figure 14**).

4. Pull one brake pad up and out of the caliper body (**Figure 15**).

5. With a wooden dowel or wedge, push the caliper piston fully back into the caliper body to gain sufficient room to install one new pad.

CAUTION
Never use a screwdriver or similar metal tool to push the caliper piston back into the caliper body or damage may result to the caliper and/or the brake disc.

6. Slide in one new brake pad. Install the pad shim so the "diamond" cutout on the shim points forward as shown in **Figure 15**.
7. Repeat Steps 4 through 7 for the other pad.
8. Install the retainer pins and secure with the snap clips.
9. Install the plastic inspection cover.

FRONT CALIPER

Removal/Installation

Removal and installation is the same for either front caliper.
1. Remove the banjo bolt securing the brake hose to the caliper (**Figure 16**). Have a container ready to catch any dripping brake fluid.

NOTE
It is not necessary to remove the brake hose if the caliper is being removed only for brake pad replacement.

2. Remove the bolts securing the caliper to the fork leg (**Figure 17**) and slide the caliper off the brake disc.
3. Installation is the reverse of these steps. Bleed the brake system if the brake hose was removed. Torque the caliper mounting bolts and the brake hose banjo bolt as specified in **Table 1**.

Disassembly/Assembly

Refer to **Figure 18** or **Figure 7** for this procedure.

11

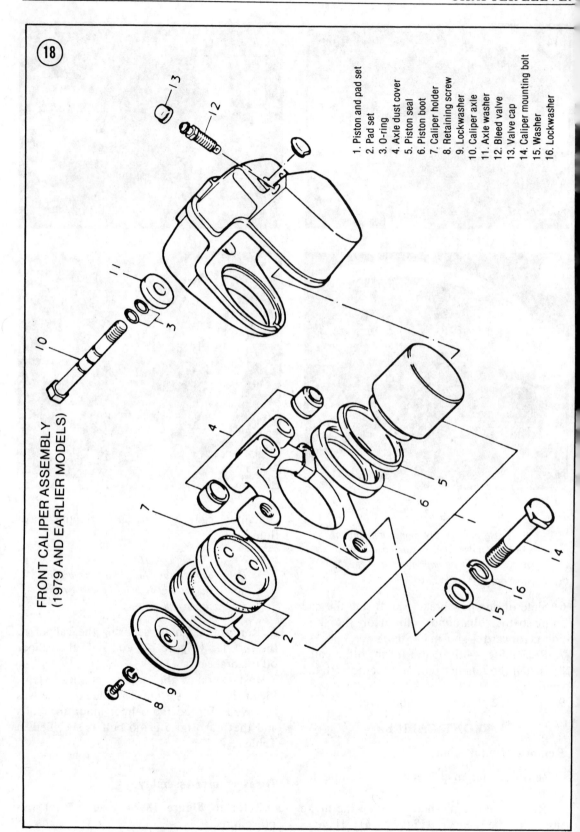

(18)

FRONT CALIPER ASSEMBLY
(1979 AND EARLIER MODELS)

1. Piston and pad set
2. Pad set
3. O-ring
4. Axle dust cover
5. Piston seal
6. Piston boot
7. Caliper holder
8. Retaining screw
9. Lockwasher
10. Caliper axle
11. Axle washer
12. Bleed valve
13. Valve cap
14. Caliper mounting bolt
15. Washer
16. Lockwasher

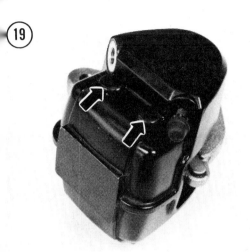

NOTE
The calipers used on 1979 and earlier models differ from those used on TSCC models, however, disassembly/assembly techniques for both style calipers are nearly identical.

1. Remove the brake pads as outlined under *Brake Pad Replacement.*

2. On TSCC models, remove the caliper axles and separate the caliper body from the caliper holder.

3. On 1979 and earlier models, perform the following:

    a. Remove the plugs covering the caliper bolts (**Figure 19**).

    b. Remove the bolts securing the caliper body (**Figure 20**).

    c. Remove the caliper holder and separate the caliper halves.

4. Remove the rubber boot from the piston (**Figure 21**).

5. Carefully remove the caliper piston (**Figure 22**). Inject compressed air, if available, into the fluid inlet to help force out the piston.

6. Remove the large O-ring from the piston

and the seal from the piston bore (**Figure 23**).

7. Perform *Inspection*.

> *CAUTION*
> *Do not clean brake components in any substance other than clean brake fluid.*

8. Assembly is the reverse of these steps. Keep the following points in mind:

   a. Lubricate the new seals and O-rings, as well as the piston and caliper bore, with clean, fresh brake fluid.

   b. Install a new seal in the groove in the caliper body as shown in **Figure 23**.

   c. Carefully install the piston in the caliper body.

   d. Install the dust cover over the piston. Make sure the dust cover fits over the shoulder on the caliper and engages the groove in the piston. Wipe off all excess brake fluid that may attract dust.

   e. Lubricate and install new dust boots on the caliper axle bolts or the caliper holder (**Figure 24**). Torque the caliper axle bolts as specified in **Table 1**. Install the plugs over the caliper bolts (**Figure 25**) on models so equipped.

   f. Install brake pads as outlined under *Brake Pad Replacement*.

Inspection

1. Clean all brake components in clean, fresh brake fluid.

2. Use a bore gauge and measure the caliper bore as shown in **Figure 26**. Refer to **Table 2** for specifications. If the piston bore exceeds the specified diameter, the entire caliper assembly must be replaced.

3. Measure the caliper piston diameter with a micrometer as shown in **Figure 27**. Replace the piston if it is worn beyond the specified limits (**Table 2**).

REAR CALIPER

Removal/Installation

1. Remove the banjo bolt securing the brake hose to the caliper (**Figure 28**).

2. Remove the cotter pin securing the torque link nut (**Figure 29**). Remove the bolt and nut securing the torque link to the caliper and disconnect the end of the torque link.

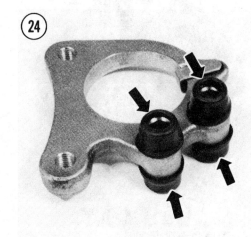

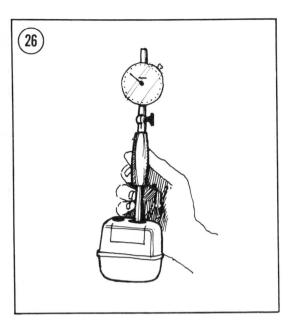

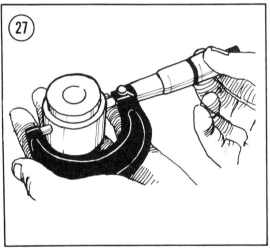

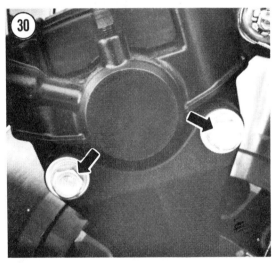

11

3. Remove the bolts securing the caliper to the mounting bracket (**Figure 30**) and carefully lift off the caliper.

4. Installation is the reverse of these steps. Torque the banjo bolt and caliper mounting bolts as specified in **Table 1**. Bleed the brake system as outlined in this chapter.

Disassembly/Assembly

Refer to **Figure 31** for this procedure.

1. Remove the brake pads as outlined under *Brake Pad Replacement.*

2. Remove the Allen bolts securing the caliper halves together and carefully separate the caliper body.

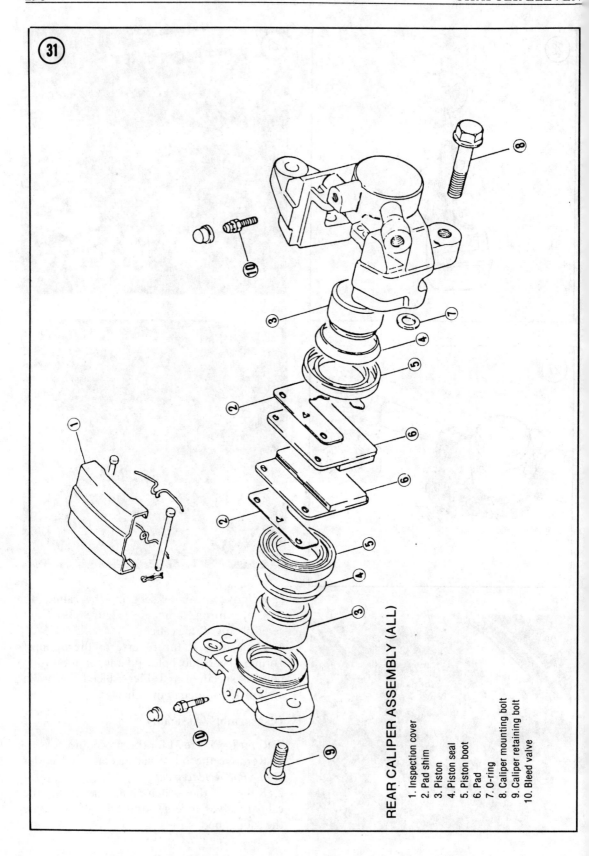

REAR CALIPER ASSEMBLY (ALL)

1. Inspection cover
2. Pad shim
3. Piston
4. Piston seal
5. Piston boot
6. Pad
7. O-ring
8. Caliper mounting bolt
9. Caliper retaining bolt
10. Bleed valve

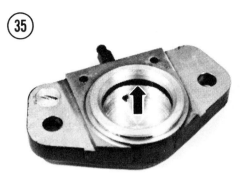

CAUTION
Do not clean brake components in any substance other than clean brake fluid.

7. Assembly is the reverse of these steps. Keep the following points in mind:

    a. Lubricate the new seals and O-rings, as well as both pistons and caliper bores with clean, fresh brake fluid.

    b. Install a new seal in the groove in each half of the caliper body as shown in **Figure 35**.

    c. Carefully install the pistons in each half of the caliper body.

    d. Install the rubber boots over each piston. Make sure the boots fit over the shoulder on the caliper and engage the groove in each piston (**Figure 36**). Wipe off any excess brake fluid that may attract dust.

    e. Install new O-rings in the inner caliper half as shown in **Figure 37**. Make sure the O-rings are not lost or misaligned as the caliper halves are assembled.

3. Remove the rubber boot from each piston (**Figure 32**).

4. Inject compressed air, if available, into the fluid inlet to help force out each piston. Remove the piston seal from each piston (**Figure 33**).

5. Carefully remove the seal from the bore in each half of the caliper body (**Figure 34**).

6. Perform *Inspection*.

f. Torque the caliper retaining bolts as specified in **Table 1**.

g. Install brake pads as outlined under *Brake Pad Replacement*.

Inspection

1. Clean all brake components in clean, fresh brake fluid.

2. Use a bore gauge and measure each caliper bore as shown in **Figure 38**. Refer to **Table 2** for specifications. If either piston bore exceeds the specified diameter, the complete caliper unit must be replaced.

3. Measure each caliper piston diameter with a micrometer as shown in **Figure 39**. Replace the entire caliper assembly if either piston is worn beyond the specified limits (**Table 2**).

MASTER CYLINDERS

A separate hydraulic master cylinder is used on the front and rear brake systems. Minor differences exist between some models, however, the disassembly and repair of all units is nearly identical.

The rear master cylinder on all 1977 models uses an integral fluid reservoir. All later models are fitted with a remote reservoir connected to the master cylinder by a hose. The repair procedures are the same for all units.

> *CAUTION*
> *While performing the following procedures, do not allow brake fluid to contact any painted surfaces or the paint will be damaged.*

Front Master Cylinder
Removal/Installation

1. Remove the cotter pin, bolt and nut securing the front brake lever and remove the lever.

2. Remove the banjo bolt securing the brake hose to the master cylinder (**Figure 40**). Have a few rags or a container ready to catch any fluid drips.

3. Remove the bolts securing the master cylinder to the handlebar (**Figure 41**). Carefully remove the cylinder.

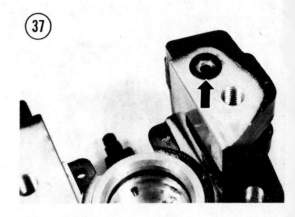

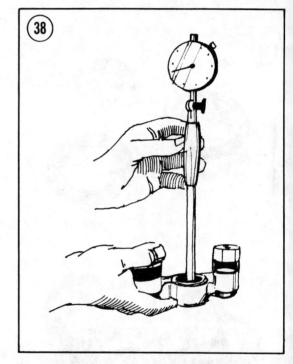

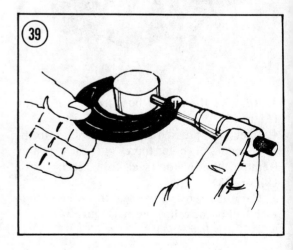

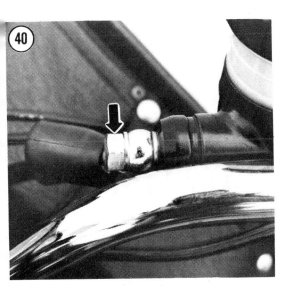

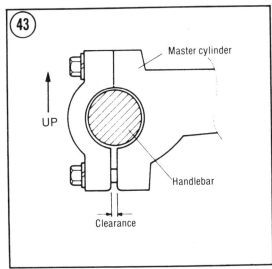

4. Installation is the reverse of these steps. Keep the following points in mind:

   a. Install the brake lever on the cylinder before installing the cylinder on the handlebar.

   b. Make sure at least 2 mm (3/16 in.) clearance is maintained between the master cylinder and the handlebar switch assembly (**Figure 42**).

   c. On TSCC models, tighten the upper clamp bolt first as shown in **Figure 43**.

   d. Torque the mounting bolts and banjo bolt as specified in **Table 1**.

   e. Bleed the brake system as outlined in this chapter.

**Rear Master Cylinder
Removal/Installation**

1. Remove the cotter pin and clevis pin securing the brake pedal linkage to the master cylinder (**Figure 44**).

2. Remove the banjo bolt securing the brake hose to the master cylinder (**Figure 45**). Have a few rags or a container ready to catch any fluid drips.

3. On all 1978 and later models, remove the bolt securing the reservoir to the frame (**Figure 46**).

4. Remove the bolts securing the master cylinder to the frame (**Figure 47**) and remove the cylinder.

5. Installation is the reverse of these steps. Keep the following points in mind:

11

a. Torque the mounting bolts and banjo bolt as specified in **Table 1**.

b. Secure the linkage clevis pin with a new cotter pin.

c. Bleed the brake system as outlined in this chapter.

Disassembly/Assembly
(Front and Rear Master Cylinders)

Refer to **Figure 48** or **Figure 49** for this procedure.

1. Drain the old brake fluid into a container. Use snap ring pliers with an angled tip and remove the snap ring securing the piston and cup set (**Figure 50**).

2. Carefully withdraw the piston and cup set from the cylinder bore.

3. On models so equipped, if reservoir removal is desired, remove the screws securing the reservoir plate (**Figure 51**).

4. Perform *Inspection*.

> *CAUTION*
> *Do not clean brake components in any substance other than clean brake fluid.*

5. Assembly is the reverse of these steps. Keep the following points in mind:

a. Lubricate the new piston and cup assembly, as well as the cylinder bore, with clean, fresh brake fluid.

b. Carefully install the new piston and cup assembly and secure it with the snap ring. Make sure the snap ring is fully seated in the cylinder bore groove.

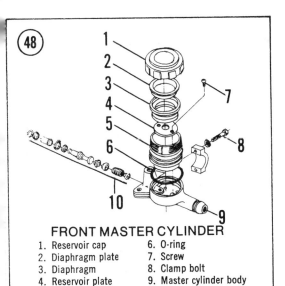

FRONT MASTER CYLINDER

1. Reservoir cap
2. Diaphragm plate
3. Diaphragm
4. Reservoir plate
5. Reservoir
6. O-ring
7. Screw
8. Clamp bolt
9. Master cylinder body
10. Piston and cup set

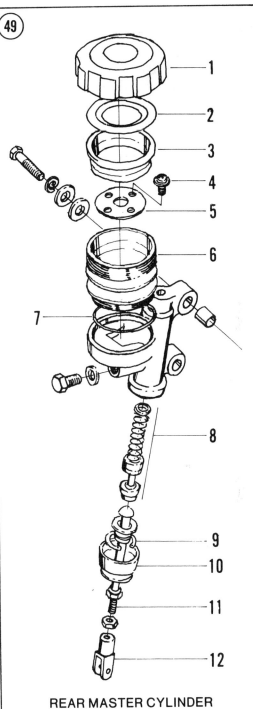

REAR MASTER CYLINDER

1. Reservoir cap
2. Diaphragm plate
3. Diaphragm
4. Screw
5. Reservoir plate
6. Reservoir
7. O-ring
8. Piston and cup set
9. Circlip
10. Boot
11. Pushrod
12. Clevis

11

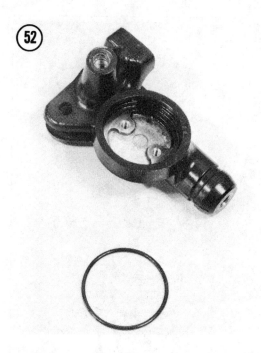

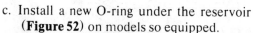

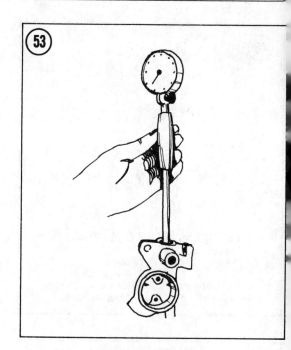

c. Install a new O-ring under the reservoir (**Figure 52**) on models so equipped.

Inspection

1. Clean all brake components in clean, fresh brake fluid.
2. Use a bore gauge and measure the cylinder bore as shown in **Figure 53**. Refer to **Table 2** for specifications. If the cylinder bore exceeds the specified diameter, the complete master cylinder assembly must be replaced.
3. Carefully inspect the cylinder bore for signs of scuffing or scoring. Replace the master cylinder if the bore is less than perfect.

BRAKE PEDAL ADJUSTMENT

> *CAUTION*
> *The brake pedal free play must be properly adjusted or the rear brake pads may drag, causing excessive friction and wear.*

1. Loosen the locknut on the rear master cylinder pushrod (**Figure 54**).
2. Loosen the locknut securing the pedal stopbolt (**Figure 55**).
3. On 1979 and earlier models, perform the following:
   a. Carefully adjust the master cylinder pushrod until the top of the brake pedal

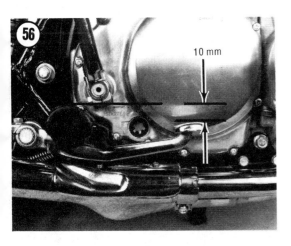

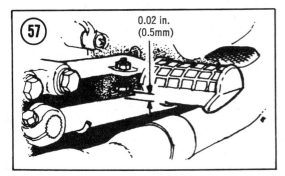

is 10 mm (3/8 in.) below the top of the footrest as shown in **Figure 56**.

b. Adjust the pedal stopbolt until there is 0.5 mm (0.02 in.) of free play between the stopbolt and the tab on the frame (**Figure 57**).

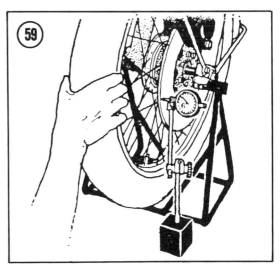

c. Secure the pushrod and stopbolt with the locknuts. Recheck the pedal and stopbolt free play and readjust if necessary.

4. On TSCC models perform the following:

a. Carefully adjust the master cylinder pushrod until the top of the brake pedal is 20 mm (3/4 in.) below the top of the footrest.

b. Adjust the pedal stopbolt until there is no clearance between the stopbolt and the tab on the frame.

c. Secure the pushrod and stopbolt with the locknuts. Recheck the pedal and stopbolt free play and readjust if necessary.

BRAKE DISC

The brake discs should be routinely inspected for scoring, abrasion and runout. Replace any disc that is scored or grooved deep enough to snag a fingernail.

Runout Inspection

NOTE
This inspection procedure can be performed with the wheels still installed on the motorcycle.

1. Raise the wheel being checked and position a dial indicator against the surface of the disc as shown in **Figure 58** or **Figure 59**.

2. Slowly rotate the wheel and check the runout on the dial indicator. If the runout

11

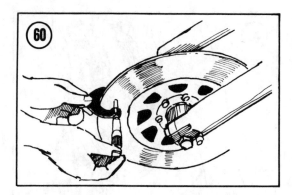

exceeds the limit specified in **Table 3**, the disc is warped and must be replaced.

3. Measure the thickness of the disc in several places (at least 8) with a micrometer (**Figure 60**). If the disc thickness is not as specified in **Table 3**, the disc must be replaced.

Removal/Installation

1. Refer to Chapter Nine or Chapter Ten to remove the front or rear wheel.
2. Straighten the locking tabs on the disc bolts (**Figure 61**).
3. Remove the bolts and remove the disc.
4. Installation is the reverse of these steps. Torque the disc bolts as specified in **Table 1**. Secure all the disc bolts with the locking tabs.

BLEEDING AND CHANGING
BRAKE FLUID

Bleeding

The hydraulic brake systems must be bled to remove all air and contamination. Bleeding the system is necessary any time a line or hose is disconnected, a cylinder or caliper is removed and disassembled, or when the brake "feel" in the lever or pedal is spongy, indicating the presence of air in the system.

1. Fill the master cylinder reservoir with fresh brake fluid to the upper line. Install the reservoir cap.

> *WARNING*
> *When adding brake fluid to either master cylinder reservoir, only use brake fluid marked DOT 3 or DOT 4. All GS750 models use a glycol-based brake fluid. Mixing a glycol-based fluid with any other type of fluid, whether petrolelum-based or*

> *silicon-based, may cause brake component damage leading to brake failure.*

2. Refer to **Figure 62** for the location of the front bleeder valves and **Figure 63** for the rear bleeder valves. Remove the dust cap from each bleeder valve and connect approximately a 2-foot length of clear plastic tubing to the valve as shown in **Figure 64**. Place the other end of the tubing in an empty can.

3. Pump the brake lever or pedal several times until resistance is felt. Hold the lever or pedal and open the bleeder valve about 1/4 turn. Continue to squeeze the lever or pedal until it reaches the limit of travel. Hold it in this position and close the bleeder valve.

4. Release the pedal or lever and repeat the previous step as many times as necessary until the fluid passing through the tubing is clean and free of air bubbles.

NOTE
Do not allow the reservoir to empty during the bleeding process or more air will be drawn into the system. Always keep the reservoir topped up.

5. When the brake fluid is clean and free of air, tighten the bleeder valve and remove the tubing. Replace the dust cap on the valve.

6. Top up the reservoir to the upper limit line. Hold the pedal or lever down and check all the brake line connections for leaks. Correct any leaks immediately.

Changing Fluid

Each time the reservoir cap is removed a small amount of contamination and moisture enters the reservoir. The same thing occurs if there is a leak or any part of the system is loosened or disconnected. Dirt can clog the system and moisture can lead to corrosion of internal brake components.

To keep the brake system as clean and free of contamination as possible, completely change the brake fluid at least every 2 years.

To change the fluid, perform *Bleeding* and continue adding new fluid until the fluid bled out is visibly clean and without air bubbles.

11

Table 1   BRAKE COMPONENT TORQUE SPECIFICATIONS

Item	mkg	ft.-lb.
Rear brake caliper mounting bolts		
1979 and earlier models	2.0-3.0	15-22
TSCC models	2.5-4.0	18-29
Front brake caliper mounting bolts		
All models	2.5-4.0	18-29
Front caliper axle bolts		
1979 and earlier models	2.5-3.5	18-26
TSCC models	1.5-2.0	11-15
Brake disc bolts	1.5-2.5	11-18
Brake hose union bolts	2.0-2.5	15-18
Front master cylinder clamp bolts		
1979 and earlier models	0.6-1.0	5-7
TSCC models	0.5-0.8	4-6
Rear master cylinder mounting bolts	1.5-2.5	11-18
Caliper bleeder valves	0.7-0.9	5-7

Table 2   HYDRAULIC BRAKE COMPONENT SPECIFICATIONS

	Standard	Service Limit
Front master cylinder bore diameter		
Single disc models	14.00 mm (0.551 in.)	14.05 mm (0.553 in.)
Double disc models	15.870-15.913 mm (0.6248-0.6265 in.)	15.925 mm (0.6270 in.)
Front master cylinder piston diameter		
Single disc models	13.96 mm (0.550 in.)	13.94 mm (0.549 in.)
Double disc models	15.811-15.838 mm (0.6225-0.6235 in.)	15.799 mm (0.6220 in.)
Rear master cylinder bore diameter (all models)	14.000-14.043 mm (0.5512-0.5529 in.)	14.05 mm (0.553 in.)
Rear master cylinder piston diameter (all models)	13.957-13.984 mm (0.5496-0.5506 in.)	13.94 mm (0.549 in.)
Front caliper bore diameter (1977-1979 models)		
Single disc models	42.85 mm (1.687 in.)	42.89 mm (1.689 in.)
Double Disc models	38.180-38.219 mm (1.5031-1.5047 in.)	38.230 mm (1.5051 in.)
Front caliper piston diameter 1977-1979 models		
Single Disc	42.82 mm (1.686 in.)	42.77 mm (1.684 in.)
Double Disc models	38.116-38.148 mm (1.5006-1.50019 in.)	38.105 mm 1.5002 in.
Rear caliper bore diameter (1977 models)	38.15 mm (1.502 in.)	38.19 mm (1.504 in.)
Rear caliper bore diameter (1978 and 1979 models)	38.180-38.219 (1.5031-1.5047)	38.230 mm (1.5051 in.)
Front and rear caliper bore diameter (TSCC models)	38.180-38.256 mm (1.5031-1.5061 in.)	—
Rear caliper piston diameter (1977 models)	38.18 mm (1.503 in.)	38.13 mm (1.501 in.)
Rear caliper piston diameter (1978 and 1979 models)	38.116-38.148 mm (1.5006-1.5019 in.)	38.105 mm (1.5002 in.)
Front and rear caliper piston diameter (TSCC models)	38.098-38.148 mm (1.4999-1.5019 in.)	—

Table 3   BRAKE DISC SPECIFICATIONS

	Standard	Service limit
Disc runout	0.1 mm (0.004 in.)	0.3 mm (0.012 in.)
Front disc thickness		
GS750B,C,N	6.7 mm (0.264 in.)	6.0 mm (0.236 in.)
GS750EC,EN,LN	6.0 mm (0.236 in.)	5.5 mm (0.217 in.)
TSCC models	5.0 mm (0.197 in.)	4.5 mm (0.177 in.)
Rear disc thickness		
All models	6.7 mm (0.264 in.)	6.0 mm (0.236 in.)

SUPPLEMENT

1981 AND LATER SERVICE INFORMATION

> This supplement provides service information unique to 1981 and later models. All other service information remains unchanged.
>
> The chapter headings in this supplement correspond to those in the main portion of this book. If a chapter is not included in this supplement, there are no changes affecting 1981 and later models.

CHAPTER THREE

PERIODIC MAINTENANCE

Rear Brake Pedal Free Play Adjustment

Turn the adjustment nut (**Figure 1**) on the end of the brake rod until there is 20-30 mm (3/4-1 1/4 in.) of free play.

Free play is the distance the pedal travels from the at-rest position to the applied position when the pedal is lightly depressed.

Rotate the wheel and check for brake drag. Also operate the pedal several times to make sure it returns to the at-rest position immediately after release.

Front Fork Oil

Refer to **Table 1** for fork oil specifications for 1981 and later models.

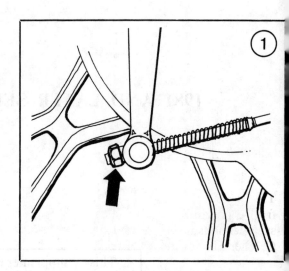

Table 1 CAPACITIES

Fuel tank	liters	U.S. gal.	Imp. gal.
LT, LX	15	4.0	3.3
TZ	16	4.2	3.5
ET, EX, EZ	19	5.0	4.2
Front fork oil	**cc**	**U.S. oz.**	**Imp. oz.**
ET, LT, LX	237	8.0	8.3
EX	191	6.5	6.7
TZ	209	7.1	7.4
EZ	214	7.2	7.5
Fork oil level*	**mm**		**in.**
ET, LT, LX	229		9.0
EX	227		8.9
EZ	201		7.9
TZ	180		7.1

* Remove spring and measure oil level from top of fork leg with fork leg held vertically and fully compressed.

CHAPTER FIVE

TSCC ENGINES

Perform the following additional procedures for 1981 and later models. All other disassembly and repair procedures are the same as for earlier models. Refer to **Tables 2-5** for engine specifications that differ from previous years. For all engine specifications not listed in **Tables 2-5** refer to Chapter Five of the main book.

ENGINE

**Engine Installation and
External Assembly**

On all 1982 and later models, torque the engine sprocket nut as specified in **Table 2**.

CAMSHAFTS

Installation

*NOTE
Replacement camshafts for 1982
models from Suzuki are supplied with 3*

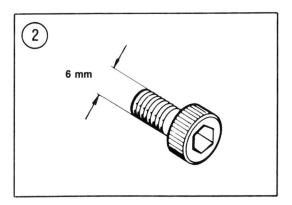

different sized shims to adjust the end play of the camshaft in the cylinder head. Proper installation of these camshaft shims can help eliminate camshaft knocking noises at low engine speeds. These replacement camshafts and shims can be installed in earlier machines; however, the shims cannot be used with original equipment camshafts.

1. Carefully lay the camshaft in the cylinder head bearings and shift the camshaft as far as possible to one side.
2. Use a feeler gauge and measure the clearance between the shoulder on the camshaft and the inside edge of the bearing journal in the cylinder head.
3. Install each one of the supplied shims in turn, on the right-hand side of the engine, until a clearance of 0.05-0.20 mm (0.002-0.008 in.) is achieved. Ensure that the loop of the shim is installed under the camshaft and each end is secured under a camshaft bearing bolt.

Inspection

1. Remove and replace the camshaft sprockets as outlined in Chapter Five.

*NOTE
Three types of fasteners are used to secure the sprockets to the camshafts on TSCC engines. Most earlier engines use 6 mm Allen bolts (**Figure 2**) or 6 mm hex head bolts with a folding*

12

*locking washer (**Figure 3**). On most later engines and replacement part camshafts, the camshaft sprockets are secured with 7 mm hex head flange bolts.*

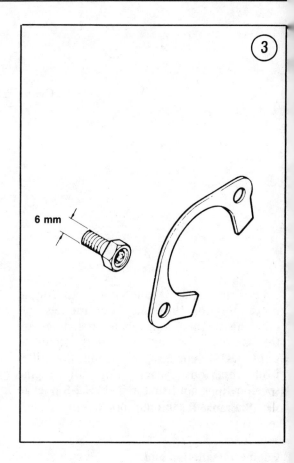

2. Apply a couple of drops of blue Loctite (Lock N' Seal No. 2114) to the bolts before installation.

3. On camshafts with 6 mm hex head bolts, always use new folding locking washers.

4. Torque the camshaft mounting bolts as follows:

    a. 6 mm Allen bolts–0.8-1.2 mkg (6.0-8.5 ft.-lb.).

    b. 6 mm hex head bolts with folding locking washer–1.5-2.0 mkg (11.0-14.5 ft.-lb.).

    c. 7 mm hex head flange bolts–2.4-2.6 mkg (17.5-19.0 ft.-lb.).

5. Fold the locking washer against the bolt head on models so equipped.

Crankshaft and Connecting Rod Inspection

NOTE
On GS750 engines No. 152574 and subsequent, a thrust bearing is installed in the crankcase to control the lateral thrust of the crankshaft. This change also affects earlier models if the crankcases are changed, as only new style crankcases with the thrust bearings are stocked as replacement parts by Suzuki.

1. Refer to Chapter Five and perform Steps 1 through 5 of *Crankshaft and Connecting Rod Inspection*. If the clearance exceeds the specified tolerance, measure the width of No. 2 crankshaft main journal and No. 2 crankcase main journal as described in Step 5 and write down the information for future reference. Do not be concerned if the measured dimensions exceed the specifications of Table 8 in Chapter Five. After obtaining the crankshaft and crankcase bearing width dimensions, perform the following steps to determine the correct thrust bearing.

    a. Remove the existing thrust bearing. Note the color code (if any) on the outside edge of the existing bearing. In most cases replacing the stock thrust bearing will correct the excessive end play.

    b. If the stock thrust bearing is incorrect or if the crankshaft and/or crankcases have been replaced, the correct size thrust bearing will have to be computed as described in the following steps.

2. Subtract the width of the crankcase main bearing journal from the width of the crankshaft main bearing journal to obtain the size of the bearing space. Refer to **Table 3** to select the correct thrust bearing for the bearing space.

    a. For example, suppose the width of the crankshaft No. 2 main bearing is 24.00 mm and the width of the crankcase No. 2 main bearing is 21.00 mm.

    b. Subtract 21.00 mm from 24.00 mm; the result is 3.00 mm bearing space.

c. The correct thrust bearing for this example, as specified in **Table 3**, is color-coded black.

3. Install the new thrust bearing into the locating groove in the crankcase. Ensure that the oil groove on the bearing surface faces the alternator side of the engine.

4. Recheck the bearing clearance. Apply a thin film of molybdenum disulfide lubricant (such as Bel-Ray Moly Lube) to the thrust bearing to protect the bearing surface during initial engine start-up.

5. Perform Step 6 of *Crankshaft and Connecting Rod Inspection* in Chapter Five of the main book.

Connecting Rod Bearing Insert Selection and Installation

1. Perform Steps 1 through 6 of *Connecting Rod Bearing Insert Selection and Installation* in Chapter Five of the main book.

2. If any crank pin measurements taken during inspection do not fall within the tolerance range for the stamped number code, the serviceability of the crankshaft must be carefully examined. If the crank pin journal in question is not tapered, out-of-round or scored, the crankshaft may still be used; however, the bearing selection will have to be made based on the measured diameter of the crank pin journal and not by the stamped number code. If the crank pin journal is damaged, it may be possible to avoid the expense of a new crankshaft by having the damaged journal ground undersize by a machine shop. Undersize connecting rod bearing inserts are available in 0.25 mm and 0.50 mm sizes as specified in **Table 4**.

NOTE
All engines No. 153402 and earlier are equipped with early style connecting rod bearing inserts manufactured from an aluminum-based alloy. All later model engines, No. 153403 and subsequent, are fitted with improved connecting rod bearing inserts manufactured from a copper-based alloy. The later style components can be distinguished by the light silver-colored back on the bearing inserts. On older models, if any new bearings are to be installed, it is recommended that all connecting rod bearings be replaced with the new style inserts.

CAUTION
Never use both style bearing inserts on the same connecting rod or engine damage may result.

3. Refer to Chapter Five of the main book and perform Steps 8 and 9 of *Connecting Rod Bearing Insert Selection and Installation*.

Crankshaft Main Bearing Insert Selection and Installation

1. Perform Steps 1 through 6 of *Crankshaft Main Bearing Insert Selection and Installation* in Chapter Five.

2. If any main bearing journal measurements taken during inspection do not fall within the tolerance range for the stamped letter codes, the serviceability of the crankshaft must be carefully examined. If the main bearing journal in question is not tapered, out-of-round or scored, the crankshaft may still be used; however, the bearing selection will have to be made based on the measured diameter of the bearing journal and not by the stamped letter code. If the bearing journal is damaged, it may be possible to avoid the expense of a new crankshaft by having the damaged journal ground undersize by a machine shop. Undersize main bearing inserts are available in 0.25 mm and 0.50 mm sizes as specified in **Table 5**.

NOTE
*On engines No. 142943 and earlier, grooved main bearing inserts are installed in both upper and lower positions (**Figure 4**). On engines No. 142944 and subsequent, the upper main bearing inserts are plain with no oil groove or oil holes (**Figure 5**); the lower inserts are unchanged. On 1982 and*

12

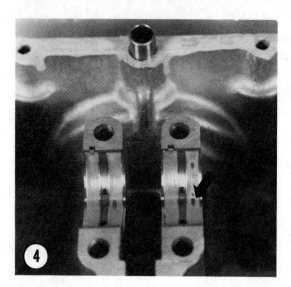

later models, to improve oil flow, grooved bearing inserts are installed in the two center main bearing journals of the upper crankcase half. When replacing main bearing inserts for all models, use **non-grooved** bearing inserts in all upper positions, except the two center bearings. Use **grooved** bearing inserts in the two center upper positions as well as all lower bearing journals.

CAUTION
Do not use a non-grooved bearing insert in the lower bearing position or the oil flow to the bearing journal will be blocked, resulting in crankshaft bearing journal damage.

3. Refer to Chapter Five of the main book and perform Steps 8 and 9 of *Crankshaft Main Bearing Insert Selection and Installation.*

Table 2 TORQUE SPECIFICATIONS

Item	mkg	ft.-lb.
Engine sprocket nut (1982)	10.5-15.0	72.5-108.5
Camshaft sprocket bolts		
6 mm Allen bolt	0.8-1.2	6.0-8.5
6 mm hex head bolt	1.5-2.0	11.0-14.5
7 mm hex head flange bolt	2.4-2.6	17.5-19.0
Anti-dive modulator valve		
Allen mounting bolts	0.6-0.9	
		4.5-6.5
Anti-dive hose banjo bolt	2.0-2.5	14.0-18.0
Anti-dive bleeder valve	0.6-0.9	4.5-6.5

Table 3 CRANKSHAFT THRUST BEARING SPECIFICATIONS

Bearing space* (mm)	Part No.	Color Code	Thickness (mm)
3.05-3.10	12228-45401	no color	2.95-2.98
3.01-3.05	12228-45402	green	2.91-2.95
2.97-3.01	12228-45403	black	2.87-2.91

Crankshaft thrust bearing clearance
  Standard
  Service limit
		0.08-0.24 mm (0.003-0.009 in.)
		0.50 mm (0.020 in.)	

* Bearing space is the width of the No. 2 crankshaft main bearing journal minus the width of the No. 2 crankcase journal.

Table 4 CONNECTING ROD BEARING SELECTION

	Crank pin code and diameter		
	Number 1 33.992-34.000 mm (1.3383-1.3386 in.)	Number 2 33.984-33.992 mm (1.3380-1.3383 in.)	Number 3 33.976-33.984 mm (1.3376-1.3380 in.)

Connecting rod code and diameter
  Number 1
  37.000-37.008 mm
  (1.4567-1.4570 in.)
	Green	Black	Brown

Number 2
  37.008-37.016 mm
  (1.4570-1.4573 in.)
	Black	Brown	Yellow

Bearing color code	Suzuki part No.	Bearing thickness
Green	12164-45510-010	1.484-1.488 mm (0.0584-0.0586 in.)
Black	12164-45510-020	1.488-1.492 mm (0.0586-0.0587 in.)
Brown	12164-45510-030	1.492-1.496 mm (0.0587-0.0589 in.)
Yellow	12164-45510-040	1.496-1.500 mm (0.0589-0.0591 in.)
None	12164-45510-025	undersized 0.25 mm
None	12164-45510-050	undersized 0.50 mm

12

Table 5 CRANKSHAFT MAIN BEARING SELECTION

	Crankshaft main bearing journal code and diameter		
	Letter A 35.992-36.000 mm (1.4170-1.4173 in.)	Letter B 35.984-35.992 mm (1.4167-1.4170 in.)	Letter C 35.976-35.984 mm (1.4164-1.4167 in.)
Crankcase journal **code and diameter**			
Letter A 39.000-39.008 mm (1.5354-1.5357 in.)	Green	Black	Brown
Letter B 39.008-39.016 mm (1.5357-1.5361 in.)	Black	Brown	Yellow

Bearing color code (non-grooved)	Suzuki part No.	Bearing thickness
Green	12229-45410-010	1.486-1.490 mm (0.0585-0.0587 in.)
Black	12229-45410-020	1.490-1.494 mm (0.0587-0.0588 in.)
Brown	12229-45410-030	1.494-1.498 mm (0.0588-0.0590 in.)
Yellow	12229-45410-040	1.498-1.502 mm (0.0590-0.0591 in.)
None	12229-45410-025	undersized 0.25 mm
None	12229-45410-050	undersized 0.50 mm

Bearing color code (grooved)	Suzuki part No.	Bearing thickness
Green	12229-45400-010	1.486-1.490 mm (0.0585-0.0587 in.)
Black	12229-45400-020	1.490-1.494 mm (0.0587-0.0588 in.)
Brown	12229-45400-030	1.494-1.498 mm (0.0588-0.0590 in.)
Yellow	12229-45400-040	1.498-1.502 mm (0.0590-0.0591 in.)
None	12229-45400-025	undersized 0.25 mm
None	12229-45400-050	undersized 0.50 mm

CHAPTER EIGHT

ELECTRICAL SYSTEMS

INSTRUMENTS (GS750EZ)

Instrument Cluster
Removal/Installation

1. Carefully remove the headlamp from the headlamp housing and remove the headlamp housing.
2. Disconnect the speedometer and tachometer cables from the instruments.
3. Remove the small rubber plugs covering the back cover screws and remove the screws securing the back cover (**Figure 6**). Carefully remove the back cover. If only indicator bulb replacement is desired, further disassembly is unnecessary.

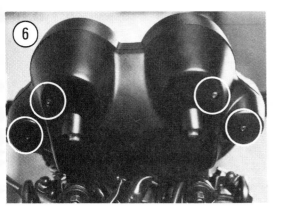

NOTE
*Refer to **Figure** 7 and perform continuity tests to isolate a defective indicator bulb or wiring fault.*

4. Disconnect the electrical connectors from the instrument cluster.
5. Remove the bolts securing the complete instrument cluster and carefully lift the cluster clear of the motorcycle (**Figure 8**).
6. Installation is the reverse of these steps.

Oil Temperature Gauge Unit Test

1. Remove the seat and disconnect the pink oil temperature gauge wire.
2. Turn on the ignition and ground the gauge side of the wire to the motorcycle frame. If 320° is indicated on the gauge, the gauge is operating properly.
3. If the gauge tests properly but the gauge malfunctions when the engine is running, replace the oil temperature gauge sending unit.
4. If the gauge unit is defective, remove the instrument cluster and replace the oil temperature gauge.

Oil Temperature Gauge Sending Unit
Removal/Installation

1. Remove the nuts securing the cover over the oil pressure/oil temperature sending units.
2. Remove the wire from the end of the temperature sending unit.
3. Carefully unscrew and remove the temperature sending unit.
4. Installation is the reverse of these steps. Keep the following points in mind:
   a. Apply a small amount of Bond No. 4 or equivalent to the threads on the sending unit before installing the unit.
   b. Tighten the oil temperature sending unit to 1.3-1.7 mkg (9.5-12.5 ft.-lb.).

12

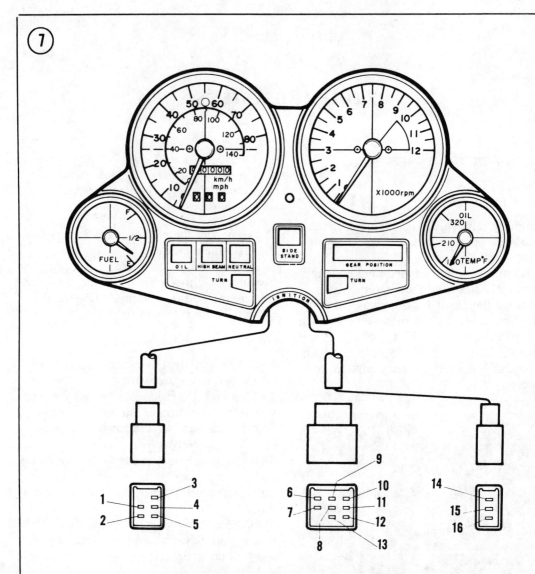

INSTRUMENT PANEL CONNECTORS (GS750EZ)

1. Brown/red–5th gear
2. Yellow/blue–4th gear
3. White/yellow–1st gear
4. Red/black–2nd gear
5. Green/blue–3rd gear
6. Blue–neutral
7. Green/white–side stand (-)
8. Green/yellow–oil pressure (-)

9. Black/white–ground
10. Yellow–high beam
11. Black–left turn (+)
12. Light green–right turn (+)
13. Gray–meter indicator lights
14. Orange–+ 12 volts
15. Yellow/black–fuel gauge
16. Pink–oil temperature gauge

Sidestand Switch Test/ Replacement/Adjustment

Refer to **Figure 9** for this procedure.
1. Pull back the rubber boot and disconnect the wires from the switch.
2. Connect an ohmmeter to the switch terminals. The ohmmeter should indicate continuity when the stand is down and no continuity when the stand is retracted.
3. If the ohmmeter indication is incorrect, loosen the locknuts securing the switch and adjust the position of the switch. If the switch will not operate after adjustment, it must be replaced.
4. Adjust the locknuts on the switch so that the sidestand indicator light on the instrument panel comes on when the

sidestand is in any position but fully retracted.

INSTRUMENTS (1982)

Fuel Gauge Accuracy Test

The fuel gauge on 1982 and later models is an electromagnetic oil damped unit. It differs from earlier type gauge systems in that the gauge will not return to "E" when the ignition switch is turned off.

To check the operation of the fuel gauge and sending unit, perform the *Fuel Gauge Test* as outlined in Chapter Eight of the main book. To check the accuracy of the gauge unit, perform the following procedure.
1. Disconnect the fuel gauge wires as outlined under *Fuel Gauge Test* in Chapter Eight of the main book.
2. Connect a 3 ohm resister between the black/white and yellow/black wires from the gauge unit (not the tank sending unit).
3. *Turn on the motorcycle ignition.* The gauge unit should indicate "F".
4. Turn off the ignition and connect a 110 ohm resistor between the gauge unit wires.
5. *Turn on the ignition.* The gauge unit should indicate "E."
6. If the gauge unit indications are not correct, replace the gauge unit.

CHAPTER NINE

FRONT SUSPENSION AND STEERING

12

FRONT FORKS (GS750TZ)

All internal components of the front forks on this model are the same as the fork assembly outlined in Chapter Nine of the main book. The fork assembly used on the GS750TZ is a straight fork leg.

Refer to **Figure 10A** for an exploded view drawing of this fork and to Chapter Nine for all service procedures.

ANTI-DIVE FRONT FORKS

Removal/Installation

1. On models equipped with anti-dive forks, remove the banjo bolt securing the brake hose to the anti-dive valve assembly (**Figure 10B**). Have a container ready to catch any dripping brake fluid.

CAUTION
Do not allow any brake fluid to drip on painted parts or the paint will be damaged.

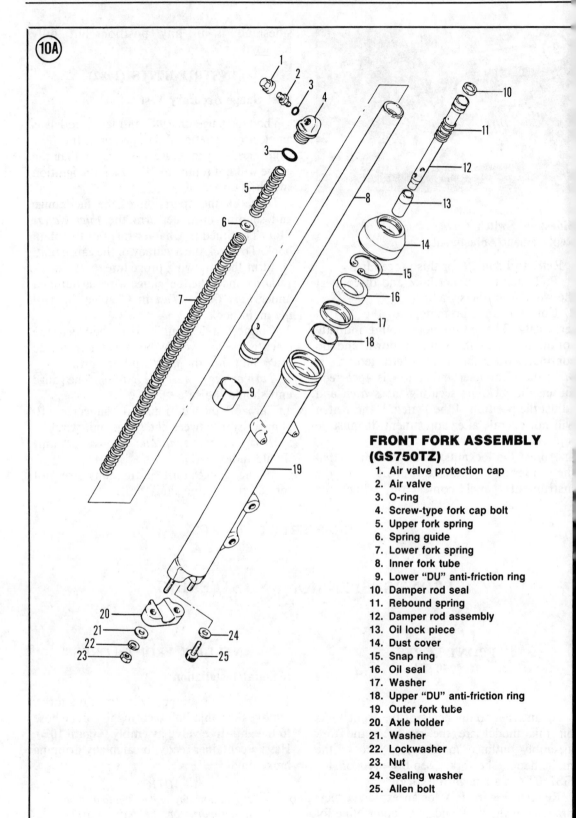

10A

FRONT FORK ASSEMBLY (GS750TZ)

1. Air valve protection cap
2. Air valve
3. O-ring
4. Screw-type fork cap bolt
5. Upper fork spring
6. Spring guide
7. Lower fork spring
8. Inner fork tube
9. Lower "DU" anti-friction ring
10. Damper rod seal
11. Rebound spring
12. Damper rod assembly
13. Oil lock piece
14. Dust cover
15. Snap ring
16. Oil seal
17. Washer
18. Upper "DU" anti-friction ring
19. Outer fork tube
20. Axle holder
21. Washer
22. Lockwasher
23. Nut
24. Sealing washer
25. Allen bolt

2. Complete removal and installation of the front forks as outlined in Chapter Nine of the main book. Bleed the brake system as outlined in the Chapter Eleven section of this supplement.

Disassembly/Assembly

Refer to **Figure 11** for this procedure.

Each fork inner tube contains 2 Teflon coated metal "DU" rings. These "DU" rings decrease the internal friction between the inner fork tube and the outer slider unit, allowing the forks to operate more smoothly. The Teflon surface of these "DU" rings is often damaged when the inner fork tubes are removed; therefore, Suzuki recommends replacing these rings each time the forks are disassembled.

> *NOTE*
> *Suzuki specifies that the anti-dive modulator valve assembly mounted on the front of each fork tube is a non-repairable item. Should the anti-dive mechanism fail to operate properly, the modulator valve must be replaced. Refer any suspected modulator valve failure to your local Suzuki dealer.*

Preparation should be made prior to starting the disassembly as an impact tool (air or electric) or a special holding tool is necessary to remove the Allen retaining bolt in the bottom of each fork leg. The Allen bolt is secured with a thread locking compound (such as Loctite) and is often difficult to remove because the damper rod will turn inside the fork tube. If an impact tool is not available, remove the Allen bolts with an Allen wrench and the special Suzuki holding tool Attachment "D" (Suzuki part No. 09940-34561). The special holding tool is used inside the fork tube to hold the damper rod. Attachment "D" can be used with the Suzuki handle (Suzuki part No. 09940-34520) or with one or two long 3/8 in. drive socket extensions equaling approximately 18 inches.

1. Remove the front forks as outlined in this supplement and Chapter Nine of the main book.

2. If removal if the anti-dive modulator assembly is desired, remove the Allen bolts and the assembly from the fork tube (**Figure 12**).

> *NOTE*
> *It is not necessary to remove the anti-dive modulator valve assembly to disassemble the forks.*

3. If an impact tool is to be used to remove the Allen retaining bolt in the bottom of the fork tube, leave the fork cap bolt and fork springs installed until the Allen bolt is removed. The interal spring pressure against the damper rod assembly helps hold it in place as the Allen bolt is removed. Fully extend the fork tubes and hold them extended against the rebound spring pressure while removing the Allen bolt with the impact tool (**Figure 13**).

4. Remove the fork cap bolt (**Figure 14**) from the inner tube.

5. Remove the short upper spring and the flat spring guide (**Figure 15**).

6. Remove the long fork spring (**Figure 16**). Have a few rags handy as the spring will be quite oily.

7. Tip up the fork tube and completely drain the remaining fork oil. Stroke the fork tube

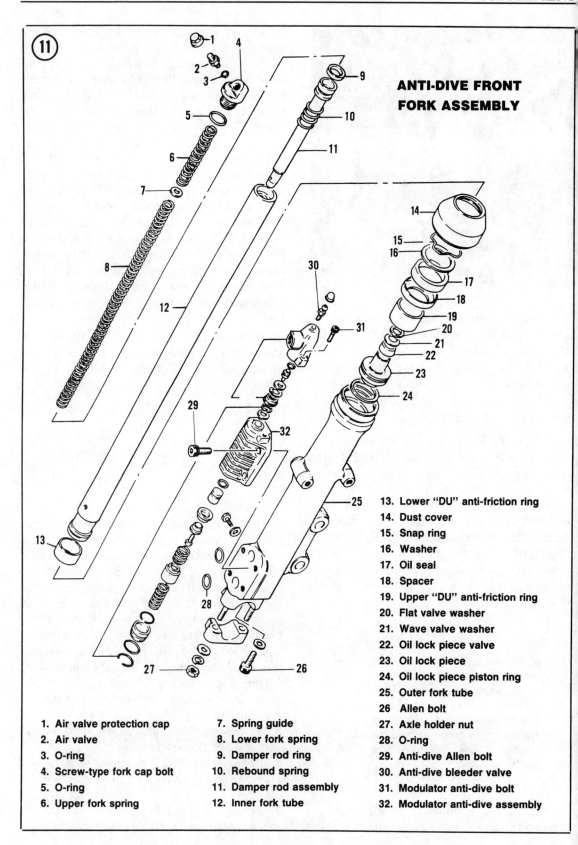

ANTI-DIVE FRONT FORK ASSEMBLY

1. Air valve protection cap
2. Air valve
3. O-ring
4. Screw-type fork cap bolt
5. O-ring
6. Upper fork spring
7. Spring guide
8. Lower fork spring
9. Damper rod ring
10. Rebound spring
11. Damper rod assembly
12. Inner fork tube
13. Lower "DU" anti-friction ring
14. Dust cover
15. Snap ring
16. Washer
17. Oil seal
18. Spacer
19. Upper "DU" anti-friction ring
20. Flat valve washer
21. Wave valve washer
22. Oil lock piece valve
23. Oil lock piece
24. Oil lock piece piston ring
25. Outer fork tube
26. Allen bolt
27. Axle holder nut
28. O-ring
29. Anti-dive Allen bolt
30. Anti-dive bleeder valve
31. Modulator anti-dive bolt
32. Modulator anti-dive assembly

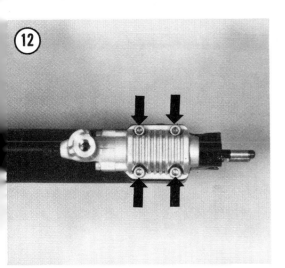

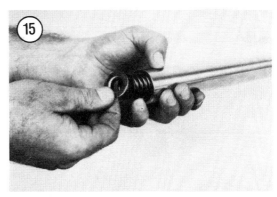

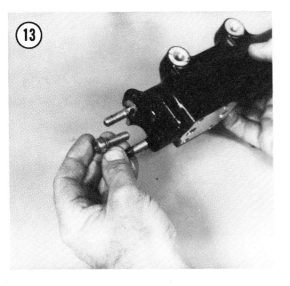

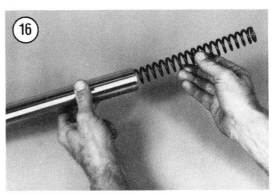

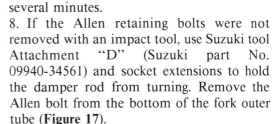

several times over a drain pan to pump out any remaining oil. Stand the fork tube in the drain pan and allow the tube to drain for several minutes.

8. If the Allen retaining bolts were not removed with an impact tool, use Suzuki tool Attachment "D" (Suzuki part No. 09940-34561) and socket extensions to hold the damper rod from turning. Remove the Allen bolt from the bottom of the fork outer tube (**Figure 17**).

9. Remove the outer dust cover to gain access to the snap ring securing the fork oil seal. Use snap ring pliers with strong tips and remove the snap ring (**Figure 18**).

NOTE
The seal in some machines is secured with a wire-type circlip. This circlip can usually be removed by prying up with a small screwdriver. Pad the edges of the outer fork tube with a rag to prevent any possible damage to the fork tube.

10. Pad the jaws of a vise with wooden blocks or soft aluminum plates. Place the fork

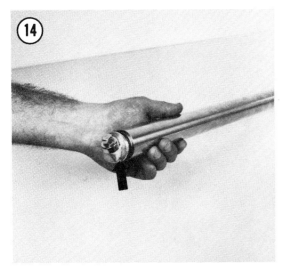

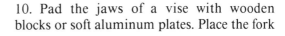

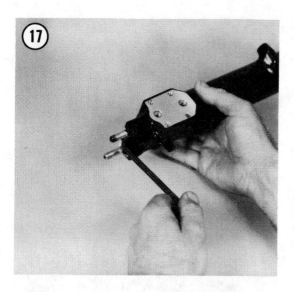

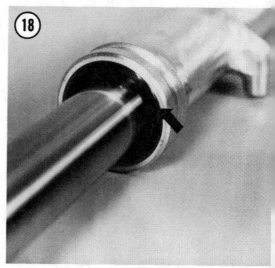

leg in the vise and clamp the vise securely on the brake caliper mounting lugs as shown in **Figure 19**.

11. Use several quick slide-hammer motions and remove the inner tube from the outer tube. The seal, seal washer and upper "DU" ring are removed with the inner tube (**Figure 20**).

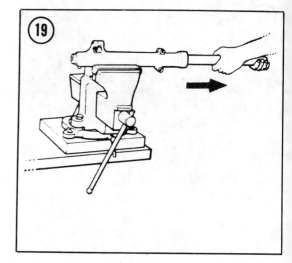

> *NOTE*
> *The oil lock piece, oil lock piece valve and valve washers may be loose in the bottom of the outer fork tube. Correct component arrangement is outlined during fork assembly.*

12. Remove the oil lock piece from the end of the damper rod (**Figure 21**).

13. Remove the oil lock piece valve (**Figure 22**). Note that the slight cone shape points toward the upper end of the fork tube.

14. Remove the wave and flat valve washers (**Figure 23**).

15. Tip up the inner tube and slide out the damper rod assembly complete with the rebound spring (**Figure 24**).

16. Use a screwdriver blade to carefully spread open and remove the "DU" ring from the end of the inner tube (**Figure 25**).

17. Perform *Inspection*.

18. Assembly is the reverse of these steps. Keep the following points in mind:

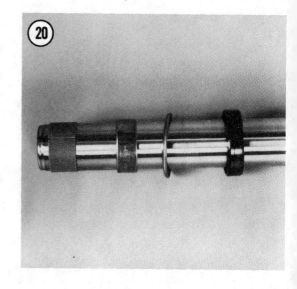

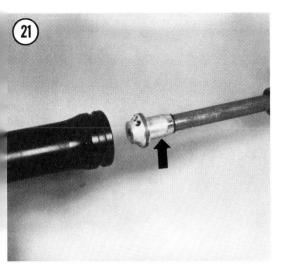

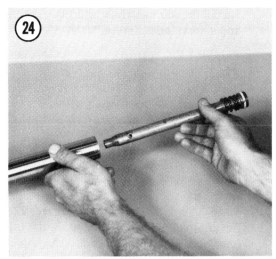

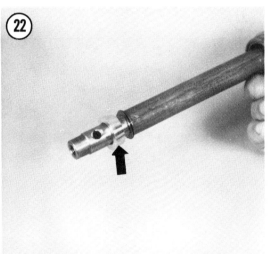

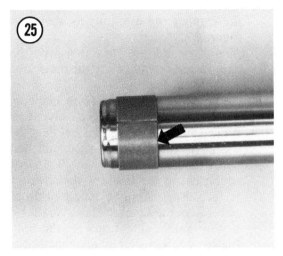

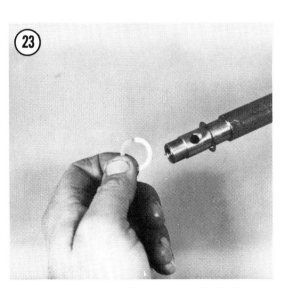

a. Ensure that all fork components are clean and dry. Wipe out the seal bore in the outer fork tube.

b. Carefully install a new "DU" ring on the end of the inner tube (**Figure 25**). Take care not to damage the Teflon surface of the "DU" ring.

c. Apply a light film of grease to the outer edge and lips of each new fork seal.

d. Slide the lower "DU" ring, seal washer and oil seal on the inner fork tube in the order shown in **Figure 20**.

e. Lightly oil the inner and outer tubes and damper rod assembly with clean fork oil before assembling the parts.

f. Make sure the rebound (top-out) spring is installed on the damper rod and

12

install the damper rod assembly into the inner fork tube (**Figure 24**).

> *NOTE*
> *Temporarily install the fork springs and the fork cap bolt. The tension of the fork springs will keep the damper rod extended through the end of the fork tube and ease the assembly process.*

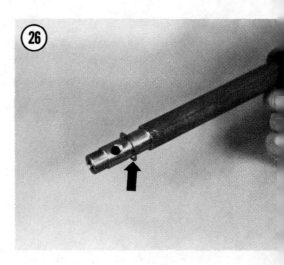

g. Install the flat valve washer on the end of the damper rod (**Figure 26**).

h. Install the wave washer and the oil lock piece valve as shown in **Figure 22**. Ensure that the "cone" shape on the oil lock piece valve points toward the upper end of the fork tube.

i. Slide the oil lock piece over the end of the damper rod assembly as shown in **Figure 27**.

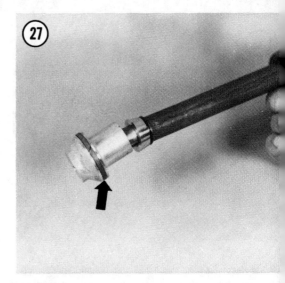

j. Carefully install the inner tube with the damper rod assembly into the outer tube as shown in **Figure 28**.

k. Clean the threads of the Allen retaining bolt thoroughly with clean solvent or spray contact cleaner. Ensure that the washer is fitted to the Allen bolt and apply Suzuki Bond No. 1215 or equivalent to the first few threads next to the washer. Apply a couple of drops of blue Loctite (Lock N' Seal No. 2114) to the remaining threads on the bolt. Install the bolt and tighten using the impact tool or Suzuki holding tool. Torque the bolt to 1.5-2.5 mkg (11-18 ft.-lb.).

l. Slide the upper "DU" ring, seal washer and seal into the outer fork tube. Use a piece of pipe over the inner tube or a seal installation tool and carefully tap the oil seal into place. Make sure that the seal is fully seated into the outer fork tube. Secure the seal with the snap ring (**Figure 18**). Ensure that the snap ring is locked into the groove in the fork tube. Install the dust cover over the top of the outer fork tube.

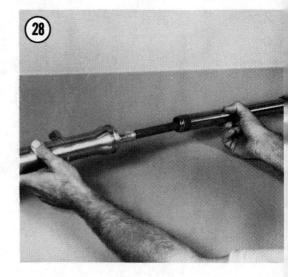

> *NOTE*
> *If Suzuki special tools are available, use the oil seal installation tool (part No. 09940-50111).*

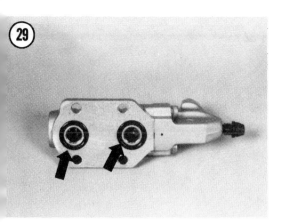

m. If the anti-dive modulator valve assembly was removed, carefully inspect the O-rings on the valve body (**Figure 29**). Replace the O-rings if less than perfect. Install the valve assembly on the outer fork tube and torque the bolts to 0.6-0.8 mkg (4.5-6.0 ft.-lb.).

19. Remove the fork cap bolt and fork springs. Refer to **Table 1** and add the specified amount and type of fork oil to each fork tube. Use a graduate or a baby bottle (**Figure 30**) to ensure the oil amount is correct for each fork tube.

20. The fork oil level can also be measured from the top of the fork tube. Use an accurate ruler or the Suzuki oil level gauge (part No. 09943-74110) to ensure the oil level is as specified in **Table 6**. The oil level must be measured with the forks completely compressed and without springs.

NOTE
*An oil level measuring device can be locally fabricated as shown in **Figure 31**. Fill the fork with a few cc more than the required amount of oil. Position the hose clamp on the top edge of the fork tube and draw out the excess oil. Oil is sucked out until the level reaches the small diameter hole. A precise oil level can be achieved with this simple device.*

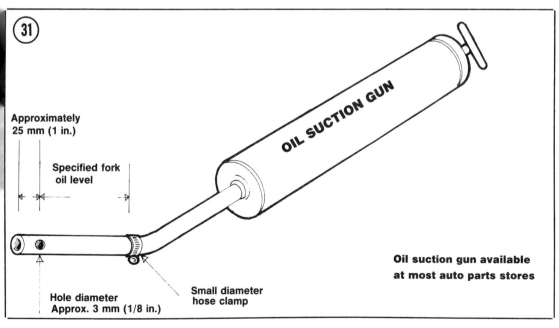

Approximately 25 mm (1 in.)

Specified fork oil level

Hole diameter Approx. 3 mm (1/8 in.)

Small diameter hose clamp

OIL SUCTION GUN

Oil suction gun available at most auto parts stores

12

21. Install the fork springs and spring guide. Make sure the closer coils on the long spring are pointed up.

22. Install the cap bolt finger-tight. The cap bolt can be tightened after the forks have been installed on the motorcycle.

Inspection

1. Thoroughly clean all parts in solvent and dry them completely. Lightly oil and assemble the inner and outer fork tubes, then slide the tubes together. Check for looseness, noise or binding. Replace any defective parts.

2. Carefully examine the area of the inner fork tube that passes through the fork seal. Any scratches or roughness on the tube in this area will damage the oil seal. If the inner fork tube is scratched or pitted, it should be replaced.

3. Inspect the damper rod assembly for damage or roughness. Check for signs of galling, deep scores or excessive wear. Replace the parts as necessary. Make sure all the oil passages are clean and free of any sludge or oil residue.

4. Carefully examine the oil lock piece valve and washers for signs of damage or wear (**Figure 32**).

5. Inspect the piston ring on the oil lock piece for damage or wear (**Figure 33**). Replace the piston ring if less than perfect.

6. Inspect the dust cover on each fork tube for holes or abrasive damage. A damaged cover will allow dirt and moisture to pack up next the fork seal. Packed-in dirt can scratch the surface of the fork tubes as well as damage the fork seal. Install new dust covers if any damage exists.

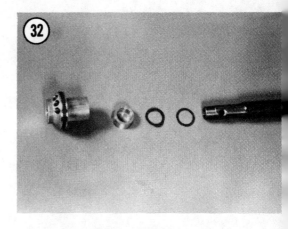

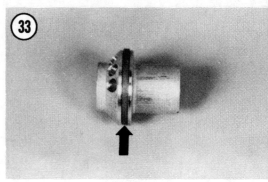

7. Accurately measure the fork springs. If any spring is shorter than the length specified in **Table 6**, replace the springs as a set.

STEERING HEAD (GS750TZ, GS750EZ)

The steering head assembly is the same as that outlined under *Steering Stem* in Chapter Nine of the main book. Refer to all portions of the procedure that relate to TSCC models and to **Figure 34**.

STEERING STEM
(GS750EZ, GS750TZ)

1. Bolt
2. Washer
3. Handlebar upper holder
4. Steering stem upper bracket
5. Rubber cushion
6. Headlight bracket
7. Front fork cover
8. Bolt
9. Washer
10. Nut
11. Lockwasher
12. Washer
13. Handlebar upper holder
14. Bolt
15. Nut
16. Lockwasher
17. Washer
18. Bolt
19. Steering stem nut
20. Dust cover
21. Upper bearing
22. Lower bearing
23. Shim
24. Steering stem

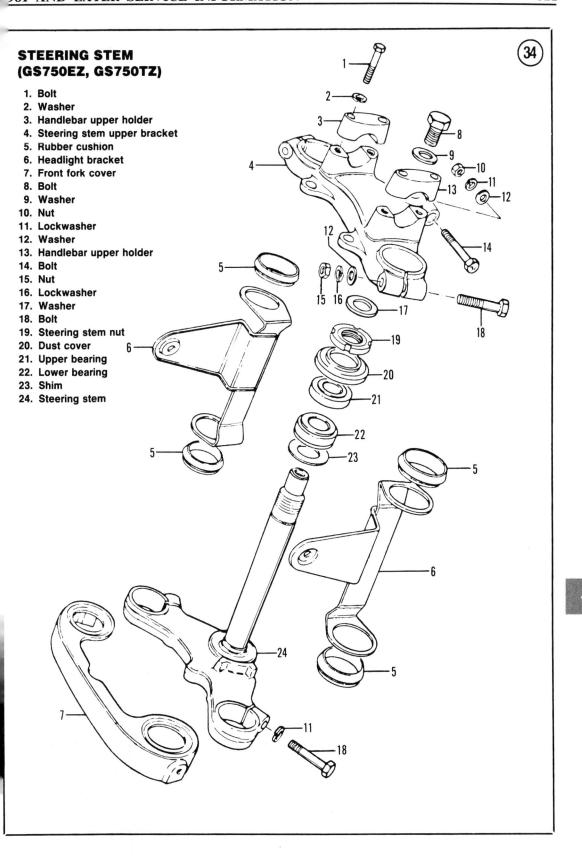

34

12

Table 6 FRONT FORK SPECIFICATIONS

Fork oil capacity[1]	cc	U.S. oz.	Imp. oz.
ET, LT, LX	237	8.0	8.3
EX	191	6.5	6.7
TZ	209	7.1	7.4
EZ	214	7.2	7.5
Fork oil level[2]	**mm**		**in.**
ET, LT, LX	229		9.0
EX	227		8.9
EZ	201		7.9
TZ	180		7.1
Fork spring length (service limit)		**mm**	**in.**
EZ			
Short spring		63	2.48
Long spring		439	17.28
TZ			
Short spring		156	6.14
Long spring		360	14.17
EX			
Short spring		62	2.44
Long spring		466	18.35
ET, LT			
Short spring		153	6.02
Long spring		451	17.76

1. Recommended fork oil is SAE10, 15, 20 or 30 fork oil or a 50/50 mix of fork oil and automatic transmission fluid.
2. The maximum allowable difference in oil level between the right and left fork tubes is 1 mm (0.04 in.). Measure oil level from the top of the fork leg with the fork leg held vertical, spring removed and fork leg fully compressed.

CHAPTER ELEVEN

BRAKES

FRONT MASTER CYLINDER (GS750EZ, GS750TZ)

Removal/Installation

1. Remove the rear view mirror from the master cylinder.
2. Pull back the rubber boot and remove the banjo bolt (**Figure 35**) securing the brake hose to the master cylinder. Have a few rags or a container ready to catch any fluid drips. Remove the brake hose and both sealing washers. Tie the end of the brake hose up and cover the end to prevent the entry of foreign matter.

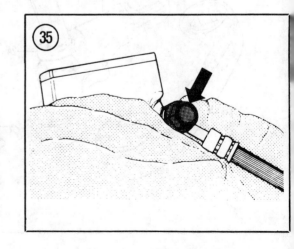

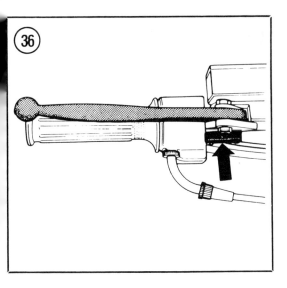

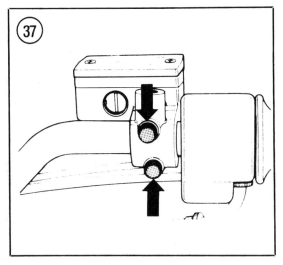

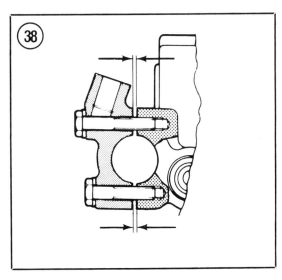

3. Remove the screws securing the brake light switch (**Figure 36**) and remove the switch from the master cylinder.

4. Remove the bolt and nut securing the front brake lever to the master cylinder and remove the lever.

5. Remove the clamping bolts (**Figure 37**), washers and clamp securing the master cylinder to the handlebar and remove the master cylinder.

6. Installation is the reverse of these steps. Keep the following points in mind:
   a. Install the brake lever onto the master cylinder before installing the cylinder on the handlebar.
   b. Install the master cylinder onto the handlebar and install the clamp, washers and bolts. Tighten the bolts evenly so that the clearance between the clamp and the master cylinder body are even at both top and bottom as shown in **Figure 38**.
   c. Install the brake hose onto the master cylinder. Be sure to place a sealing washer on each side of the fitting and install the banjo bolt. Tighten the banjo bolt to 2.0-2.5 mkg (14-18 ft.-lb.).
   d. Bleed the brake system as outlined in Chapter Nine of the main book.

Disassembly/Assembly

Refer to **Figure 39** for this procedure.

1. Remove the master cylinder as described in this chapter.

2. Remove the screws securing the cap (A, **Figure 40**) and remove the cap and diaphragm (B, **Figure 40**). Pour out the brake fluid and discard it. *Never* reuse brake fluid.

3. Remove the dust seal boot from the area where the hand lever actuates the internal piston assembly.

4. Use snap ring pliers with an angled tip and remove the internal snap ring (**Figure 41**) from the body.

5. Carefully withdraw the piston (A, **Figure 42**), primary cup (B, **Figure 42**) and the spring (C, **Figure 42**) from the cylinder bore.

6. Perform *Inspection*.

7. Assembly is the reverse of these steps. Keep the following in mind:

a. Soak the new cups in fresh brake fluid for at least 15 minutes to make them pliable.

b. Lubricate the new piston, the cups and the inside of the cylinder bore with fresh brake fluid prior to the assembly of parts.

CAUTION
When installing the piston assembly, do not allow the cups to turn inside out as they will be damaged and allow brake fluid leakage within the cylinder bore.

c. Install the spring, primary cup and piston assembly (**Figure 43**) into the cylinder together. Install the spring with the tapered end facing toward the primary cup.

d. Install the master cylinder as described in this supplement.

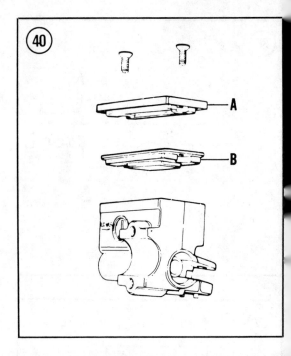

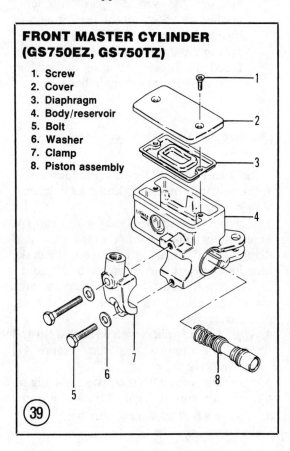

FRONT MASTER CYLINDER (GS750EZ, GS750TZ)

1. Screw
2. Cover
3. Diaphragm
4. Body/reservoir
5. Bolt
6. Washer
7. Clamp
8. Piston assembly

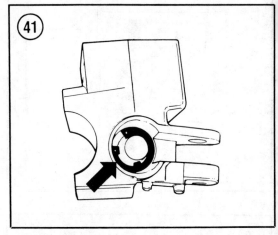

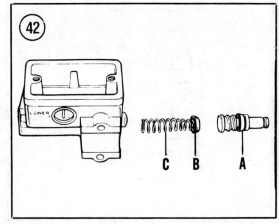

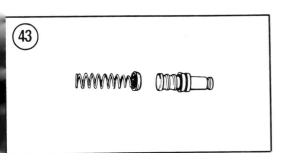

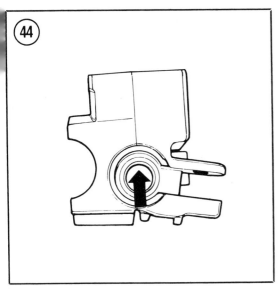

Inspection

1. Clean all brake components in fresh brake fluid.

2. Inspect the cylinder bore (**Figure 44**) and piston contact surfaces for scuffing or scoring. If either part is less than perfect, replace it.

3. Check the end of the piston for wear caused by the hand lever. Replace if worn.

4. Inspect the pivot hole in the hand lever. If worn or elongated it must be replaced.

5. Make sure the passages in the bottom of the brake fluid reservoir are clear. Check the reservoir cap and diaphragm for damage and deterioration and replace as necessary.

6. Inspect the threads in the bore for the brake line.

7. Check the hand lever pivot lugs on the master cylinder body for cracks.

8. Measure the cylinder bore (**Figure 45**). Replace the master cylinder if the bore exceeds the standard dimension specification given in **Table 7**.

9. Measure the outside diameter of the piston as shown in **Figure 46** with a micrometer. Replace the piston assembly if it is less than the standard dimension specification given in **Table 7**.

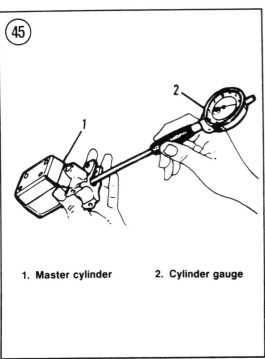

1. Master cylinder   2. Cylinder gauge

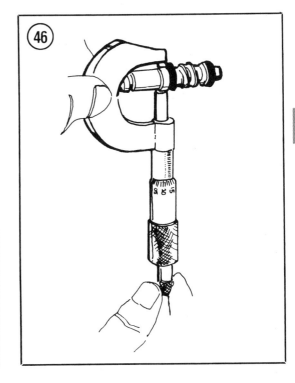

12

BLEEDING AND
CHANGING BRAKE FLUID

Bleeding

On models equipped with anti-dive front forks, use the techniques for bleeding the brakes as outlined in Chapter Eleven of the main book. Bleed the anti-dive components and front brake calipers in the following order:

    a. Left-hand anti-dive modulator valve (A, **Figure 47**).
    b. Left-hand brake caliper (B, **Figure 47**).
    c. Right-hand anti-dive modulator valve.
    d. Right-hand brake caliper.

REAR DRUM BRAKE

Pushing down on the brake foot pedal pulls the rod which in turn rotates the camshaft. This forces the brake shoes out into contact with the brake drum.

Pedal free play must be maintained to minimize brake drag and premature brake wear and maximize braking effectiveness.

Refer to the Chapter Three section of this supplement for brake free play adjustment.

Disassembly

Refer to **Figure 48** for this procedure.
1. Remove the rear wheel as described in Chapter Ten of the main book.
2. Pull the brake assembly straight up and out of the brake drum.
3. Remove the bolt and nut securing the brake arm and remove the brake arm, washer and the O-ring seal. Withdraw the camshaft from the backing plate.

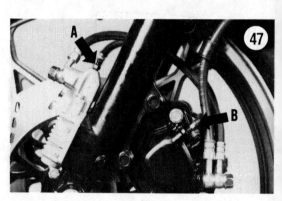

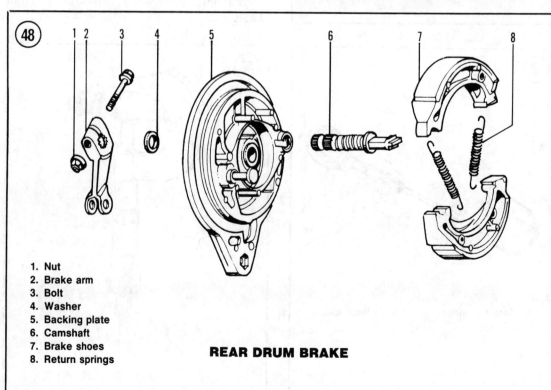

1. Nut
2. Brake arm
3. Bolt
4. Washer
5. Backing plate
6. Camshaft
7. Brake shoes
8. Return springs

REAR DRUM BRAKE

NOTE
Place a clean shop cloth on the linings to protect them from oil and grease during removal.

4. Remove the brake shoes from the backing plate by pulling up on the center of each shoe as shown in **Figure 49**.

5. Assembly is the reverse of these steps. Keep the following points in mind:

  a. Grease the camshaft with a light coat of molybdenum disulfide grease. Install the cam into the backing plate from the backside and install a new O-ring seal.

  b. From the outside of the backing plate install the washer.

  c. When installing the brake arm onto the camshaft, be sure to align the dimples on the two parts. Tighten the bolt and nut securely.

  d. Grease the camshaft and pivot post with a light coat of molybdenum disulfide grease; avoid getting any grease on the brake backing plate where the brake linings may come in contact with it.

  e. Hold the brake shoes in a "V" formation with the return springs attached and

snap them into place on the brake backing plate. Make sure they are firmly seated on it.

  f. Install the brake panel assembly into the brake drum.

  g. Install the rear wheel as described in Chapter Ten.

  h. Adjust the rear brake as outlined in the Chapter Three section of this supplement.

Inspection

1. Thoroughly clean and dry all parts except the brake linings.

2. Check the contact surface of the drum for scoring. If there are deep grooves, deep enough to snag your fingernail, the drum should be reground.

3. Measure the inside diameter of the brake drum with vernier calipers (**Figure 50**). If the measurement is greater than the service limit listed in **Table 6** the rear wheel must be replaced as the brake drum is an integral part of the wheel.

4. If the drum can be turned and still stay within the maximum service limit diameter, have the drum turned. If the drum is turned new linings will have to be installed and they must be arced to comform to the new drum contour.

5. Measure the brake linings with a vernier caliper (**Figure 51**). They should be replaced if

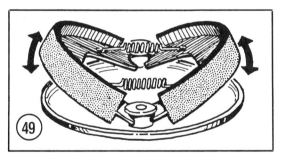
(49)

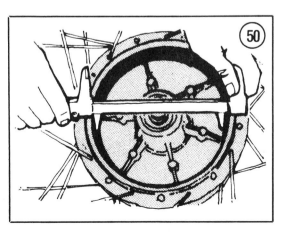
(50)

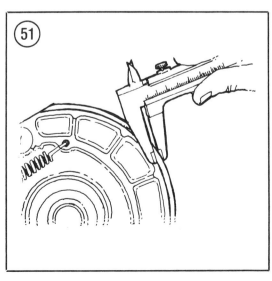
(51)

12

the lining portion is worn to the service limit dimension or less. Refer to specifications listed in **Table 7**.

6. Inspect the linings for imbedded foreign material. Dirt can be removed with a stiff wire brush. Check for any traces of oil or grease; if they are contaminated they must be replaced.

7. Inspect the cam lobe and pivot pin area of the backing plate for wear or corrosion. Minor roughness can be removed with fine emery cloth.

8. Inspect the brake shoe return springs for wear. If they are stretched, they will not fully retract the brake shoes and they will drag and wear out prematurely. Replace as necessary.

Table 7 BRAKE COMPONENT SPECIFICATIONS

	Standard	Service limit
Front master cylinder		
Bore ID	14.000-14.043 mm (0.5512-0.5529 in.)	—
Piston OD	13.957-13.984 mm (0.5459-0.5506 in.)	—
Rear drum brake		
Drum ID	—	180.7 mm (7.11 in.)
Lining thickness	—	1.5 mm (0.06 in.)

INDEX

13

References to illustrations and tables are given in boldface type.

References to illustrations and tables are given in boldface type.

13

References to illustrations and tables are given in boldface type.

References to illustrations and tables are given in boldface type.

13

References to illustrations and tables are given in boldface type.

1977 GS750B

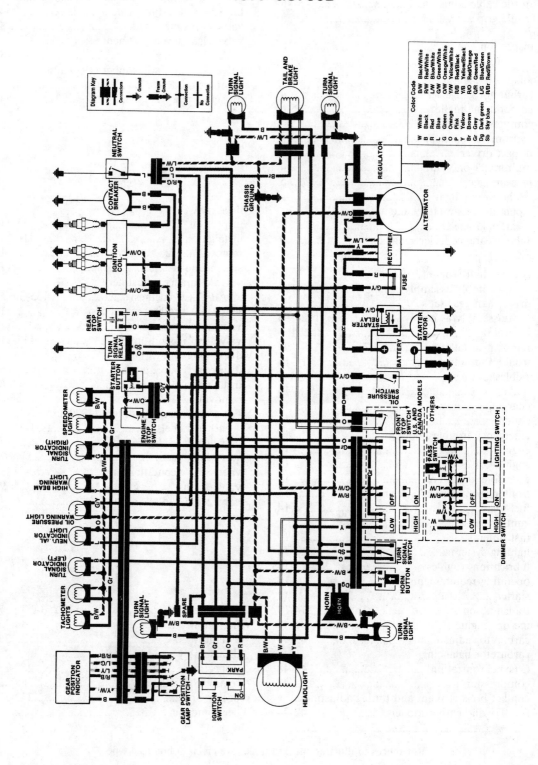

1978 GS750C & EC

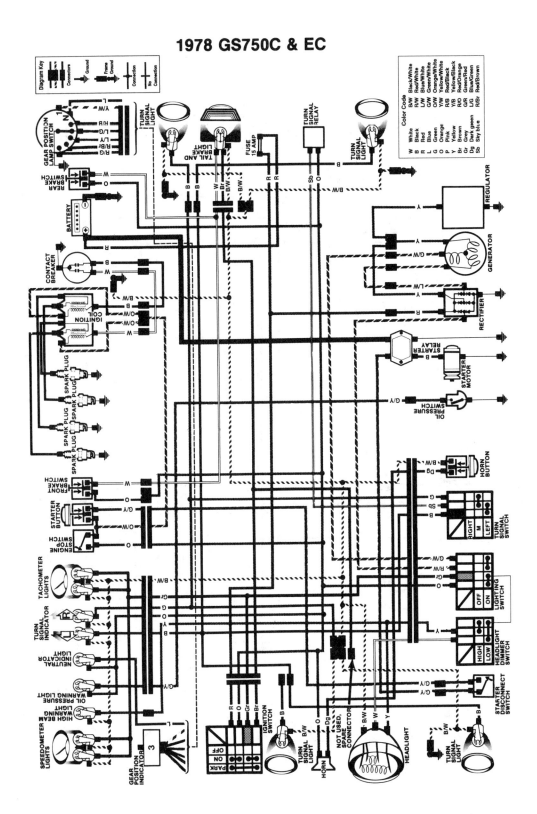

1979 GS750N & EN

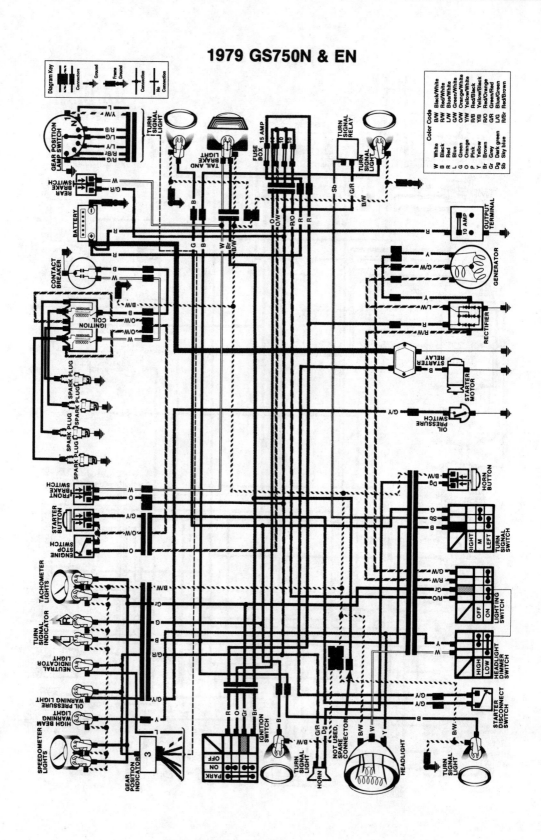

1979 GS750LN

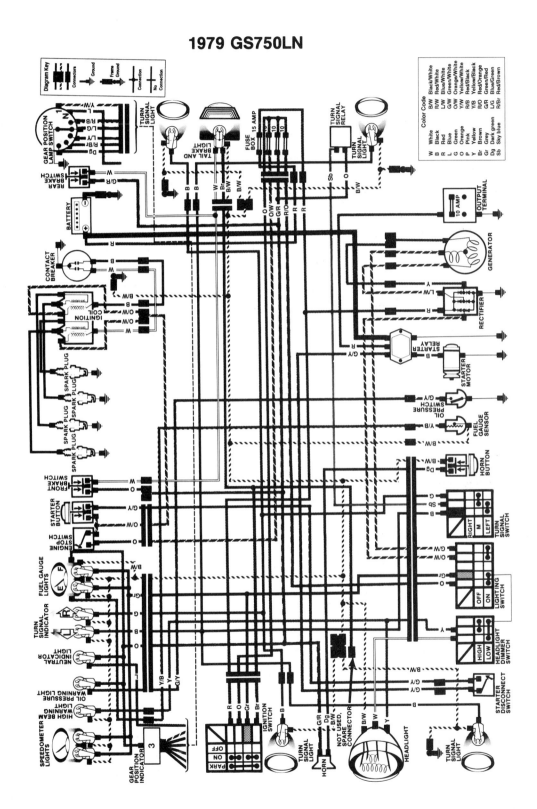

1980 GS750ET

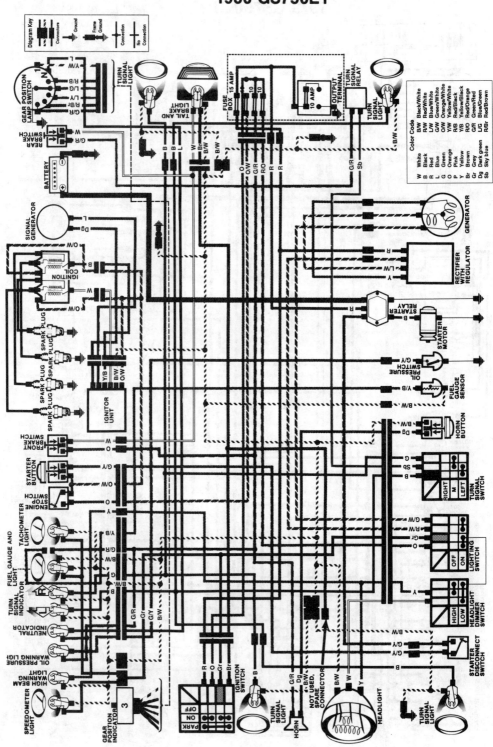

1980 GS750LT

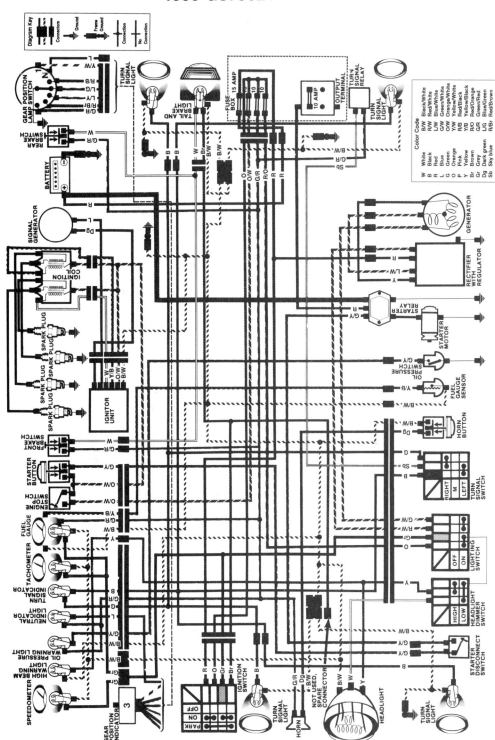

1981 GS750EX

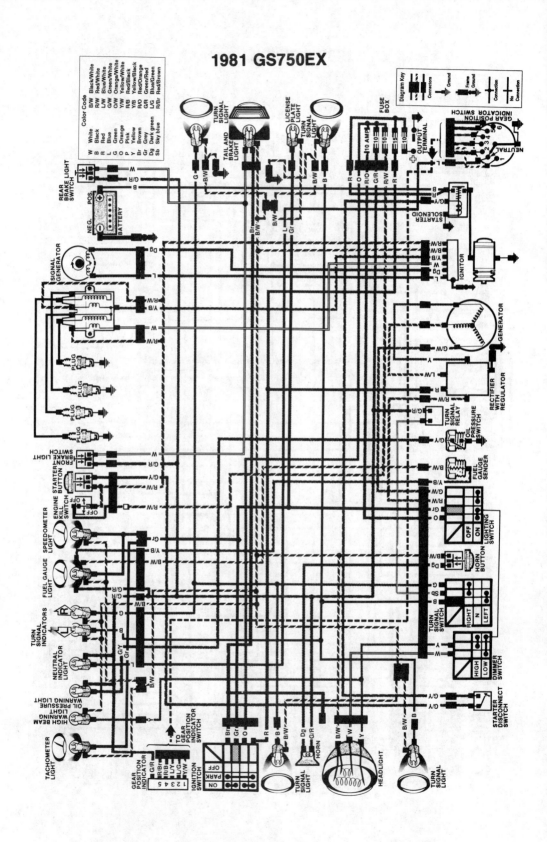

1981 GS750LX

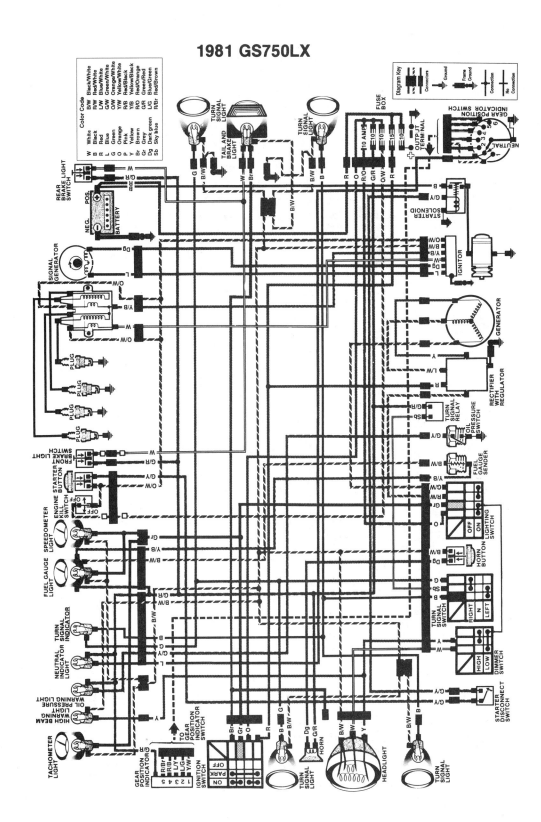

1982 GS750EZ

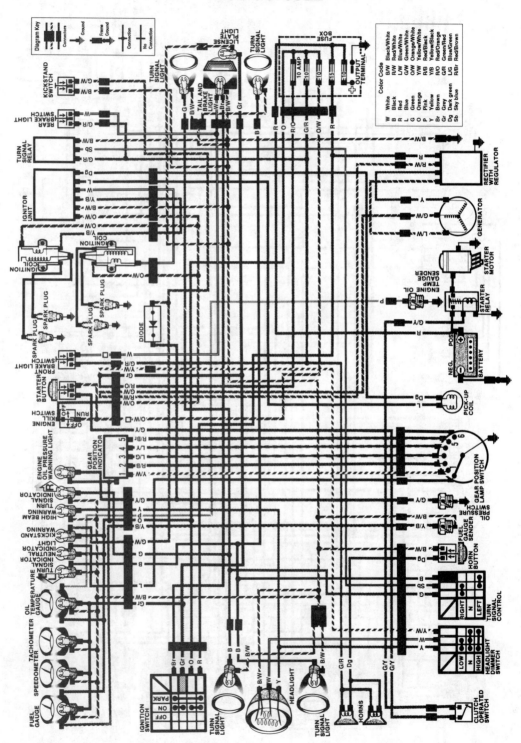

1982 GS750TZ

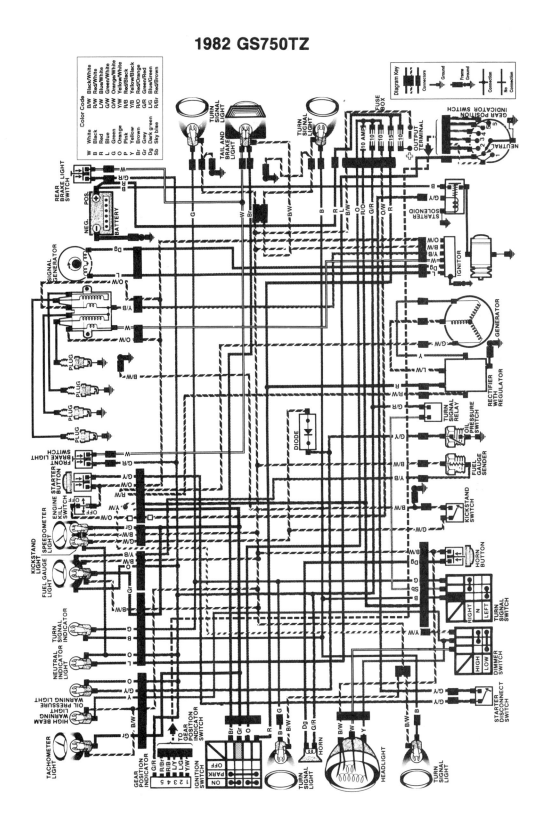

NOTES

NOTES

MAINTENANCE LOG

Date	Miles	Type of Service

BMW

M308	500 & 600cc Twins, 55-69
M309	F650, 1994-2000
M500-3	BMW K-Series, 85-97
M501	K1200RS, GT & LT, 98-05
M502-3	BMW R50/5-R100GS PD, 70-96
M503-3	R850, R1100, R1150 and R1200C, 93-05

HARLEY-DAVIDSON

M419	Sportsters, 59-85
M429-5	XL/XLH Sportster, 86-03
M427-1	XL Sportster, 04-06
M418	Panheads, 48-65
M420	Shovelheads,66-84
M421-3	FLS/FXS Evolution,84-99
M423-2	FLS/FXS Twin Cam, 00-05
M422-3	FLH/FLT/FXR Evolution, 84-98
M430-4	FLH/FLT Twin Cam, 99-05
M424-2	FXD Evolution, 91-98
M425-3	FXD Twin Cam, 99-05
M426	VRSC Series, 02-07

HONDA

ATVs

M316	Odyssey FL250, 77-84
M311	ATC, TRX & Fourtrax 70-125, 70-87
M433	Fourtrax 90, 93-00
M326	ATC185 & 200, 80-86
M347	ATC200X & Fourtrax 200SX, 86-88
M455	ATC250 & Fourtrax 200/250, 84-87
M342	ATC250R, 81-84
M348	TRX250R/Fourtrax 250R & ATC250R, 85-89
M456-3	TRX250X 87-92; TRX300EX 93-04
M215	TRX250EX, 01-05
M446-3	TRX250 Recon & Recon ES, 97-07
M346-3	TRX300/Fourtrax 300 & TRX300FW/Fourtrax 4x4, 88-00
M200-2	TRX350 Rancher, 00-06
M459-3	TRX400 Foreman 95-03
M454-3	TRX400EX 99-05
M205	TRX450 Foreman, 98-04
M210	TRX500 Rubicon, 01-04

Singles

M310-13	50-110cc OHC Singles, 65-99
M319-2	XR50R, CRF50F, XR70R & CRF70F, 97-05
M315	100-350cc OHC, 69-82
M317	125-250cc Elsinore, 73-80
M442	CR60-125R Pro-Link, 81-88
M431-2	CR80R, 89-95, CR125R, 89-91
M435	CR80R, 96-02
M457-2	CR125R & CR250R, 92-97
M464	CR125R, 1998-2002
M443	CR250R-500R Pro-Link, 81-87
M432-3	CR250R, 88-91 & CR500R, 88-01
M437	CR250R, 97-01
M352	CRF250R, CRF250X, CRF450R & CRF450X, 02-05
M312-13	XL/XR75-100, 75-03
M318-4	XL/XR/TLR 125-200, 79-03
M328-4	XL/XR250, 78-00; XL/XR350R 83-85; XR200R, 84-85; XR250L, 91-96
M320-2	XR400R, 96-04
M339-8	XL/XR 500-600, 79-90
M221	XR600R & XR650L, 91-07
M225	XR650R, 00-07

Twins

M321	125-200cc Twins, 65-78
M322	250-350cc Twins, 64-74
M323	250-360cc Twins, 74-77
M324-5	Twinstar, Rebel 250 & Nighthawk 250, 78-03
M334	400-450cc Twins, 78-87
M333	450 & 500cc Twins, 65-76
M335	CX & GL500/650, 78-83
M344	VT500, 83-88
M313	VT700 & 750, 83-87
M314-3	VT750 Shadow Chain Drive, 98-06
M440	VT1100C Shadow, 85-96
M460-4	VT1100 Series, 95-07
M230	VTX1800 Series, 02-08

Fours

M332	CB350-550, SOHC, 71-78
M345	CB550 & 650, 83-85
M336	CB650,79-82
M341	CB750 SOHC, 69-78
M337	CB750 DOHC, 79-82
M436	CB750 Nighthawk, 91-93 & 95-99
M325	CB900, 1000 & 1100, 80-83
M439	600 Hurricane, 87-90
M441-2	CBR600F2 & F3, 91-98
M445-2	CBR600F4, 99-06
M220	CBR600RR, 03-06
M434-2	CBR900RR Fireblade, 93-99
M329	500cc V-Fours, 84-86
M438	VFR800 Interceptor, 98-00
M349	700-1000 Interceptor, 83-85
M458-2	VFR700F-750F, 86-97
M327	700-1100cc V-Fours, 82-88
M340	GL1000 & 1100, 75-83
M504	GL1200, 84-87
M508	ST1100/Pan European, 90-02

Sixes

M505	GL1500 Gold Wing, 88-92
M506-2	GL1500 Gold Wing, 93-00
M507-2	GL1800 Gold Wing, 01-05
M462-2	GL1500C Valkyrie, 97-03

KAWASAKI

ATVs

M465-2	Bayou KLF220 & KLF250, 88-03
M466-4	Bayou KLF300, 86-04
M467	Bayou KLF400, 93-99
M470	Lakota KEF300, 95-99
M385-2	Mojave KSF250, 87-04

Singles

M350-9	80-350cc Rotary Valve, 66-01
M444-2	KX60, 83-02; KX80 83-90
M448	KX80/85/100, 89-03
M351	KDX200, 83-88
M447-3	KX125 & KX250, 82-91 KX500, 83-04
M472-2	KX125, 92-00
M473-2	KX250, 92-00
M474-2	KLR650, 87-06

Twins

M355	KZ400, KZ/Z440, EN450 & EN500, 74-95
M360-3	EX500, GPZ500S, Ninja 500 R, 87-02
M356-5	Vulcan 700 & 750, 85-06
M354-3	Vulcan 800 & Vulcan 800 Classic, 95-05
M357-2	Vulcan 1500, 87-99
M471-3	Vulcan 1500 Series, 96-08

Fours

M449	KZ500/550 & ZX550, 79-85
M450	KZ, Z & ZX750, 80-85
M358	KZ650, 77-83
M359-3	Z & KZ 900-1000cc, 73-81
M451-3	KZ, ZX & ZN 1000 &1100cc, 81-02
M452-3	ZX500 & Ninja ZX600, 85-97
M468-2	Ninja ZX-6, 90-04
M469	Ninja ZX-7, 91-98
M453-3	Ninja ZX900, ZX1000 & ZX1100, 84-01
M409	Concours, 86-04

POLARIS

ATVs

M496	3-, 4- and 6-Wheel Models w/250-425cc Engines, 85-95
M362	Magnum and Big Boss, 96-98
M363	Scrambler 500 4X4, 97-00
M365-2	Sportsman/Xplorer, 96-03

SUZUKI

ATVs

M381	ALT/LT 125 & 185, 83-87
M475	LT230 & LT250, 85-90
M380-2	LT250R Quad Racer, 85-92
M270	LT-Z400, 03-07
M343	LTF500F Quadrunner, 98-00
M483-2	King Quad/ Quad Runner 250, 87-98

Singles

M371	RM50-400 Twin Shock, 75-81
M369	125-400cc 64-81
M379	RM125-500 Single Shock, 81-88
M476	DR250-350, 90-94
M477	DR-Z400, 00-06
M384-4	LS650 Savage/S40, 86-07
M386	RM80-250, 89-95
M400	RM125, 96-00
M401	RM250, 96-02

Twins

M372	GS400-450 Chain Drive, 77-87
M481-5	VS700-800 Intruder, 85-07
M260	Volusia/Boulevard C50, 01-06
M482-2	VS1400 Intruder, 87-03
M261	1500 Intruder/C90, 98-07
M484-3	GS500E Twins, 89-02
M361	SV650, 1999-2002

Triple

M368	GT380, GT550 & GT750, 72-77

Fours

M373	GS550, 77-86
M364	GS650, 81-83
M370	GS750, 77-82
M376	GS850-1100 Shaft Drive, 79-84
M378	GS1100 Chain Drive, 80-81
M383-3	Katana 600, 88-96 GSX-R750-1100, 86-87
M331	GSX-R600, 97-00
M264	GSX-R600, 01-05
M478-2	GSX-R750, 88-92 GSX750F Katana, 89-96
M485	GSX-R750, 96-99
M377	GSX-R1000, 01-04
M266	GSX-R1000, 05-06
M265	GSX1300R Hayabusa, 99-07
M338	Bandit 600, 95-00
M353	GSF1200 Bandit, 96-03

YAMAHA

ATVs

M499	YFM80 Badger, 85-88 & 92-01
M394	YTM200, 250 & YFM200, 83-86
M488-5	Blaster, 88-05
M489-2	Timberwolf, 89-00
M487-5	Warrior, 87-04
M486-6	Banshee, 87-06
M490-3	Moto-4 & Big Bear, 87-04
M493	Kodiak, 93-98
M280-2	Raptor 660R, 01-05
M285	Grizzly 660, 02-07

Singles

M492-2	PW50 & PW80, BW80 Big Wheel 80, 81-02
M410	80-175 Piston Port, 68-76
M415	250-400 Piston Port, 68-76
M412	DT & MX 100-400, 77-83
M414	IT125-490, 76-86
M393	YZ50-80 Monoshock, 78-90
M413	YZ100-490 Monoshock, 76-84
M390	YZ125-250, 85-87 YZ490, 85-90
M391	YZ125-250, 88-93 & WR250Z, 91-93
M497-2	YZ125, 94-01
M498	YZ250, 94-98 WR250Z, 94-97
M406	YZ250F & WR250F, 01-03
M491-2	YZ400F, YZ426F, WR400F WR426F, 98-02
M417	XT125-250, 80-84
M480-3	XT/TT 350, 85-00
M405	XT/TT 500, 76-81
M416	XT/TT 600, 83-89

Twins

M403	XS1, XS2, XS650 & TX650, 70-82
M395-10	XV535-1100 Virago, 81-03
M495-5	V-Star 650, 98-07
M281-3	V-Star 1100, 99-07
M282	Road Star, 99-05

Triple

M404	XS750 & XS850, 77-81

Fours

M387	XJ550, XJ600 & FJ600, 81-92
M494	XJ600 Seca II/Diversion, 92-98
M388	YX600 Radian & FZ600, 86-90
M396	FZR600, 89-93
M392	FZ700-750 & Fazer, 85-87
M411	XS1100, 78-81
M397	FJ1100 & 1200, 84-93
M375	V-Max, 85-03
M374	Royal Star, 96-03
M461	YZF-R6, 99-04
M398	YZF-R1, 98-03
M399	FZ1, 01-05

VINTAGE MOTORCYCLES

Clymer® Collection Series

M330	Vintage British Street Bikes, BSA, 500–650cc Unit Twins; Norton, 750 & 850cc Commandos; Triumph, 500-750cc Twins
M300	Vintage Dirt Bikes, V. 1 Bultaco, 125-370cc Singles; Montesa, 123-360cc Singles; Ossa, 125-250cc Singles
M305	Vintage Japanese Street Bikes Honda, 250 & 305cc Twins; Kawasaki, 250-750cc Triples; Kawasaki, 900 & 1000cc Fours